ENDORSEMENTS

Dr. Ché Ahn has written what I consider to contain vital keys to seeing both individuals and nations transformed. He writes both from personal experience as well as that of seeing the results of hundreds of thousands of people crying out for a nation. It is a fascinating read and a timely message for the hour.

— Cindy Jacobs
Generals International

I have given my life in pursuit of revival. And one of the great joys on this journey is to have run alongside covenant friends and ministry partners such as Ché and Sue Ahn for over 20 years. They amaze me. Ché has carried the message in this book for as long as I've known him. His brilliant insights from the Word of God and his passion to honor the Lord in all things make transformation doable and reasonable. In *Blueprints for Transformation*, he gives us practical yet profound strategies to see the reality of heaven come to earth. My prayer is that you and I would live in such a way that the kingdom of God would be truly displayed in and through our lives. I highly recommend this book!

— Bill Johnson
Senior Leader of Bethel Church, Redding, CA
Author of *Open Heavens* and *When Heaven Invades Earth*

It has always been an honor to have as our long-term friends Ché and Sue. We have had the privilege of not only being blessed by them and their family in key decades but sometimes invited to be a contributor with them in the amazing chain of stories you can read about here with fresh revelations of our matchless Maker and Master... We all get a chance to pass on to others from giftings He invests in our lives, to please Him in what we can do in a short span before we move out, up, and on forever. Here is Ché's new gracious gift for the rest of the Bride still here to see the One we all long for.

— Winkie, Fae, and Will Pratney
GMA, New Zealand

During 50 years of ministry and upon turning 75 recently, I realized that when Abraham turned 75, God called him and told him, "I'll bless those who bless you" (Genesis 12:3). Ché has blessed me repeatedly during almost 50 years of friendship, so I'm returning the blessing with the release of this phenomenal new book. You, too, will be blessed incredibly as you read it at this defining moment in America's history. We need a download from heaven, so buckle your seatbelt and enjoy the adventure!

— Larry Tomczak
Cultural Commentator, Best-Selling Author

Let me cut to the chase: Our nation is in trouble. In fact, the nations of the world are figuratively on fire. We need answers, and we need them now. We need transformation, soon. Ché Ahn is a man of prayer, vision, and action. He is not intimidated by evil. He sees the earthly problems and provides scriptural solutions. He "runs to the roar," rather than away from it. He believes that the Spirit of the Living God can transform a person, a family, a community, a state, a nation, and a world. He resonates with the fires of revival. But more than that, he understands the underpinnings of reformation. Some understand one; few grasp the dimensions of both. This book will help you to abandon the false notion of merely "going to church" and embrace "*being* the church."

—Jim Garlow
Founder and CEO of Well Versed

I have been a friend, an intercessor, and at times a prophetic voice into the life and ministry of Dr. Ché Ahn for many years. When revelation is granted, Ché desires to partner with the Holy Spirit to see the vision come to pass. Ché is committed to the *Word* and the *will* of God according to the *ways* of God. These three components are exhibited in everything he does. This book on transformation is composed according to that blueprint.

—James W. Goll
God Encounters Ministries
Author, Consultant, Recording Artist

For nearly three decades of friendship, Ché and his wife, Sue, have been a tremendous blessing, in our personal lives and in ministry. We have seen them weather many storms, and they have remained warm, unbelievably generous, and completely devoted to the gospel regardless of life's challenges. If you hunger to see God's kingdom grow, let Ché's words strengthen you as you go out to gather the harvest that is already waiting. The hour is now!

— Heidi G. Baker, Ph.D.
Co-founder and Executive Chairman of the Board,
Iris Global

Ché Ahn's *Blueprints for Transformation* is a remarkably timely book. He captures the essence of what many prophets say the Lord is doing in this hour—taking us from personal revival into societal reformation. This isn't just theory. It's a practical road map for those called to carry the fire of the Holy Spirit into the seven mountains of culture. If you're serious about stepping up into the next level of your assignment, this book is a must-read. Ché breaks down 12 essential shifts that will position you to radically reframe not just your life but your world. Heaven has a blueprint for global transformation, and Ché Ahn has decoded it!

— Dr. Lance W. Wallnau
CEO, Lance Learning Group

For many years, the church has toyed with the idea of changing the world, but high-sounding words never turned into action. Then something happened in California. Dr. Ché Ahn sued the state for locking down the church and won. This mirrors what Paul did in Acts 16. Because of this— plus his anointing in the supernatural—Dr. Ché Ahn has the right to speak to us about changing the world. And he does it convincingly. Who are we? Why are we here? What shifts in our thinking do we need to make? Is a global miracle within our reach? *Blueprints for Transformation* not only answers those questions—it is charged with the Holy Spirit to take us to certain victory.

— Mario Murillo
Mario Murillo Ministries

It has been a joy and honor to co-labor with Dr. Ché Ahn for over 25 years. His latest book, *Blueprints for Transformation*, will take you on a compelling journey. Using 12 clear lenses, the focus of what it means to live for Jesus in this world enlarges from micro to macro. This is not theory. Ché lives what he writes. Personal restoration and wholeness is the beginning but not the end of our life in Christ! We are each here to make the world a better place.

— Dr. Charles Stock
Senior Leader, Life Center Ministries

I was so delighted to read the story of a drug pusher to a world changer and to read about the 12 things that lead to the most efficient path of transformation. This book of testimonies will warm your heart and spur you onward into action to join the ranks of those world changers whom God has raised up.

— Doris Wagner
Author of *God's Apostle:
My Adventures in Life with C. Peter Wagner*

Over the past two decades of serving WLI (Wagner University) and Harvest International Ministry, a lot has changed for me. First, Dr. Peter Wagner changed my paradigm. Second, I myself grew into a paradigm changer through Apostle Ché Ahn. I used to stay inside the four walls of the church but have become a transformer of the wider world outside of it. Through the teachings and impartations of pioneers like Ché Ahn, who is able to read the signs of the times, the traditional Korean church is gradually being transformed. I highly recommend this book, which is a must-read for churches to read the signs of the times and move into the next season of transformation.

— Dr. Jung-shik Hong
HIM Korea

I came to know Pastor Ché Ahn and love his humble but fearless stand for truth through the COVID-19 pandemic… We join with him in standing for Christ and against the darkness trying to invade our nation and world. I agree totally that we are already in a Third Great Awakening in this nation and around the world, but that will only happen as it first begins in us. Let the ministry of Pastor Ché Ahn spark that seed of revival in you and then take it to your world.

— Andrew Wommack
Andrew Wommack Ministries

In *Blueprints for Transformation*, Dr. Ché Ahn masterfully guides us through the rich history of revival and reformation, revealing how the current move of the Holy Spirit is shaping our world today. As you explore the 12 pivotal shifts necessary for personal and global change, you will discover how God is equipping you to fulfill your divine calling to bring heaven to earth. This book is an essential read for every believer who desires to be a revivalist and reformer in this generation.

— Tammy Hotsenpiller
Co-Pastor, Influence Church
Author of *Fasting for Miracles*,
Fasting for a Change, and *Fasting with God*

Blueprints for Transformation is a powerful and timely guide for anyone who senses a call to make a difference in this world. Dr. Ché Ahn masterfully combines biblical wisdom with practical insights, providing a clear path to personal and global impact. This book is a must-read for those who are ready to step into their God-given purpose and become agents of change in their communities and beyond.

— Phil Hotsenpiller
Senior Pastor, Influence Church
Author of *One Nation Without Law* and *Midnight in America*

Pastor Ché Ahn's book is a powerful call to personal and societal transformation rooted in biblical truth. Each chapter challenges believers to move from knowledge to action, embracing their role as world-changers. His insights are timely and essential for anyone passionate about living out the gospel in every sphere of life.

— Samuel Rodriguez
New Season, Lead Pastor; NHCLC President/CEO
Author of *Your Mess, God's Miracle!*
Exec. Producer, "Breakthrough" and "Flamin Hot" Movies

In this book, Ché Ahn has uncovered what I believe are the core values that we as the church have overlooked in our perspective and methodology, to fulfill the prayer of Christ in bringing heaven to earth! Each and every chapter unveils distorted ideologies that have hindered our quest, as the church, for authentic transformation. I believe that as you read his words, you will experience a dramatic paradigm shift in the way you view Scripture and understand truth. Ché Ahn's relevancy is unparalleled as he integrates current-day examples and events to historical content.

— Philip L. Liberatore
CPA, IRS Problem Solver, and Ordained Minister

As one of God's generals in this era of church reformation, Ché Ahn clearly defines the necessary paradigm shifts to bring the transformative power of the kingdom into our world. *Blueprints for Transformation* will challenge, inspire, and enlighten you to become a history maker in your generation. It is a must-read for every leader and believer who wants to be on the cutting edge of all God is doing.

— Tom and Jane Hamon
Apostles, Vision Church at Christian International,
Santa Rosa Beach, FL
Authors of *7 Anointings for Kingdom Transformation* and
The Apostolic Mantle

Pastor Ché is one of my spiritual fathers and a brilliant example of humble, faith-empowered, and courageous leadership. In *Blueprints for Transformation*, he shows that all it takes to change the world is *you*, aligned with God's heart, empowered by His Spirit, and living out 12 key biblical graces. God desires to bring not only revival but reformation into this world… Interspersed with incredible faith-building testimonials, this book will equip you into a closer walk with Jesus and prepare you to play a key part in a divine adventure with God—global transformation!

— Dr. Leanna Cinquanta
Founder and President of We Ignite Nations (WIN)
Author of *Treasures in Dark Places* and *Your Secret Calling*

A blueprint is one thing. A building is another. A builder is yet another. Pastor Ché Ahn has done it again. In *Blueprints for Transformation*, Ché has provided a blueprint, built the building, and demonstrated his gifts as a builder of transformational atmospheres. *You* can be a revivalist *and* a reformer. You were made for this moment in human history, and "Papa Ché" has provided you with everything you need to lead to the transformation of your life and the world around you for the glory of the One. Buy this book, read this book, live this book. Be part of a God-sized transformation of your life and legacy!

— Dr. John Jackson
President of Jessup University
Author of *Grace Ambassador* and 9 other books on
Leadership & Transformation

In this incredible book, Papa Ché Ahn reminds us of the divine calling on our lives through Scripture and powerful testimonies. *Blueprints for Transformation* provides hope and encouragement for believers looking to step into their God-given purpose. Papa Ché's insights help us understand how we can be part of something bigger—reviving and reforming our world with the power of the Holy Spirit. This book is a guide to living out the Great Commission in a real, impactful way.

— Shannon Grove
California State Senator

With solid biblical insight, transformative personal experience, and a heart attuned to the Father, *Blueprints for Transformation* will peel back the layers of your heart like an onion, revealing simple yet challenging revelations of what God is doing in the world for such a time as this. Having known Pastor Ché Ahn for over three decades, I can attest that this book is birthed from his life of continuous, progressive obedience. Could it be that we are living in a season where *chronos* and *kairos* converge to fulfill God's finest hour and use His remnant, the church, to bring about global transformation? Prayerfully read this book, and the Holy Spirit will unveil what you've never seen before. More, Lord!

— Dr. Paul Tan
Apostle, City Blessing Church

Dr. Ché Ahn is a true practitioner of revival and reformation... His leadership and influence have measurably impacted nations and fueled leaders with boldness to take stands for righteousness. This book is a practical guide to become a *revived reformer* in your personal sphere of influence. If God has touched your life (revival), the only way you will step into your purpose and destiny—along with experiencing a sense of sustained revival—is stepping into your calling and bringing the Holy Spirit's power, presence, and prophetic solutions to the place Heaven has assigned you. This is when you become a reformer who changes the world around you—and these pages will ignite your heart to become such a change agent wherever you are called!

— Larry Sparks, MDiv.
Publisher, Destiny Image; LM Sparks Ministries
Author of *Pentecostal Fire*

Blueprints for Transformation is a powerful and timely book that challenges believers to recognize their pivotal role in fulfilling the Great Commission. Ché Ahn brilliantly outlines how shifting our mindsets and being empowered by the Holy Spirit is key to unleashing God's transformative power in our world. As revival sparks within us, reformation must follow, bringing lasting change to our society. This book will ignite your heart with a fresh vision of how God can use you to transform the world around you. Prepare yourself for a thrilling encounter with the God of glory as you dive into its pages!

— Brian Simmons
Passion & Fire Ministries

The greatest thing I love and admire about Ché Ahn is that he's unafraid to take a risk for the sake of the gospel. In today's polarized, angry, and distracted culture, the stakes are high, and we need more leaders willing to push the boundaries and make an impact. And now, his new book, *Blueprints for Transformation*, is a masterclass in how to do precisely that. Using experiences from his own life and ministry, you'll discover what real transformation looks like and how to face the future with confidence.

— Phil Cooke, Ph.D.
Filmmaker, Media Consultant,
and Author of *Maximize Your Influence*

Blueprints for Transformation is not just a book; it's a powerful call to action for believers to embrace their God-given authority and bring the kingdom of heaven to earth. Whether you are a seasoned believer or new to your spiritual walk with the Lord, the personal shifts outlined within these pages will serve as powerful catalysts to help you navigate, influence, and impact the chaos within society and culture with the timeless truth of the gospel and authority of victorious warfare. Friends, this book will equip you to be the change agent of kingdom transformation in cities, regions, and nations.

— Rebecca Greenwood
Co-Founder, Christian Harvest International
Strategic Prayer Apostolic Network

We must cry out for revival but fight for reformation. We do not fight with clubs and fists, but with love, righteousness, and justice as Ché Ahn strongly emphasizes in his new book. It is a must-read for everyone desiring to not only do "missions work," but disciple and transform cultures, communities, cities, and nations for the kingdom of God. By using the principles Ché unfolds in his book, over the last 20 years I have personally witnessed a kingdom transformation taking place in the nation of Cuba. When we get something, it will change us. But when something gets us, it will transform us! Don't just read this amazing project, but let it read you, and thus transform you!

Dr. Leanne Goff
The Transformational Coach;
President, Leanne Goff Ministries
Author of *Missionary & Millionaire:*
Transforming Cultures as Priests and Kings

This book unveils 12 profound principles essential for the journey from revival to reformation. These are not mere words on a page, but divine truths embodied in the life of Dr. Ché Ahn. As you engage with its pages, you will be drawn into a powerful experience of personal revival and transformation. I wholeheartedly recommend this book—embrace it, read it, and let it change your life.

— Bishop Gregory Toussaint
Founder and Senior Pastor at Tabernacle of Glory

Finally, a book that has the potential to release a new generation called to take (back) their nations for God. In *Blueprints for Transformation*, Ché Ahn does an excellent job of integrating revival and reformation. What separates this book from others is that it is both theologically sound and extremely practical. This makes the transitions Ché describes easy to understand and apply. This is a game changer. *Blueprints for Transformation* is for everyone who longs to be used by God to see the church revived, the harvest come in, and righteousness and justice restored in all areas of society.

— Dick and Arleen Westerhof
Co-Lead Pastors, God's Embassy Amsterdam
Co-Founders, "By Design" Apostolic Network

Blueprints for Transformation has been published at a very timely moment, as the church of God is focusing on fulfilling the Great Commission of the Lord Jesus before His second coming. Every pastor and individual who longs for global transformation should read this book. In clear and easy-to-read language, Dr. Ché Ahn outlines 12 aspects of personal and social transformation that must take place both within individuals and the church.

— Dr. Niko Njotorahardjo
Founder and President of Gereja Bethel International

Dr. Ché believes that we are called to be revivalists and reformers for such a time as this—entering a Third Great Awakening in the history of the church... In order to bring about transformation of society, reformation needs to happen. How will we be able to do this? These 12 paradigm shifts that Dr. Ché explains to us are vital for every believer because God has always used a remnant of holy people to usher in the move of God that transformed their world. This book is a must-read for all—pastors, leaders, church members alike. It's time to awaken the Body of Christ to rise up to our calling and to really be salt and light to the depraved world, to partner with the Holy Spirit in bringing out the reformation that the world needs and bring glory to God.

— Bishop Augusto "Chito" Sanchez Jr.
& Pastor Rachel Sanchez
Commission Head of the Transformation
and Revival Ministry
Founder of Jesus Loves the
Little Children Foundation, Inc.
Overseer of River of God Churches

This is a powerful book on personal and cultural transformation. Pastor Ché begins each chapter with a fascinating personal story of God's divine intervention that resulted in his own personal shift in thinking and spiritual growth. Global transformation begins with personal transformation, and personal transformation happens in relationship to Jesus. From these 12 shifts in his life, God has miraculously worked through Pastor Ché to transform a young man who was once addicted to drugs and without hope to one of the most courageous and anointed servants of God whose influence touches every corner of the earth. Pastor Ché's servant heart and his love for the Lord is evident in the pages of this book. Pay careful attention to the profound message woven throughout *Blueprints for Transformation*, and you, too, will be transformed and equipped to transform the world around you.

— Mathew D. Staver, Esq., B.C.S.*
Founder and Chairman, Liberty Counsel

In *Blueprints for Transformation*, Dr. Ché Ahn (Papa Ché), provides a blueprint that demonstrates the active faith each believer in Jesus Christ should exhibit daily. This book answers the question that so many church leaders and believers ask ourselves: What can I do to make a difference? Now, whoever authentically seeks to transforms themselves and even the world according to the biblical mandate, after reading *Blueprints for Transformation*, we are without excuse. Digesting *Blueprints for Transformation* is not only a life-changing experience, but it also can be a world-changing experience in the hands of believers who embrace the power and authority given to us by Jesus Christ.

— Marc T. Little, Esq.
Host, "The Marc Little Show"
Pastor, Lawyer, Political Commentator

Dr. Ché Ahn's new book, *Blueprints for Transformation*, is refreshing, inspiring, and most importantly, very timely because the author is both the pastor of an influential church and an apostle with a worldwide impact. He has poured his vast experience into it to not only challenge but also equip the church to complete the Great Commission. A must-read!

— Dr. Ed Silvoso
Founder & President, Transform Our World
Author of *Ekklesia* and *Anointed for Romance*

My dear friend Ché Ahn is a powerful man of God with such a strong apostolic calling that is aligned with the thoughts of heaven. In this profound and transformative book essential for this new era we've entered, he will help you to renew your mind as you go from inferiority realities to superior realities, which you are called to live in as a son or daughter of God. He will help you to plant the powerful truths of Scripture into your world until you become more and more like Jesus. Get ready to be totally transformed!

— Jean-Luc Trachsel
President of IAHM
(International Association of Healing Ministries)
Founder & President of Europe Shall Be Saved
Co-Chairman of the Global Evangelist Alliance
& Member of Empowered21 Council

BLUEPRINTS

for

TRANSFORMATION

Bringing Revival and Reformation to the Nations

Ché Ahn

BLUEPRINTS FOR TRANSFORMATION: Bringing Revival and Reformation to the Nations
Published by Servant Leader Publishing
Pasadena, California, U.S.A.

Unless otherwise indicated, Scripture quotations are from the New American Standard Bible. Copyright © 1960, 1971, 1977, 1995, 2020 by The Lockman Foundation. Used by permission. All rights reserved. www.lockman.org

Scripture quotations identified NKJV are from the New King James Version®. Copyright © 1982 by Thomas Nelson. Used by permission. All rights reserved.

Scripture quotations identified TPT are from The Passion Translation®. Copyright © 2017, 2018 by Passion & Fire Ministries, Inc. Used by permission. All rights reserved. ThePassionTranslation.com.

Scripture quotations identified ESV are from The ESV® Bible (The Holy Bible, English Standard Version®), copyright © 2001 by Crossway, a publishing ministry of Good News Publishers. Used by permission. All rights reserved.

Scripture quotations identified NLT are from the Holy Bible, New Living Translation, copyright © 1996, 2004, 2015 by Tyndale House Foundation. Used by permission of Tyndale House Publishers, Carol Stream, Illinois 60188. All rights reserved.

Scripture quotations identified NIV are from the Holy Bible, New International Version®, NIV®. Copyright © 1973, 1978, 1984, 2011 by Biblica, Inc.™ Used by permission of Zondervan. All rights reserved worldwide. www.zondervan.com

Scripture quotations identified AMPC are from the Amplified Bible, Classic Edition. Copyright © 1954, 1958, 1962, 1964, 1965, 1987 by The Lockman Foundation.

Scripture quotations identified BSB are from the Holy Bible, Berean Standard Bible, produced in cooperation with Bible Hub, Discovery Bible, OpenBible.com, and the Berean Bible Translation Committee. Public domain.

All italics in Scripture verses quoted have been added by the author.

Cover design by Carolyn Covell.

AHN, CHÉ, Author
BLUEPRINTS FOR TRANSFORMATION
DR. CHÉ AHN

ISBN: 979-8-9908059-6-5, 979-8-9908059-8-9 (paperback)

ISBN: 979-8-9908059-7-2 (eBook)

Cataloging-in-Publication Data is on file with the Library of Congress.
Interior & eBook Design: Amit Dey (amitdey2528@gmail.com)
Publishing Management: Susie Schaefer (finishthebookpublishing.com)

QUANTITY PURCHASES: Schools, companies, professional groups, clubs, and other organizations may qualify for special terms when ordering quantities of this title. Visit www.harvestim.org

I dedicate this book to my wife and best friend, Sue Ahn,
who has had the greatest impact on my life besides Jesus Christ.
I love you with all my heart.
Thank you for loving me these past 45 years.
I also dedicate this book to my ten grandchildren.
May you bring revival and reformation to your generation.

TABLE OF CONTENTS

ACKNOWLEDGMENTS

I want to thank six revivalists and reformers who greatly impacted my life and helped shape this book:

- The late C. Peter Wagner, my friend, mentor, apostle, and spiritual father.

- Lou Engle, prophet and friend, for his tireless life of prayer for revival and reformation around the world.

- Cindy Jacobs, my sister, who has given me more significant prophetic words than any others who have impacted my life and ministry.

- Bill Johnson, a covenant friend, who became my pastor and my apostle when Peter Wagner and Jack Hayford went home to be with Jesus.

- Winkie Pratney, who gave me my theology and love for revival.

- Larry Tomczak, my first pastor, mentor, and friend.

Further thanks: I want to thank the members, pastors, and elders of Harvest Rock Church for releasing me to go on a three-month sabbatical to write this book and for being the best church.

I want to thank Pastor Rebecca Lee, my personal assistant, who has helped me to redeem my time to do all that God has called me to do.

Thanks to Mark Miller, a spiritual son and my editor.

And thanks to all the leaders who gave me an endorsement for this book. You guys are my heroes!

Foreword By

LOU ENGLE

*C*hé Ahn and I have, at the time of this writing, just gathered with 370,000 Esthers and Mordecais at the Washington, D.C. Mall on October 12, 2024 (the Day of Atonement), to fast and pray for America. There are profound indications that history shifted that day. Derek Prince writes in his classic book *Shaping History Through Prayer and Fasting* that in the last days of the crisis of nations, collective solemn assemblies will be the holy prescription to avert the crises and turn nations back to God. The books of Joel and Esther speak concerning the power and efficacy of this kind of prayer and fasting.

The book of Esther is particularly interesting. Whereas the outcome promised by Joel was the restoration of the land of Israel and worldwide *revival*, the outcome of Esther was the raising up and bringing down of queens and kings, the dismantling and removal of false ideologies and evil infrastructures, and the complete reversal of the Persian public policy concerning the Jews. This is *reformation*! One changes millions of hearts; the other changes culture.

It is my conviction that the ancient demonic spirit of hatred of the Jews, the very spirit possessing the wicked Haman, was broken by the Esther Fast. However, the decree of destruction would have still been carried out had Esther not gone public, risked her life, and appeared before the king. The point is this: You can pray all you want, but if you don't vote, you lose. If you don't stand publicly against transgenderism in schools, you lose your children. If you remain silent, you lose your freedoms and get totalitarianism and persecution. This is why this most urgent and timely book by my friend and apostle Ché Ahn is so needed. It arrives for such a time as this.

Ché and I were both radically saved in the Jesus Movement of the 1970s. It seemed like everywhere we looked, everyone was being saved. Sadly, a theology of what I call "Beam me up, Scotty" from the Star Trek days ran rampant, paralleling the revival. Everybody was looking to be raptured into heaven at any moment to escape the Tribulation. The devil was, in our thinking, "alive and well on planet earth" instead of being focused on "how great is our God." We all thought that we were the terminal generation, so why reform the earth? *It's all going up in flames anyway...* We were on a Star Trek to heaven when we should have been singing that 70s song, "These Boots Are Made for Walking." We should have been treading the earth with transformational kingdom ideas, thus reforming its institutions into kingdom colonies where we could ring out freedom and hammer out justice. Instead, we sang out love songs of revival, which were needed and glorious, but we vacated the public square. While we slept, the enemy sowed seeds of ideological destruction, put purveyors of poisonous thought into positions of influence, and thereby created power centers through which the devil could control the earth.

Now we are reaping the whirlwind of our "don't get involved in politics" appeasement and passivity! Such statements by "politically correct" pastors and preachers are more cowardly than correct. Give us prophets who can subpoena the conscience of America as Martin Luther King Jr. spoke. And what about this accusation of being so-called "Christian nationalists"? I don't get this. I'm not a nationalist—I'm fighting for my grandchildren!

We discipled individuals instead of discipling nations as Jesus commanded us (Matt. 28:19). Now, our kids are discipled by drag queens and transgender groomers. Now, the Big Brother government seeks to become the Big Parent government. Now, more children are being killed than before *Roe* was reversed by the abortion pill and candidates pushing abortion to the moment of birth as the main campaign agenda. We need reformation! Indeed, I see a new civil-rights revival movement emerging called "Don't Mess with Our Kids." Through this book, you can hear the rising roar and rumble, along with relevant ideas to explode such a reversal.

Ché Ahn, my pastor for 40 years, is not speaking theory. During the LA riots of 1992, he united pastors to reconcile in the intense atmosphere of racial tension. Pasadena was transformed through the labors and prayers of Harvest Rock Church (HRC) and many others. A worldwide cult headquartered in Pasadena was dismantled and became an evangelical church; HRC bought and now meets in its world-renowned auditorium. Revival broke out in 1994, and tens of thousands around the world came to be transformed in protracted meetings for several years.

But what I perhaps love the most is Ché's courage and leadership in refusing to bow to the arrogant overreach of Governor Gavin Newsom in the days of COVID. While churches shut down, Ché, like Mordecai of old, refused to bow down to the governor's and the city's threats of imprisonment and destructive fines. In the end, the U.S. Supreme Court backed Pastor Ché, and Gavin Newsom had to pay all the court and legal fees in the $1.35 million settlement. Ever since, I've seen a fire and faith burning in Ché's soul declaring, "If God be for us, who can be against us?" (Rom. 8:31 KJV).

God commands us to subdue the earth and bring it into submission (Gen. 1:28). In this book, with 12 governmental visionary and practical lenses, I see Daniel's stone being slung from David's sling, the stone hewn without human hands striking and crumbling the mountain of man's rebel kingdoms, and that stone becoming an exceedingly great mountain that fills the earth (Dan. 2:34–35). That striking stone is not reserved only for the time of the eschaton. The strike of reformation is now. Dear Apostle Ché, thank you for throwing forth this rock of reformation revelation, for on this rock Christ will build His *Ekklesia*, and the gates of hell will not prevail against it (Matt. 16:18).

Foreword By

DUTCH SHEETS

It has always been God's plan that we humans be His change agents on earth. Initially, the change was always from good to better. "Bad" didn't exist. In the beginning, the great Creator released His creative genius for six days, ending each day by stating that the finished product was "good." And the good that He made had some amazing surprises hidden in it.

God concealed in earth's creation the potential for humans to release additional creativity. In the planet's unseen elements, along with its laws of mathematics, physics, and science, were hidden airplanes, skyscrapers, phones, clothing, computers, fire, and a million more discoveries. The Creator had obviously determined that He would create creators! (I know, but sometimes redundancy just seems to make the point more powerfully!)

Of course, we humans don't actually create objects from nothing. Only God can create matter. We *transform* creation through the implementation of His scientific laws. Dictionary.com says *transform* means "to change in form, appearance, or structure—*metamorphose*; to change in condition, nature, or character—*convert*; to change into another substance—*transmute.*"

I often chuckle when imagining some of the conversations God and his new student may have had. "Adam, one day you'll *metamorphose* aluminum into a tube, *convert* earth's resources into rubber, bolts, screws, fabric, and instrumentation, and *transmute* it all into an airplane."

"And what will I do with this 'airplane?'" Adam would likely have asked through a blank stare. The conversations they must have had! No question about it—God created humans to be transformers. "Develop the planet" was His plan for us.

God's original intent was also for Adam and his offspring to reveal His image and likeness, and they were assigned the responsibility of governing the entire planet. Through them, God intended to establish an outpost of His heavenly kingdom here on earth. For Adam, "heaven on earth" was not just a wishful idiom; it was a reality.

Then hell came to earth.

When Adam sinned, the transformation and development of earth went in reverse. The world was plunged into chaos. Our bodies began to age and decay, some of earth's beautiful plants morphed into thornbushes, animals began to fight, and food spoiled. Worst of all, the now sinful nature of the human race made us capable of horrible actions. Genesis 6:5 (KJV) tells us, "And God saw that the wickedness of man was great in the earth, and that every imagination of the thoughts of his heart was only evil continually." The Creator had to send the great flood to stop the decline.

God's change agents now needed to be changed; His transformers needed transforming. So, to the shock of all but Himself, God transformed His Son into one of them and restored humankind back into His image: "But we all, with unveiled faces, looking as in a mirror at the glory of the Lord, are being transformed into the same image from glory to glory, just as from the Lord, the Spirit" (2 Cor. 3:18).

Then the great Creator re-commissioned us:

> *"Go ye therefore, and teach all nations, baptizing them in the name of the Father, and of the Son, and of the Holy Ghost: Teaching them to observe all things whatsoever I have commanded you: and, lo, I am with you always, even unto the end of the world"* (Matt. 28:19–20 KJV).

God's kids, His redeemed family on earth, would begin global transformation, once again qualified to expand His kingdom throughout the world. *"On earth, as it is heaven"* could now continue (Matt. 6:10).

Blueprints for Transformation: Bringing Revival and Reformation to the Nations is more than just a title. It is a prophetic declaration, an announcement that God's plan has been restored *and* is now going to a new level. Transformation will not be limited only to a congregation or community but will now become global!

Not many people could have written this masterpiece; great revelation was needed. Ché makes it clear that he had to personally experience the Holy Spirit's transformation in 12 areas of his thinking before he could fully understand and participate at a global level. The 12 paradigm shifts he reveals are critical for us, as well. Ché lays out the biblical truths beautifully and strategically, causing them to become even more clear through his personal testimonies.

The greatest expansion of God's kingdom on earth has begun. *Blueprints for Transformation* is one of its textbooks! Without a doubt, this is one of the most important books of our time.

Introduction:

A DIVINE BLUEPRINT

You were born to be a revivalist and reformer. Out of all the epochs in human history, you are alive today—in this specific time and season—for a purpose that only you can fulfill. God planned your life with a divine blueprint in mind: *to transform your world.*

"How on earth am I supposed to transform the world?" you may be wondering. The answer is simple. If you are a born-again follower of Jesus Christ, *He* is the answer to all the world's deepest and darkest problems. His Spirit now lives inside you, and you carry Him with you wherever you go. You are His ambassador, His change agent. *Christ in you* is the "hope of glory" (Col. 1:27) that creation itself is yearning "in eager expectation" to see revealed (Rom. 8:19).

Whether you realize it or not, you are the key to seeing the Great Commission fulfilled. Shortly before His ascension into heaven, Christ gave His disciples this mandate:

> All authority has been given to Me in heaven and on earth. Go therefore and make disciples of all the nations, baptizing them in the name of the Father and the Son and the Holy Spirit, teaching

them to observe all that I commanded you; and lo,
I am with you always, even to the end of the age.
(Matt. 28:18–20 NASB1995)

In His sovereignty and infinite wisdom, God has chosen us to be the sons and daughters who will carry out His commission, but He has not left us to fulfill it on our own. He has given each of us the power (Acts 1:8) and the authority (Luke 10:19) to do our part in transforming the world. That's why it can be called the Great *Co-mission*.

I have ministered in 94 countries over the last 45-plus years, and everywhere I travel, my desire is to see the Body of Christ fall more deeply in love with Jesus. A passive and powerless church is not going to fulfill the Great Commission effectively. Nominal Christians are not going to bring historic revival and reformation to society.

God is looking for passionate, sold-out Jesus followers— His laid-down lovers—whose lives have been changed from the inside out. The Father is seeking sons and daughters whose testimonies of transformation will spark that same transformation in the lives of countless others.

The beautiful thing about transformation is that it is transferable. When we are filled with the Holy Spirit's life-changing power, we become super-spreaders of supernatural transformation. And as we will see in this book, *transformed lives lead to the transformation of society.*

MY STORY OF REDEMPTION

On May 25, 2023, I celebrated 50 years as a follower of Jesus Christ. When the Lord saved me in 1973, I was a long-haired,

17-year-old drug dealer and addict living in open rebellion to God. Much to my Korean parents' shame, I had dropped out of high school, and despite being the son of a Southern Baptist pastor, I had no qualms about sleeping with the girls I dated. I was drifting through life with no hope and no sense of purpose, and no doubt I'd be dead if the Lord had not saved me in His mercy.

To give you an idea of how radically God has transformed my life since that day in 1973, Sue and I just celebrated our 45th wedding anniversary! Our four children—Gabe, Grace, Joy, and Mary—all love the Lord, and we have the ten cutest grandkids in the world! Together, Sue and I are the senior leaders of Harvest Rock Church, Pasadena, which began as a prayer meeting in our home in April 1994. I also have the privilege of serving as International Chancellor of Wagner University and President of Harvest International Ministry (HIM), a global network with a Christ-honoring presence in over 70 countries.

Though I was a high school dropout whose mind was severely damaged through drug usage, thanks to God's restoration, I was able to obtain two graduate degrees, including a Doctor of Ministry, from Fuller Theological Seminary. While I feel blessed to have studied under professors and mentors of the caliber of Dr. C. Peter Wagner, I believe my academic progress really came from the discipline of memorizing Scripture, which I learned to do early in my walk with Christ. And although my teenage vocabulary was limited to a three-letter word I could say backward—"*wow*"—this is my 16th book!

I share all this not to boast but to glorify God and give you hope. If He could redeem my life to such an extent, He can do it for anyone! Because of His amazing grace and mighty power, this transformation is available to anyone who believes, from individuals to families to communities to nations.

TRANSFORMATION: A CHANGED HEART AND A CHANGED MIND

When Jesus appeared on the scene in public ministry, the first words out of His mouth were, "Repent, for the kingdom of heaven is at hand" (Matt. 3:2). The Greek word for repent, *metanoeo*, means to have "a change of heart" (TDNT)[1] and "a change of mind" (DNTT)[2]. Today, we would call this having a paradigm shift.

These two shifts—a changed heart and a changed mind—are essential to reforming individuals and societies. It takes a changed heart to truly love God and our neighbor as ourselves, which Jesus said are the two greatest commandments (see Matt. 22:37–40). And it takes a transformed mind to transform society. As Romans 12:2 famously says, we are transformed by the renewing of the mind.

Another thing we need to transform society is a biblically accurate worldview. A worldview is our perceived reality, and everyone has one. As Charles Kraft writes in *Christianity and Culture*:

Worldview is the major influence on how we perceive REALITY. In terms of its worldview

---

[1] Gerhard Kittel and Gerhard Friedrich, *Theological Dictionary of the New Testament*, Vol. IV. Eerdmans, 1967, p.626.
[2] Colin Brown, *Dictionary of New Testament Theology*. Zondervan, 1986, p.357.

assumptions, values, and commitments, a society structures such things as what its people are to believe, how they are to picture reality, and how and what they are to analyze. People interpret and react on this basis reflexively without thinking.[3]

To obtain a biblical worldview, we need "the whole counsel of God" (Acts 20:27 NKJV). If we cherry-pick what we like or find easy in the Bible, our worldview will never fully align with God's.

I have written this book to equip you to do your part in transforming the world. I will share some of the life-changing paradigm shifts in the areas of a transformed heart, mind, and worldview. I trust they will serve as blueprints for you, no matter your history, current situation, or what God has called you to do.

Specifically, we will look at 12 aspects of personal and social transformation. In each chapter, I back up the Scriptures with real-life testimonies of how God is supernaturally involved with us as we "seek first His kingdom and His righteousness" (Matt. 6:33).

One of the Bible's final chapters tells us that "the *testimony* of Jesus is the spirit of *prophecy*" (Rev. 19:10). We should never apologize for sharing the testimonies that God has given to us, for a testimony, by its nature, brings encouragement to those who hear it. Similarly, prophecy is a spiritual gift intended to build up, exhort, and strengthen fellow believers

---

[3] Charles H. Kraft. *Christianity and Culture*. Maryknoll, NY: Orbis Books, 1979, p.20. Capitals in original.

(1 Cor. 14:3). Any testimonies we have are only by God's grace and goodness, and we should give Him all the glory and honor.

I pray that my personal testimonies will encourage you and embolden your faith. Again, if God could do it for me, He can do the same for you—wherever you may be, in any city or nation around the world!

Let's begin our journey together with this prayer:

"Heavenly Father, thank You that I was born for such a time as this. I believe You have called me to be a revivalist and a reformer. Transform me from the inside out. Make me more like Jesus so that I think like Jesus, act like Jesus, and do the works of Jesus. Fill me with Your Holy Spirit. Empower me and prophetically lead me to transform my world for Your glory, in Jesus' mighty name!"

Chapter 1:

FROM REVIVAL TO REFORMATION

Righteousness and justice are the foundation of Your
throne; mercy and truth go before Your face
(Ps. 89:14 NKJV).

"Your kingdom come. Your will be done,
on earth as it is in heaven" (Matt. 6:10).

In the wee hours of a Sunday morning in May 1995, my wife unlocked the doors of the dark and empty Mott Auditorium, little realizing what she was about to behold. With Sue were our young daughters, Grace, Joy, and Mary, and their friend Christine. As the doors swung open, the five of them gasped in unison as they immediately beheld an unparalleled vision of the manifest glory of heaven. They stood transfixed, trying to take it all in.

Through the white mist filling the building, they saw thousands of translucent doves resting on the chairs and lining the rafters. Bright colors of heaven, previously unknown, flooded their eyes. The entire floor was covered in a carpet of luminous grass dressed with celestial flowers in brilliant hues that blazed like jewels. The refrain of magnificent music filled the room, and it thrilled them to realize it was the flowers singing. Hundreds of majestic angels of every size and ethnicity were visible throughout the vast auditorium, many towering 30 to 40 feet toward the ceiling.

Harvest Rock Church, which began in our home on April 4, 1994, was only a year old at the time. We had earnestly sought a visitation from the Lord during that first year and took a major step of faith to rent Mott Auditorium in north Pasadena for our services. At $35,000 a month, the rent was a huge stretch, but we were willing to pay the price for revival. We had been holding special meetings at Mott almost nightly for over a month, and our congregation was experiencing wonderful encounters with the Holy Spirit.

Earlier on this particular Saturday night, after everyone in the house had been tucked into bed and my wife was drifting off, I was having no success getting to sleep. Joy and her friend Christine were camped out in the living room, which happened to be right next to our bedroom, and we could hear their laughter continuing on for quite some time. After tossing and turning a while longer, I finally asked Sue if she would help the girls quiet down. She sleepily complied and rolled out of bed.

As she entered the living room, Sue realized that both girls had been overcome with holy laughter. Shaking under the power of the Holy Spirit, Christine cried out to Sue, "Mott, Mott, we've got to go to Mott!" Joy immediately chimed in, "Yes, Mother, we've got to go to Mott!"

It was nearly one in the morning, yet Sue sensed strongly that God was moving on the children, so she decided to take them to Mott Auditorium. She loaded the two girls, along with Grace and Mary, into the family van and drove over to the large, old building.

As they stood amazed by the glorious sights surrounding them, one of the girls exclaimed, "We have to get Pastor Lou!" Lou Engle, one of our pastors at Harvest Rock, lived just across the street from Mott. He and his wife, Therese, had chosen that location so Lou could walk to the early morning prayer meetings that he led daily.

Quickly turning around and crossing the street, Sue and the girls roused Lou with a knock at the door and urged him to come and behold the glory-filled scene. He rushed back with them, and upon entering the auditorium, he felt a heaviness in the air but couldn't see anything. Sue and the girls, however, continued to behold the vision that had surprised them earlier.

Because the children were describing such spectacular things, including giant angels, Lou decided to separate Joy and Christine and interview each girl alone. He had a microcassette tape recorder on hand so he could verify each detail they shared without one girl hearing the other. After his detailed questioning, Lou was astounded that both Joy and Christine continued to describe the incredible sights and sounds in the same way. He was convinced the teenagers were witnessing a bona fide visitation of the glory of God.

Another unexpected part of this encounter was that the girls had a vision of the football legend Vince Lombardi as they began to prophesy, "Mott's too small. Stadiums will be

3

filled." The girls were utterly convinced we would have to move to a stadium. What they didn't know was that the first Super Bowl was held in the LA Coliseum in 1967, and Vince Lombardi was the coach of the Green Bay Packers, who won that first championship. None of us could have foreseen back in May 1995 that Lou and I would stand together in the LA Coliseum on April 9, 2016, as The Call "Azusa Now" prayer gathering took place in fulfillment of this prophetic word.

I learned of what had happened at Mott while on my way to the church a few hours later. When I stepped foot into the auditorium, I also felt an increased presence of God in the building, though I saw nothing. Yet the meeting that evening, which was conducted as usual, was clearly different. It marked the beginning of a period of angelic visitation and manifest glory in our services.

For the next six months, the girls—along with other children in the church—continued to see angels during our meetings. It was as if heaven had descended on us. Extraordinary healings took place. People smelled the fragrance of heaven, and gold dust even appeared in spontaneous manifestations of God's glory. I loved each and every testimony that we witnessed. Through these experiences, I reached this conclusion: *This is what God's glory is—heaven coming to earth!*

THE PRAYER OF REFORMATION: HEAVEN ON EARTH

After those supernatural encounters, I felt led by the Holy Spirit to study the biblical theme of heaven on earth. In that season, I discovered an extremely important truth that had been in the Disciple's Prayer (commonly called "the Lord's Prayer") all along.

In Matthew 6:10, Jesus instructs His disciples to decree these words in prayer: "Your kingdom come. Your will be done, *on earth as it is in heaven.*" This is a revival prayer! For the past 2,000 years, the church has been praying for the kingdom of heaven—the rule and reign of God—to be established and manifested on earth. In essence, we have been praying for Revival with a capital "R." But this is also a prayer for reformation. It's not only for us individually or for our families; it's a prayer for our nations.

Cindy Jacobs offers an insightful comment on this passage in her book *The Reformation Manifesto*:

> After studying Matthew 6:9-13, I realized that this was an intercessory prayer for the one who is called not only to make disciples of individuals but of nations ... If part of this prayer is for the here and now, that we work to see God be the Lord not only for our family affairs but our cities and nations— then the rest of the prayer must be understood in the same vein. It is not only for the individuals; it is also a prayer of intercession for the nations.[4]

The more I delved into the reality of seeing heaven on earth, the verse that really gripped me was Psalm 89:14 (NKJV), where the psalmist declares, "Righteousness and

---

[4] Cindy Jacobs, *The Reformation Manifesto: Your Part in God's Plan to Change Nations Today.* Bethany House, 2009, p.66.

justice *are* the foundation of Your throne; mercy and truth go before Your face." This verse will act as a primer for the sections below and the recurring themes throughout this book.

In praying the Disciple's Prayer and meditating on Psalm 89:14, I learned that we are actually praying for *God's* righteousness, *God's* justice, *God's* love, and *God's* truth to invade our lives and permeate society. Heaven on earth is asking God to invade the earth. Yes, with supernatural salvations, healings, and deliverance—the revival component of His kingdom—but also with His attributes of righteousness, justice, love, and truth, which bring reformation to earth as it is in heaven. For *that* is what heaven looks like.

REVIVAL AND REFORMATION: A THIRD GREAT AWAKENING

Since the events of 2020, I have been sharing that we are living in an extraordinary time of global shaking and greater glory. From the onset of the COVID-19 lockdowns to skyrocketing inflation, the extreme progressive Left agenda, and escalating global conflicts everywhere we look, all the nations of the globe have gone through an unprecedented time of shaking. This ancient biblical prophecy is being fulfilled right before our eyes:

> 'I will shake all the nations; and they will come with the wealth of all nations, and I will fill this house with glory,' says the Lord of hosts. 'The silver is Mine and the gold is Mine,' declares the Lord of hosts. 'The latter glory of this house will be greater

than the former,' says the Lord of hosts, 'and in this place I will give peace,' declares the Lord of hosts. (Hag. 2:7–9 NASB1995)

In my previous book, *Turning Our Nation Back to God Through Historic Revival*, I share how God is using the darkness we are witnessing today as a backdrop for the great light of revival and reformation to break out. In my 50-plus years of walking with Jesus, I have never seen such a stark contrast between the darkness covering the nations and the greater glory of God being revealed, as Isaiah had prophesied centuries ago.

Arise, shine; for your light has come, and the glory of the LORD has risen upon you. For behold, darkness will cover the earth and deep darkness the peoples; but the LORD will rise upon you and His glory will appear upon you. Nations will come to your light, and kings to the brightness of your rising. (Isa. 60:1–3 NASB1995)

I believe with all my heart that we are entering into a Third Great Awakening, which will encompass both the darkness getting darker and the light getting brighter. I define a Great Awakening as a national revival and reformation of society. In this case, the revival and reformation will spread throughout the world to other nations.

It is interesting to note the First Great Awakening of 1738 and the Second Great Awakening of 1801 were set against the dark backdrop of two of the most significant wars in

America: the Revolutionary War (1775–1783) and the Civil War (1861–1865). I am not prophesying another global conflict like WWII (1939–1945), but the truth is that signs of war are everywhere. As I write this, Russia and Ukraine are at war, and Israel is at war with Hamas, Hezbollah, and Iran. And civil war is threatening to tear apart countries like the UK and Ireland. Nevertheless, one reason I am so optimistic about the move of God is that a global revival is underway *right now!*

I recently had the privilege of speaking at two campuses of Gereja Bethel Indonesia (GBI). Under the able leadership of Senior Pastor Niko Njotorahardjo, GBI has 1,200 campuses and a combined membership of 300,000. While numbers alone don't signify revival, this is a body of Spirit-filled, on-fire believers who are making a difference in their society.

Indonesia is now 35 percent born-again believers.[5] To put that in context, despite being the world's largest Muslim nation, Indonesia has some of the world's largest churches! The move of the Holy Spirit is truly turning the tide in this island nation. Other places experiencing genuine revival range from Brazil and Latin America to Nigeria, India, China, and the underground church throughout the Middle East. My friends Rolland and Heidi Baker are transforming Mozambique, another Muslim nation, through Iris Ministries.

---

[5] See: David Barrett. *World Christian Encyclopedia*. Oxford University Press, 2001; Ché Ahn. *Turning Our Nation Back to God Through Historic Revival*. Wagner Publication, 2022, p.175–176.

The World Christian Database (WCD), one of the most authoritative sources on religious statistics, offers invaluable reference materials on all parts of the world. Its figures on China are particularly startling. According to the WCD, the country's Christian population exploded from under 1 million in 1970 to around 120 million today. That's over 9 percent of the country's entire population, which is expected to grow to 220 million by 2050.[6]

If these numbers are even close to accurate, it would make the story of Chinese Christianity probably the greatest harvest in church history—and that is just one nation. Tens of thousands of souls are being born again every day, primarily in the Global South. From a macro-global perspective, I believe that we are near the end of the last days, *and God is on the move like never before!*

Along with the harvest of souls, the Third Great Awakening is bringing about righteousness and justice in different areas of society. We are already seeing nations being transformed economically, a sure sign of reformation. Be sure to read the essay "How the Protestant Reformation Broke the Spirit of Poverty" later in this book for more on this topic.

FOUNDATIONS OF THE KINGDOM

If we want to see revival and reformation, we must focus on bringing the kingdom of heaven to earth. The way we bring about reformation is by bringing God's righteousness (*tzedeq*), justice (*mishpat*), lovingkindness or mercy (*chesed*), and truth

---

[6] Philip Jenkins, "Who's counting China?" *The Christian Century.* August 10, 2010. https://www.christiancentury.org/article/2010-08/who-s-counting-china

(*emeth*) to the nations. These four words in Psalm 89:14—the values of righteousness, justice, truth, and mercy—are repeated over and over again. The word *righteousness*, including its respective Hebrew and Greek words and their derivatives, appears 277 times in the Bible. The word *justice* is used 135 times. The word *chesed* appears 197 times, and its Greek equivalent, *agape*, appears 112 times. *Truth* is mentioned 235 times in the Bible.

The throne is a symbol of kingship, and it represents the rule and reign of God. Throughout Scripture, the phrases "kingdom of heaven" and "kingdom of God" are used interchangeably. Thus, understanding righteousness and justice is foundational to knowing what heaven and God's kingdom are like. And God's nature and character include all four: God is absolutely righteous, just, merciful, and truthful.

We need to realize the greater implications of Matthew 6:10 when we pray these words: "Your kingdom come; Your will be done, on earth as it is in heaven." Jesus taught us to pray for His kingdom to come on earth, and His kingdom embodies righteousness and justice. Therefore, God wants righteousness and justice to be on earth as it is in heaven. Heaven's throne is built on God and these principles, and so should our society. To me, that's what a Great Awakening looks like.

As we see from verses like Psalm 33:5, God absolutely loves righteousness and justice. "To do righteousness and justice is more acceptable to the LORD than sacrifice" (Prov. 21:3 NKJV), and this is what the prophet Amos wrote concerning God's desire for society: "Hate evil, love good, and establish *justice* in the gate … But let *justice* roll down like waters and *righteousness* like an ever-flowing stream" (Amos 5:15, 24 NASB1995).

In the famous passage that opens Genesis 12, God calls Abraham to leave his father's house and his country, saying, "I will make you into a great nation ... And in you all the families of the earth will be blessed" (vv. 2–3). God handpicked Abraham to be the father of a nation that was intended to model righteousness and justice to the other nations, and He paid him this tremendous compliment:

> For I have known him, in order that he may command his children and his household after him, that they keep the way of the LORD, to do righteousness and justice, that the LORD may bring to Abraham what He has spoken to him. (Gen. 18:19 NKJV)

No wonder he became known as "the friend of God" (James 2:23)! The Lord even refers to him as "My friend" (Is. 41:8).

Notice how the Lord revealed Himself to Abraham as the God of righteousness (Dan. 9:14) and the God of justice (Deut. 32:4) and instructed him to teach righteousness and justice to his household. These are the ways of God. Even though Abraham did not have the Bible to teach him these truths, he had a *relationship* with the God of the Bible, and he received a *revelation* of Him. This is how he was able to lead others to do what is just and right and how he became a great nation, a prototype for other nations. And as Proverbs 14:34 famously says, "Righteousness exalts a nation."

Conversely, as the rest of this verse warns, a nation is disgraced and brought down if righteousness and justice are not permeating its society.

A conservative Jewish writer and speaker named Dennis Prager, who has dedicated his life to producing a commentary on the Torah (the first five books of the Bible) from the original Hebrew, says:

> God Himself explains here what exactly 'the way of the Lord' is: doing what is right and just. For the first time, the Torah explicitly states God's purpose for Abraham and his descendants: to do what is just and right and, implicitly, to teach it to the world.[7]

RIGHTEOUSNESS

Our key verse, Psalm 89:14, opens with a reference to God's righteousness: *"Righteousness* and justice are the foundation of Your throne."

Righteousness is foundational to God's kingdom because God is righteous. He is holy, and there is no sin in Him. Righteousness can be defined as obedience to God's will. It means doing what is right. While God does require righteousness from us, according to 2 Corinthians 5:21 and Romans 14:17, He also gives us His righteousness as a gift!

Jesus, the only one who ever walked in perfect obedience to God the Father, is Himself our righteousness (1 Cor. 1:30). Now seated at the right hand of the Father, He is the source of all righteousness. And as He told His disciples, "I am the

---

[7] Dennis Prager, The Rational Bible: Genesis. Regnery Faith, 2019, p.215.

vine, you are the branches ... apart from Me you can do nothing" (John 15:5).

A well-rounded view of righteousness is both positional and practical. Positionally, the moment you are born again, you are in right standing with God. Practically, God now gives you the grace to put His truth into practice and do what is right. Thus, we can grasp more clearly these words of the Apostle Paul:

> So then, my beloved, just as you have always obeyed, not as in my presence only, but now much more in my absence, work out your salvation with fear and trembling; for it is God who is at work in you, both to will and to work for His good pleasure. (Phil. 2:12–13 NASB1995)

The key to walking in righteousness is reliance on the Holy Spirit. He is at work in us and wants to see us practice righteousness even more than we do. In John 16:8, Jesus says the Holy Spirit would do three things: (1) Convict the world of *sin*, that is to bring us to salvation; (2) Convict the world of *righteousness*, that is to bring us into personal revival; and (3) Convict the world of *judgment*, that is to bring about the reformation of society.

We need a revival of righteousness to be restored to the church and society. When he had an encounter with God and was called to end the slave trade in his nation, the English reformer William Wilberforce (1759–1833) was also called to bring about a revival of righteousness. He termed it a restoration of "manners" or morals: "God Almighty has set before me two great objects, the suppression of the slave trade and the reformation of manners [morality or righteousness]."[8]

Christian reformers like Wilberforce show us that *to bring heaven down to earth is to bring God's righteousness to earth as it is in heaven* (Matt. 6:10).

THREE CHARACTERISTICS OF HISTORIC REVIVAL

Before we look more closely at reformation, we have to be on the same page when it comes to understanding historic revival. Today, God wants His people to experience a fresh outpouring of His Spirit. He wants us to be spiritually refreshed and revived so we can steward the harvest of souls and transformation of society that will follow.

> Repent therefore and be converted, that your sins may be blotted out, so that times of refreshing may come from the presence of the Lord, and that He may send Jesus Christ, who was preached to you before, whom heaven must receive until the times of restoration of all things, which God has spoken by the mouth of all His holy prophets since the world began. (Acts 3:19–21 NKJV)

In Acts 3:19, the Greek word for "refreshing" (*anapsuxis*) literally means a cooling or recovery of breath, and it is used

---

[8] https://christianhistoryinstitute.org/uploaded/50b649ccc5e960.06979983.pdf

here to refer to revival.[9] Thus, we must recognize in context that repentance is an indispensable condition for revival (see Acts 2:38; Joel 2:12, 28). With this in mind, let's look at the three core characteristics of historic revival based on Scripture and church history.

1. The church is revived.

The first characteristic of historic revival is that the church is revived by the Spirit of God. Throughout church history, every revival began when an individual or a group of people experienced a fresh consecration to the Lord, were filled with the power of the Holy Spirit, and the church became holy and righteous. During the outpouring of revival, the church also received a massive revelation of God the Father's love.

One of the most powerful revivals, historically known as the First Great Awakening, began on May 24, 1738. John Wesley wrote in his journal:

> Mr. Hall, Hinching, Ingham, [George] White-field, Hutching, and my brother Charles were present at our love feast in Fetter Lane with about 60 of our brethren. About three in the morning as we were continuing instant in prayer, the power of God came mightily upon us, insomuch that many cried out for exulting joy and many *fell to the ground.* As soon as we were recovered a

---

[9] Blue Letter Bible, "Lexicon: Strong's G403 - *anapsyxis*," accessed July 23, 2024, https://www.blueletterbible.org/lexicon/g403/nasb20/tr/0-1/

little from the awe and amazement at the presence of his Majesty, we broke out with one voice,
'We praise thee O God, we acknowledge thee to
be Lord.'[10]

When revival hit Toronto on January 20, 1994, the
revival was characterized by the power of God falling
mightily upon people, as many fell over and were on the
floor for a significant time, even hours. By the time I got
there with Lou Engle in October 1994, I had come into the
Regal Constellation Hotel Ball Room walking, and I had
left crawling, unable to get up. But I felt I was "born again"
again. I was personally revived as I experienced the Father's
love and fell more in love with Jesus. Revival always begins
with the church.

Toronto wasn't just experiencing the power and joy
of the Holy Spirit. There was deep repentance that took
place. In my first book, *Into the Fire*,[11] I write about my
repentance and forgiveness toward my dad and other
leaders that I carried an offense against in the previous movement, and I share about my deep repentance
of hurting my wife by shutting her off from my emotions
and depression during the 80s. I am firmly convinced that
repentance must begin with the house of God, with God's
people. 1 Peter 4:17 says, "For it is time for judgment to
begin with the household of God; and if it begins with
us first, what will be the outcome for those who do not

---

[10] John Wesley, *The Works of John Wesley* (Peabody, MA: Hendrickson Publishers, 1984), vol.1, p.170 (emphasis added).
[11] Regal, 1998.

obey the gospel of God?" Everything rises and falls with the church. A classic example of this is the Pyongyang Revival of 1907, which was sparked when church leaders entered an intensive season of fasting, prayer, and public repentance. The Pyongyang Revival was called the "repentance revival." All *genuine* revivals bring a restoration of righteousness and holiness.

In 2 Chronicles 7:14 (NKJV), the Lord promises, "If My people who are called by My name will humble themselves, and pray and seek My face, and turn from their wicked ways, then I will hear from heaven, and will forgive their sin and heal their land." Notice that God says, "If *My* people humble themselves and pray..." He doesn't call out the lost in the world. He doesn't name a political party or corrupt government officials. He says it starts with His people. God says revival begins with *you and me.*

2: Souls get saved.

When the church is revived and has tasted God's glory, the next phase in any true revival is when the harvest comes in. It is necessary for us as Christians to be revived in our spiritual walk with the Lord, but we must also get our nets ready to bring in a great harvest of souls. To see our nation return to God through historic revival, we must contend not just for God's people but for the lost.

This same pattern is displayed from the birth of the church. On the day of Pentecost, when the Spirit was poured out, Peter stood up to preach to the crowds, and 3,000 people were saved in one day (Acts 2:41). Among those who were baptized on Pentecost were Jews representing 15 or more language groups and up to 70 nations in the Jewish dias-pora.[12] Revival started in Jerusalem, but God intended it to spread to the ends of the earth.

The Welsh Revival of 1904 is an example of how the harvest comes in tremendously during true historic revival. As the church in Wales was starting to be revived by the Holy Spirit, 20,000 people were saved in just five weeks. Within the first six months of the revival, 100,000 came to Christ out of Wales' overall population of around 2 million. The press was covering the revival in such detail that many people became followers of Jesus simply after reading about the move of God in their daily newspapers![13]

3. Society is transformed.

In any historic revival, first, the church is revived, and second, a harvest of souls comes in. The third necessary component of historic revival is that society is transformed, and a major way is through biblical justice being restored. When the transformation of a nation takes place, we know that revival has truly come. This took place in the First Great Awakening when slavery, arguably the number-one injustice of that time, was abolished in all the British Commonwealth nations. In the Second Great Awakening, we see this justice displayed when slavery came to an end in America as a result

---

[12] C. Peter Wagner, *The Book of Acts: A Commentary* (Minneapolis, MN: Chosen Books, 2017), 64-65.

[13] G. Campbell Morgan, "The Revival: Its Power and Source," in *The Welsh Revival: A Narrative of Facts* by W.T. Stead (Boston: The Pilgrim Press, 1905), 83.

of this move of God with Charles Finney, Jeremiah Lanphier, and others.

The sad truth is that during the Jesus People movement going into the Toronto Blessing and her aftermath, we didn't see much reformation in society. I remember celebrating the tenth anniversary of the Toronto Blessing in 2004 when Sue and I went out to a late dinner with John and Carol Arnott after one of the evening services. The only restaurant that was open was at a bar. During the meal, John said something very significant and humbling: "We impacted millions of people from around the world, but we didn't transform a bit of Toronto."

Unfortunately, we had no teaching or revelation for reforming society during the Jesus People movement and very little during the Toronto Blessing. In fact, some of the worst Supreme Court decisions took place during that same time frame. *Roe v. Wade* was passed in 1973, legalizing abortion. Then, in 2015, the *Obergefell v. Hodges* decision legalized same-sex marriage after the Toronto Blessing and Brownsville Revival came to an end. That is part of the reason I am writing this book. I believe that we will see another wave of souls being saved—even greater than the Jesus People movement and the Toronto and Brownsville revivals—but it has to be unto the transformation of society!

Jesus said, "[I have] come to seek and to save that which was lost" (Luke 19:10). I believe He was referring to "that which was lost" in the garden—perfect union and fellowship with God and heaven or paradise on earth. Jesus came to destroy the works of the devil and to restore all that was lost in the garden (1 John 3:8).

REFORMATION

Reformation—the third component of historic revival—plays a key role in God's kingdom coming to earth. It's what produces social transformation. I love this definition by Cindy Jacobs:

> I would define reformation as an amendment to repair what is corrupt, to build up institutions of our government and society according to their God-ordained order and organization. It means to institutionalize God's will in how we do our daily business, deal with the poor, administer justice, make our laws, teach our children, and generally live our lives.[14]

This definition calls all believers in Jesus to be reformers. We are called to make all wrongs around us right.

Reformation is to bring biblical values and justice to society and her institutions. By extension, reformers are those who make changes and improvements to social, political, or economic practices or constructs. If we are seeking heaven's culture for our day and age, we must partner with God's desire to reform society for His glory. Biblical justice in society is a significant sign of reformation taking place.

God's Pure Justice

Justice is the second key component of the kingdom dyad: "Righteousness and *justice* are the foundation of Your throne"

---

[14] Cindy Jacobs, *The Reformation Manifesto: Your Part in God's Plan to Change Nations Today*. Bethany House, 2009, p.18.

(Ps. 89:14a). As with righteousness, justice also reflects a crucial aspect of God's nature, and He is revealed to us a just Judge in the second chapter of the Bible:

> And the LORD God commanded the man, saying, 'Of every tree of the garden you may freely eat; but of the tree of the knowledge of good and evil you shall not eat, for in the day that you eat of it you shall surely die.' (Gen. 2:16–17 NKJV)

By laying down the law and punishing those who break it, God is acting in His capacity as Judge. Without understanding His justice, we cannot appreciate God's love and mercy or understand why Jesus had to take our place on the cross before God could extend mercy and forgiveness to us.

"There is much beautiful and uplifting talk about God's loving us and being loved by us," writes Dennis Prager. "But when Moses describes God, he first describes Him as a judge. This is a gift of the Torah to humanity: The Creator judges every nation and every individual."[15]

Most people who view God as a judge think that fact implies He is mean, but nothing could be further from the truth! God's justice brings safety and security to our world. As everyone will agree, the stricter the traffic laws, the safer it is to drive.

Jesus is not only just; He is our justice. The Old Testament teaches that God is pure justice, with no qualifier before the word. For example, "social justice" is not in the Bible. It's redundant even to add the adjective "biblical." Still, we have

---

[15] Dennis Prager, *The Rational Bible: Deuteronomy*. Regnery Faith, 2022, p.189.

so watered down the truth by including abortion, same-sex marriage, transgenderism, and LGBTQ+ issues as justice issues that it seems necessary to add such a qualifier at times. But the foundation of heaven's throne is no earthly issue. It's God's justice.

"Justice, and only justice, you shall follow," says Deuteronomy 16:20 (ESV), "that you may live and inherit the land that the LORD your God is giving you." Whenever the Bible repeats a word twice, it is making a very important emphasis. It is also rare in the Torah to repeat a noun, but here, the noun "justice" is literally used twice. The original verse reads: "Justice, justice, you shall follow." Why? Because God is *pure* justice.

As Matthew 12:18 (NASB1995) reminds us, He fulfilled this prophecy: "Behold, My Servant whom I have chosen; My Beloved in whom My soul is well-pleased; I will put My Spirit upon Him, and *He shall proclaim justice* to the Gentiles" (see Isa. 42:1). Thus, Jesus was filled with the Holy Spirit for the central task of proclaiming God's justice and truth to the nations.

In His opening message from Isaiah 60:1–2, Jesus declares,

> The Spirit of the LORD is upon Me, because He has anointed Me to preach the gospel to the poor; He has sent Me to heal the brokenhearted, to proclaim liberty to the captives and recovery of sight to the blind, to set at liberty those who are oppressed; to proclaim the acceptable year of the LORD. (Luke 4:18–19 NKJV)

In every respect, this message sums up revival and reformation.

For example, good news to the poor is that Jesus came to eradicate systemic poverty. "To proclaim the acceptable year of the Lord" is about a perpetual Jubilee, which again refers to economic favor and blessings. There is no poverty in heaven, hence the prayer for God's will to be done "on earth as it is in heaven."

The most basic understanding of justice has to do with biblical truth and just laws, and these laws come from God. In Matthew 23:23 (TPT), Jesus states:

> Great sorrow awaits you religious scholars and Pharisees—frauds and pretenders! For you are obsessed with peripheral issues, like insisting on paying meticulous tithes on the smallest herbs that grow in your gardens. These matters are fine, yet you ignore the most important duty of all: to walk in the love of God, to display mercy to others, and to live with integrity [or "truth"] ...

Here, Jesus is alluding to the Torah—the laws that God gave to His people through Moses—as revealed in Genesis, Exodus, Leviticus, Numbers, and Deuteronomy. These commandments are characterized by justice and truth. As Nehemiah 9:13 (NKJV) says, "You came down also on Mount Sinai, and spoke with them from heaven, and gave them *just* ordinances and *true* laws, good statutes and commandments."

Everything God has decreed is holy, just, and good (Rom. 7:12). The law by itself cannot save us—only Jesus can do that (Gal. 2:20–21; Eph. 2:4–10)—but you cannot have true reformation without justice and truth.

God cares so much about our society that He wants us to bring pure, biblical justice to our world. We must be activists for His kingdom, "for not the hearers of the law are just in the sight of God, but the doers of the law will be justified" (Rom. 2:13 NKJV). Those who walk in obedience to God's Word will be proponents of His justice and righteousness, not only in their individual lives but also in their spheres of influence.

Examples of Reformation Through Just Laws

The first example of godly reformation is the Act for the Abolition of the Slave Trade of 1807. This act was passed in British Parliament due to the determination of William Wilberforce and his apostolic network, the Clapham Group. Wilberforce and his colleagues fought for 11 years straight to mobilize enough support to pass legislation that would abolish slavery in England. The members of Wilberforce's network, also known as the Clapham Circle, were all ardent followers of Jesus and had strong convictions that society should reflect God's justice for those bound by the slave trade.

The catalyst behind the abolition movement in England was the First Great Awakening of 1738, led by revivalists like George Whitefield and John Wesley, who was an ardent abolitionist. It was not so much the case for Whitefield, but many who came to Christ in the Great Awakening became abolitionists, like John Newton and William Wilberforce. The momentum from that move of God merged with the breakout of the Second Great Awakening of 1801, which preceded the Slave Trade Abolition Act by six years. Three decades later, in 1833, slavery was finally made illegal in the entire British Empire upon the passing of the Slavery Abolition Act.

The second example resonates deeply with the first, as it is tied to America's road toward abolishing slavery. It was primarily the Evangelicals, including the great revivalist Charles Finney and the Methodist movement, who helped spearhead the abolition movement in the United States, denouncing the evils of slavery and advocating reform. Following the surge of the Second Great Awakening, the 1857 Prayer Revival was the primary revival that hit Northern America during this time, bringing in a massive harvest of souls into the kingdom. Most of these converts were abolitionists.

Not long afterward, the issue of slavery came to a head as the first shots of the Civil War were fired in the spring of 1861. After four excruciating years, the war ended with the surrender of the Confederate South on April 9, 1865. Though it came at a high price—over half a million lives lost in battle—the social transformation that took place after the Civil War turned a new page in American history. The way was paved for the passing of the 13th Amendment in December 1865, which fully abolished slavery in our nation. Within the next five years, the 14th and 15th Amendments to the Constitution were ratified to declare civil rights for every individual born in the United States—including former slaves—and to affirm voting rights for men of all races.

As for today, I believe the Third Great Awakening has begun—bringing both revival and reformation in its wake. One of the signs pointing to this epic season of transformation was *Dobbs v. Jackson Women's Health Organization*, the 6-3 landmark decision of the U.S. Supreme Court on June 24, 2022. In this ruling, the court held that the Constitution of the United States does not confer a right to abortion. This reversed the curse of *Roe v. Wade*, whereby 63 million innocent lives had been taken by the silent killer of abortion since 1973.[16] We cannot underestimate the importance of *Dobbs v. Jackson* in light of the lives that will be spared in the coming generations of Americans.

Dennis Prager, in his wonderful commentary on Deuteronomy, writes:

> In the Torah's view, civilization rests on justice. No justice, no civilization … And justice rests on truth. Therefore, the purpose of the courtroom is first to establish what is true. Did the defendant commit the crime of which he is accused? Compassion can never play a role in determining the truth. Truth is objective, and because justice is rooted in truth to the best of our ability, justice, too, must be objective. Only once truth is established and a just verdict rendered may a judge exercise compassion in assigning punishment. Prior to that point, justice (that is truth) must be sought.[17]

---

[16] "The State of Abortion in the United States." National Right to Life Committee. May 5, 2022. http://www.nrlc.org/uploads/communications/stateofabortion2022.pdf

[17] Dennis Prager, *The Rational Bible: Deuteronomy*. Regnery Faith, 2022, p.271-272.

He concludes, "Individuals can be guided by compassion in their personal dealings, but society must be guided by justice."[18]

HOW TO BRING ABOUT REVIVAL AND REFORMATION

We know that God desires us to bring heaven to earth through revival and reformation, but what does that involve? Our foundational verse, Psalm 89:14, gives us three key concepts in this regard: (1) It's about *God's face*; (2) It's about *mercy*; and (3) It's about *truth*.

1: The Face of God (His Presence)

In his book *Face to Face with God*, Bill Johnson says, "The quest for the face of God has two central dimensions—the quest for His presence and the quest for His favor."[19]

Heaven invades earth through the presence and working of the Holy Spirit. I believe the psalmist is speaking about the manifest presence of God, the Spirit of God, or the Holy Spirit. As I have always said at Harvest Rock Church, God's presence is not the icing on the cake—it *is* the cake! We prioritize both the Word of God and the presence of God in our church family, and He never ceases to amaze us as we continue to experience glimpses of heaven on earth.

"The kingdom of God is not eating and drinking, but righteousness and peace and joy in the Holy Spirit" (Rom. 14:17). The Holy Spirit is central to seeing the kingdom of

---

[18] Ibid.
[19] Bill Johnson, *Face to Face with God*. Charisma House, 2007, p.18.

God advance. We cannot do this in our own strength. "'Not by might nor by power, but by My Spirit,' says the LORD of hosts" (Zech. 4:6 NASB1995). We are not going to see revival and reformation without the presence and power of the Holy Spirit.

2: Mercy (Love)

The word *mercy* in Psalm 89:14 is the Hebrew term *chesed*, which some versions translate as "lovingkindness" or "steadfast love." It is best defined as God's mercy and compassion for people. It is really out of a heart of compassion and mercy that God the Father gave His only Son for the redemption of the world. As the Bible's most famous verse says, "For God so *loved* the world, that He *gave...*" (John 3:16).

Chesed encapsulates the kind of deep compassion that God wants us to walk in toward others. I believe that Jesus appropriated a rare Greek word, *agape*, to express what was communicated through *chesed* in the Old Testament, and thus, I use "love" interchangeably with mercy.

We must never forget that love is a verb, and verbs are action words! The Bible makes it abundantly clear that we must love in action and in truth.

> By this we know love, because He laid down His life for us. And we also ought to *lay down our lives for the brethren.* But whoever has this world's goods, and sees his brother in need, and shuts up his heart from him, how does the love of God abide in him? My little children, let us not love in word or in tongue, but *in deed and in truth.* (1 John 3:16–18 NKJV)

I define love as "the unselfish choice for the greatest good of the greatest number of people." This definition specifies "the greatest number of people" because we need to have a focus to enact true reformation. The world is rife with diverse needs, and we should be strategic about our efforts. To bring about tangible, positive change, we must ask ourselves, "What are the greatest injustices impacting the most people? What can we do to make a difference?" See Appendix A for further discussion on this topic.

3: Truth

Biblical truth is indispensable for reformation and revival. To be people of righteousness and justice, we require absolute truth. Righteousness and justice have to be based on the reality that God exists, that He is a moral God, and that He has given us His commandments and standards of righteousness and justice based on absolute truth. The truth is based on His commandments and His written Word, the Bible, the ultimate source of truth. As such, it is the bedrock of a successful society.

Revival happens when the truth of Jesus Christ penetrates the human heart. This, in turn, revives the church, which then draws in the lost. Likewise, there's a natural progression from truth to reformation, and this is what it looks like:

- Truth changes one's *values.*
- Values lead to a change in *culture.*
- Culture changes *institutions* like family, government, education, and media.

- A changed culture based on truth will lead to *justice* and just *laws.*

- Restored justice and truth in society will reform a *nation.*

- Transformed nations will lead to *global transformation!*

Changing Culture Begins Through the Restoration of Truth

In the landmark book *After the Ball*, two Harvard gay activists, Marshall Kirk and Hunter Madsen, laid the groundwork for how the world can use language to shape culture. Through writing a book like this in 1989, Kirk and Madsen delineated their goal of changing the vocabulary surrounding homosexuality.[20] Instead of calling these people "homosexuals," they deliberated to use the word *gay* because they wanted to give the impression that they were happy with their sexuality instead of being depressed, which was the perception of reality by the non-gay community.

Changing culture began for them by redefining words and using euphemisms in place of known truths. Instead of abortion, it is "women's reproductive rights." Instead of the gay and lesbian club at high schools, it is now the "Just Be You" club.

Death and life are in the power of the tongue, and those who love it will eat its fruit. (Prov. 18:21 ESV)

---

[20] Marshall Kirk and Hunter Madsen, *After the Ball: How America Will Conquer Its Fear and Hatred of Gays in the '90s* (New York: Doubleday, 1989), p.163, 189-190.

It is interesting to note that the first night of the 2024 Democratic National Convention in Chicago was taking place as I was writing this portion of the book, and practically all the Democrats speaking at the convention used a euphemism instead of abortion, for example, "reproductive freedom."[21] Jesus said that the sons of this age are wiser than the sons of the kingdom (see Luke 16:8). Reformation begins when we restore biblical truth in the public arena, for example, that abortion is the murder of an innocent baby. It may not be politically correct, but it is the truth. God hates the hands that shed innocent blood (Prov. 6:16).

I also believe that the restoration of truth in society begins with pastors preaching the truth in love from the pulpits. Something greatly lacking in America today is the proclamation of truth from church leaders—the very ones who should know the truth most intimately.[22] Every pastor and church should be preaching the whole counsel of God every week. We cannot shy away from speaking the truth in love, especially concerning pro-life, pro-family values that are close to the heart of God. I believe God has chosen the foolishness of preaching to transform the world. When truth and biblical values are embraced, they lead to a kingdom culture that influences all institutions. This includes promoting righteousness and justice, not just in the government but

---

[21] Ben Johnson. "The 6 Most Notable Moments from Day 1 of the DNC." *The Washington Stand.* August 20, 2024. https://washingtonstand.com/commentary/the-6-most-notable-moments-of-the-dnc-day-1

[22] I highly recommend reading *Reversed* by James Garlow, the best book on the market to equip pastors to knowledgeably preach on hot-topic issues in our culture. James holds six degrees, and yet he has a pastor's heart with years of experience in the pastorate.

in every mountain of culture. For example, these values are reflected when we eliminate sexual harassment, embezzlement, and foul language from the workplace, whether in business, education, or any other vocational setting.

A culture rooted in biblical truth ensures that the transformation of society can be upheld and maintained for the long run. This is what distinguishes a Great Awakening from mere revival. Revival impacts the church, but a Great Awakening includes reformation of society. True reformation will impact every facet of life, and I believe that is God's heart for this generation. We are praying for lasting societal transformation where godly, just laws prevail and cultural values align with biblical principles.

PUTTING IT ALL TOGETHER

This is a working list of characteristics of revival vs. reformation. These are not absolutes, but they reflect a *propensity* for each characteristic to fall primarily in one category or the other.

REVIVAL

1. Righteousness
2. Personal
3. Individual
4. Personal Values
5. Personal Sanctification
6. Christlike Character
7. Morals

REFORMATION

Biblical Justice
Corporate
Institutional
Cultural Values
Social Transformation
Just and Godly Laws
Social Virtues

8. Personal Prayer	Corporate, United Prayer
9. Priests	Kings
10. Saving Souls	Discipling Nations
11. Being Filled with the Spirit	Holy Spirit's Power
12. Personal Wisdom	Wise Leadership
13. Judgment Seat	Judgment Day
14. Gospel of Salvation	Gospel of the Kingdom
15. Mercy	Truth
16. Church Apostles	Marketplace Apostles
17. Personal Transformation	Global Transformation
18. Church	Kingdom
19. Sunday Preaching	Discipleship and Training
20. Gentiles Will Be Saved	All of Israel Will Be Saved

Let's pray together as we wrap up this chapter:

"Father God, You are the God of revival and reformation. Make me a catalyst for Your kingdom—to bring righteousness, justice, mercy, and truth in my sphere of influence. Lord, send revival to my nation, and empower Your Ekklesia to be stewards of revival unto the transformation of society. In Jesus' mighty name, amen!"

Chapter 2:

FROM NARCISSISM TO LOVING GOD AND OTHERS

Jesus said to him, "'You shall love the LORD your God with all your heart, with all your soul, and with all your mind.' This is the first and great commandment. And the second is like it: 'You shall love your neighbor as yourself.' On these two commandments hang all the Law and the Prophets" (Matt. 22:37–40 NKJV).

I still weep in gratitude for how Jesus delivered me from drug addiction in one day—on May 25, 1973, when I walked out of a Deep Purple concert at the Baltimore Civic Center. Just mentioning the rock band Deep Purple gives you an idea of what my life was like before Jesus saved me. I often joked that I may have been one of the first Korean hippies in the USA.

Honestly, my encounter with God began two weeks prior when, in frustration, my one-year dabbling in Zen Buddhism came to an end when I simply prayed, "God, I don't know if You exist. But if You do exist and what my parents told me is true—that there is a heaven and a hell, and Jesus is the way to heaven—then show me. I want to know the truth! And I don't want to go to hell!"

I didn't expect God to reveal Himself to me there. I had been going on a spiritual journey for the year prior, dropping LSD, meditating on my mantra, trying to find God, and I was at a dead end. *But God, being rich in mercy, because of His great love with which He loved me* (Eph. 2:4) opened up heaven and poured His liquid love over me. I began to sob profusely, and at the same time, by revelation, I *knew* it was Jesus releasing the Holy Spirit over me. Truly, the love of God was being poured into my life through the Holy Spirit (Rom. 5:5). Simultaneously, I was shocked that my Southern Baptist pastor dad and my godly mom had been right all this time. The answer was always Jesus, but I had never believed them nor accepted Him.

This tangible encounter of God's love stayed with me for three days. Off and on, the manifest presence of God came over me, and I would weep and sob. Jesus became incredibly real to me, but there was still a problem: I wasn't saved. I was still doing drugs daily. I was still sleeping with my girlfriend. I didn't repent of my sins. However, I *was* getting convicted of my sin. I knew without anyone telling me that I had to change, but I didn't have any concept of repentance until two weeks later at the Deep Purple concert.

My buddies and I had the best seats in the house. My best friend Jon Mazur, the son of an orthodox Jew, was also a hippie party animal and had bought us tickets for the concert. An Irish phenomenon guitarist named Rory Gallagher and his band performed before Deep Purple came on. During the intermission, my two other friends decided to see if they could pick up three "chicks" to party with after the concert. I stayed back so no one would come up and take our seats at the front of the auditorium. (Keep in mind, this was a heavy-metal concert and not a Michael W. Smith Christian concert.)

While sitting there, the presence of God came over me, just like it had two weeks before. I didn't cry, but I *did* come under conviction. I was not only a drug user, but according to the daughter of the Montgomery County Sheriff, I was the biggest drug dealer in our county. I was primarily selling pounds of marijuana and thousands of tablets of LSD per month, but I sold everything from cocaine and quaaludes to speed and large quantities of weed. You get the picture.

So, right there at the concert, under the conviction of the Lord, I started to make a deal with God. I said, "I will stop selling drugs, and I will stop taking the heavy drugs: speed, cocaine, etc. But God, is it OK just to smoke pot?" I didn't get an answer, but I came to my own conclusion that it was all right to smoke pot, even though it was illegal.

Then I made a deal with God concerning sex: "God, I won't pick up girls and sleep with them," which was my goal almost every weekend, "but I will only have sex with my girlfriend." Frankly, I felt smug with my newfound theology and the deal I made with God. Looking back, I thought I was saved and had already repented.

At that exact moment, two long-haired hippies came up and sat down in my friends' seats. I was ready to tell them, "These are taken," but before I got a word out of my mouth, the one who sat next to me said these shocking words: "You think you are right with God right now, but the truth is that you are still far from Him. You have to show Him that you are really serious in following Him." Just as quickly as they had appeared, the two got up and walked away, leaving the piercing words hanging in the air behind them.

To this day, I don't know if they were two angels or two believers giving me a prophetic word of knowledge, but I knew that he was telling me the truth. Immediately, I cried out to God, "OK, what do You want me to do?"

It was at that moment that I heard the inner voice of God for the first time. I heard Jesus say, "Throw away your drugs," (I had half a pound of marijuana in a large zip-lock baggie, several tablets of quaaludes, my favorite drug, and a water pipe I had snuck in under my army jacket) "and leave this concert." In a flash, the Lord showed me that the concert represented all the sin I was in bondage to and that it was evil.

Right after this conversation with Jesus transpired, my friends came back, and Deep Purple simultaneously appeared on stage. Strobe lights started flashing in all directions, and smoke came billowing out of the backdrop. Screaming fans rushed the front where we stood as the opening notes rang out to their number-one hit, "Smoke on the Water." I was instantly trapped by a wall of people. Again, I heard God distinctly say, "Leave this concert and come follow Me."

But it wasn't easy. I had to intentionally fight my way through a sea of crazed fans to make it out. Finally breaking through the crowd, I walked out of the Baltimore Civic Center into a crisp May night. I didn't want to wait for my friends to finish the concert, so I stuck out my thumb to hitchhike back home. The first car to stop was being driven by two gay men who thought they could party with me, but they were the first two people with whom I ever shared my testimony of what had just happened at the Civic Center. They ended up taking me to my door an hour away in Rockville, Maryland.

That was on May 25. That night, I was totally delivered from drug addiction by God's grace. And by His grace, I have not once gone back to smoking pot or anything else I used to do. You can't make this up! Glory to God!

I didn't know then that I was in a revival called the Jesus People Movement or Jesus Revolution. I soon found other "hippies" like me who were set free from major drug addiction, totally changed by the power of the Holy Spirit. In essence, we were transformed by a revelation of God's love.

THE REVELATION OF GOD'S *AGAPE* LOVE

In the quest for true reformation, the first thing we must consider is how we love. It was the greatest commandment, after all. Thus, the first shift that must happen in reformation is going from loving self, or selfishness, to loving God and loving others. True *agape* love, God's unconditional love, constitutes the foundation of all other virtues. Love is the unselfish choice of giving all of oneself to God. God's essence is love (1 John 4:8, 16). To love is to be self-giving, which is intrinsically Christlike.

During the Last Supper, Jesus said, "Greater love has no one than this, than to lay down one's life for his friends (John 15:13 NKJV). That is exactly what Jesus did for the world. He laid down His life out of love for all of humanity. Love is God manifest; love is God incarnate.

Love begins with God. First John 4:19 says, "We love because He first loved us." Notice how God is the One who initiates. It all begins with receiving His love. A revelation of the love of God the Father is essential to being inwardly transformed and leading a victorious life of faith. It provides the bedrock upon which your relationship with Jesus will grow and thrive.

Love is the heart of a rich, meaningful life. Practicing love draws us closer to the divine. There is a beautiful synergy of love revealed in Scripture. Jesus demonstrated His love for us that while we were sinners, He died for us (Rom. 5:8). When we give 100 percent of our lives in love to Jesus, He then turns around and pours His love into our hearts by the Holy Spirit (Rom. 5:5). By being a recipient of God's love, you will be empowered beyond your natural ability to love. In that place of overflow, you can love God and others freely.

THE GREAT COMMANDMENT: TO LOVE GOD

We began this chapter with Jesus' words from the Gospel of Matthew after He was asked, "What is the greatest commandment in the Law?" (Matt. 22:36). Jesus' reply contains the two most important things you can ever learn to do in this life: love God and love others.

> And He said to him, "'You shall love the Lord your God with all your heart, and with all your soul, and with all your mind.' This is the great

and foremost commandment. The second is like it, 'You shall love your neighbor as yourself.' On these two commandments depend the whole Law and the Prophets." (Matt. 22:37–40 NASB1995)

Loving God is called the "Great Commandment" for a reason. It is our highest and greatest calling. It is the reason God created us in the first place—to be in loving relationship with Him. According to the biblical pattern, we start by loving God and then love our neighbor as we love ourselves.

The command to love God is foremost, making it preeminent above every other love in our lives. We are told to love God with *all our heart, soul, mind, and strength* (Mark 12:30). This is an impossible task when attempting to love God entirely in our own will. Again, we must receive His love first, and by His grace, we will be empowered to fully love Him with our whole being. When you give Jesus 100 percent of your life, the rest will fall into place.

Consider this analogy: When you get married, you would never say to your new spouse on your wedding day, "I vow to give you 99 percent of my life. But in that remaining 1 percent, I reserve the right to have sex with someone else if I want to." What kind of covenant would that be? And yet, that is, unfortunately, the attitude that many people have toward Jesus. We give only part of our lives to God. We might know how to say the right words, sing the right worship songs, and go through the motions at church on Sunday. But once Monday morning hits, we are wishy-washy Christians again, not giving Jesus our 100-percent devotion that only He is worthy to receive.

RETURN TO YOUR FIRST LOVE

I feel the need to emphasize loving Jesus because He alone is "the image of the invisible God" (Col. 1:15). Jesus said, "The one who has seen Me has seen the Father" (John 14:9). In short, it is not about us. It is about Jesus and His kingdom. We have to move from self-focus to focus on Jesus and others. Living a life infused with the love of God makes this possible.

Time Magazine has described Millennials as the most narcissistic generation among those currently living.[23] If you visit a Baby Boomer's house, you will typically see framed photographs of their entire family, including a school portrait and wedding photo for good measure. Enter a Millennial's house, on the other hand, and you'll find myriads of selfies. Despite the Millennials' proclivity to be self-centered, they have the potential to become the greatest generation. Their main strength is their sense of justice. If they get saved, God can turn their passion into a zeal for biblical justice.

Society is desperate for answers, and I believe it begins with the church, regardless of the generation, needing to return to her first love. In Revelation 2, Jesus issues a stern warning to believers who started out in revival but had grown cold in their love for Him: "Nevertheless I have this against you, that *you have left your first love*. Remember therefore from where you have fallen; *repent and do the first works*, or else I will come to you quickly and remove your lampstand from its place—unless you repent" (Rev. 2:4–5 NKJV).

---

[23] Time Staff. "Millennials: The Me Me Me Generation." *Time Magazine*. May 20, 2013, https://time.com/247/millennials-the-me-me-me-generation/

Much of the church today, like the church in Ephesus, has lost her first love. The only way we can live a transformational life is by continually renewing our love for God. We are called to live in perpetual personal revival. The practical side of this is to "repent and do the things that you did at first" (v.5 NIV). So, what did you do when you first came to Christ?

1. Spend time in the Word every day.

If you love God, you will love His Word and stay hungry for it. As we will further see in chapter 7, immersing yourself in the Word of God is paramount to personal transformation.

2. Spend time with God in prayer.

Before the fall, Adam and Eve walked with God in the cool of the day (Gen. 3:8). God's desire for intimacy and fellowship with us has not changed since Genesis. Cultivating our prayer life is crucial to keeping our love for Jesus burning in our hearts.

3. Be an active member of a local church.

God never created us to be lone rangers. It is not enough to simply have a relationship with God. He created us for relationship with others. Even for Adam, although he had intimacy and fellowship with God, God said, "It is not good that man should be alone; I will make him a helper comparable to him" (Gen. 2:18 NKJV).

Loving Jesus means loving the church, rightfully called His Body, "the Body of Christ." Staying actively connected to the Body will keep you in a community where you can give and receive God's love amongst other believers. Sadly, many who come to know the Lord do not get involved in a local church.[24] However, I feel that a good follower of Jesus will be a good follower within the context of the local church. If you are not part of "gathering" in accord with Jesus, you are by default "scattering" and out of alignment with the Lord's agenda (Matt. 12:30). If you are not involved in church now, you can take the step to get involved and rekindle your first love.

4. Share your faith regularly.

Let people know that you are a follower of Jesus. Sharing your testimony will renew your confidence in God as you tell of what He has done in your life, and it will sow seeds of faith in others to come to know Jesus. I love doing this, and I even carry around a personal tract that I use to share my testimony whenever I am on the road.

"THE SECOND IS LIKE IT": THE CALL TO LOVE OTHERS

If loving God is our highest call, loving others is a close second. Specifically, Jesus calls you to "love your neighbor as yourself." Loving yourself comes as naturally as breathing; you do this instinctively as you seek the greatest good for your

---

[24] "Why Americans Go (and Don't Go) to Religious Services." Pew Research Center. August 1, 2018. https://www.pewresearch.org/religion/2018/08/01/why-americans-go-to-religious-services/

health, well-being, and success. God wants us to take the love He has given us and love others with that same divine love.

The apostle Paul writes, "Therefore be imitators of God as dear children. And walk in love, as Christ also has loved us and given Himself for us, an offering and a sacrifice to God for a sweet-smelling aroma" (Eph. 5:1–2 NKJV). As God's sons and daughters, we were reborn into His family in order to be like our heavenly Father. Because Jesus perfectly represents the Father, we are to imitate His model of selfless, sacrificial love. *Agape* love is the unselfish choice of the greatest good of others—laying down your life to serve others (John 15:13; Gal. 5:13b). That is how we can fulfill the command to "walk in love."

I once heard a well-known speaker assert that we are not obligated to love our parents but to honor them, explaining that God never commanded us to love them. While I respect the person who said this, I disagree with this statement because loving your neighbor *begins* with your family. When you think about it, your family members are actually your nearest neighbors. God wants us to practice the lifestyle of loving others well by learning to love our family well. This truth resounds throughout all of Scripture, but we see this spelled out clearly in chapter 5 of Ephesians. The husband and wife are called to be the model for the family unit by loving each other and submitting to one another (Eph. 5:21).

Husbands, love your wives, just as Christ also loved the church and gave Himself for her. (Eph. 5:25 NKJV)

...husbands ought to love their own wives as their own bodies. He who loves his wife loves himself. (Eph. 5:28b NKJV)

...each one of you also must love his wife as he loves himself, and the wife must respect her husband. (Eph. 5:33b NIV)

As the head of the home, fathers are to set the tone and turn their hearts toward their children (Mal. 4:6). Fathers and mothers alike are given these timeless instructions to love the next generation by teaching them to walk in God's ways: "Train up a child in the way he should go, even when he is old he will not depart from it" (Prov. 22:6 NASB1995). There is no greater gift that parents can give their children than a legacy of loving God first and loving their family well. I have heard it said, "The best thing you can do for your children is to love your spouse well." In that place, children are nurtured and raised in an environment where loving and honoring their parents becomes second nature.

Children, obey your parents in the Lord, for this is right. 'Honor your father and mother,' which is the first commandment with promise: 'that it may be well with you and you may live long on the earth.' (Eph. 6:1–3)

God cares about your family and wants them to be marked by His love. At the end of the day, we can transform society by loving and transforming our family. When a family is transformed by the love of God, each member of that family will be empowered to bring transformation to their spheres of influence.

When it comes to parenting and loving your children, as mentioned earlier, God expects parents to be the primary teachers of righteousness and justice to their children. Abraham, who is the father of our faith, was told by God that he needed to instruct his family and his household in the ways of God by teaching them what is right and just (see Gen. 18:19).

I believe that when Proverbs 22:6 (NKJV) says, "Train up a child in the way he should go, even when he is old he will not depart from it"—the text is not teaching us as parents to simply help our kids to fulfill their destiny and God-given potential. Of course, we are to do that. But we are to teach "the ways" of God: justice and righteousness.

Psalm 25 says, "Show me Your ways, O LORD; teach me Your paths. Lead me in Your truth and teach me ... Good and upright *is* the LORD; therefore He teaches sinners in the way. The humble He guides in justice, and the humble He teaches His way. All the paths of the LORD *are* mercy and truth, to such as keep His covenant and His testimonies" (Ps. 25:4–5, 8–10 NKJV).

In this particular Psalm, David is declaring that the ways of God are righteousness (v.8), justice (v.9), mercy, and truth (v.10). This is what we need to teach our children. This is the way of the Lord, and of course, Jesus is *the* Way, *the* Truth, and *the* Life, and no one comes to God the Father but through Him (John 14:6)! Reformation and revival is *Jesus* manifesting His Character of righteousness, justice, love, and truth to a broken and lost world.

CALLED TO A MINISTRY OF LOVE

I believe God called me into full-time service in 1974, one year after my conversion. I had just received the baptism of the Holy Spirit, an encounter that I describe later in this book.

I knew that I was called by God, but I didn't know specifically what my calling was. At that time, I knew there were three options for me: 1) called to be an evangelist; 2) called to be a missionary; 3) called to be a pastor, like my dad. I was so determined to know that I made a commitment to go into a large closet in my home in Rockville, Maryland, and not leave the closet until I heard from Jesus what my calling was. I was hoping that He would call me to be an evangelist, specifically the next Billy Graham. After what seemed like interminable minutes, I heard the Lord say, "I have called you to a ministry of love!"

I was shocked and disappointed at once. I knew this was God speaking to me because this was the last thing on my radar. First of all, I had never heard of a ministry of love. Secondly, I knew how selfish I was. I knew I was "the chief of sinners," and *sin* is basically *selfishness.* Yes, many people are deceived by their sins. But I was so selfish; I knew and saw it for what it was, and I felt it would be a monumental task for me to move from selfishness to a "ministry of love."

There is a big difference between loving our neighbors as ourselves and selfishness. What Jesus is saying in Matthew 22:39—"You shall love your neighbor as yourself"—is that we don't think twice about taking care of ourselves. We wake up, shower, dress, eat, sleep, and so forth. Jesus expects us to care for our neighbor as we see the needs in his or her life.

Selfishness, however, is sin. It is being narcissistic, focusing on yourself and what you want above what God wants and the wants of others in your life. One of the greatest truths that has set me free (John 8:32) is that this life is not about me or you but about Jesus and others!

LOVING YOUR ENEMIES

As we touched on briefly in Chapter 1, love is central to the idea of *mercy* in Psalm 89:14, our foundational text for understanding revival and reformation. In Romans 12:9–16, Paul begins by giving specific ways to love other believers, paralleling the aphorisms of the great chapter on love in 1 Corinthians 13. Then, from Romans 12:17–21, Paul gives clear instructions on how we are to love our enemies, paralleling the teachings of Jesus in the Sermon on the Mount (Matt. 5:43–48).

Living in California, with the majority (76 percent) of Californians being Democrats or Independents,[25] I am constantly challenged by Jesus' commandment to love my enemies in spite of the people approving Prop 1, which codified abortion into our state constitution (see Appendix A for more details). I have to hate this evil, but I am commanded to love the people who created and signed off on this bill.

You have heard that it was said, 'You shall love your neighbor and hate your enemy.' But I say

---

[25] "154-Day Report of Registration." California Secretary of State. Accessed August 30, 2024. https://elections.cdn.sos.ca.gov/ror/154day-presprim-2024/historical-reg-stats.pdf

to you, love your enemies, bless those who curse you, do good to those who hate you, and pray for those who spitefully use you and persecute you, that you may be sons of your Father in heaven; for He makes His sun rise on the evil and on the good, and sends rain on the just and on the unjust. For if you love those who love you, what reward have you? Do not even the tax collectors do the same? And if you greet your brethren only, what do you do more than others? Do not even the tax collectors do so? Therefore you shall be perfect, just as your Father in heaven is perfect. (Matt. 5:43–48 NKJV)

The simple truth is that we are not going to transform our nation unless the tipping point of our nation is being transformed by God's Spirit and His Word. Transformed lives lead to transformation of our society. And no transformation is going to be of significance without the greatest force in the universe—God's *agape* love!

I want to especially highlight the statement that true biblical love must be sincere or without hypocrisy. Also, true followers of Jesus must not tolerate evil in our lives or society, but we are to embrace all the *good* in our lives and society. For example, when I mentioned that we are to love our parents earlier, the question arises, "What if my parents are evil?" I actually heard about a parent who is involved in human trafficking and wanted to sell their daughter. Fortunately, she ran away and found Jesus and is now overseeing an orphanage in a third-world nation. The truth is that we don't love the evil that anyone practices, but we are still commanded to love them as fallen, lost people (which is the majority of the world), yet to hate the sin and evil committed by them.

It is interesting that Paul uses Jesus' teachings from the Sermon on the Mount of loving our enemies in his two great chapters on love, 1 Corinthians 13 and Romans 12:9–21. He qualifies that "Love does not rejoice in unrighteousness, but rejoices with the truth" (1 Cor. 13:6) and begins his great chapter on loving one's enemies with: "Let love be without hypocrisy. Abhor what is evil, cling to what is good" (Rom. 12:9 NKJV). Both verses emphasize that true love hates evil and unrighteousness and loves truth and what is good. Paul then gives instructions on how to love our enemies.

> Repay no one evil for evil. Have regard for good things in the sight of all men. If it is possible, as much as depends on you, live peaceably with all men. Beloved, do not avenge yourselves, but rather give place to wrath; for it is written, 'Vengeance is Mine, I will repay,' says the Lord. Therefore 'if your enemy is hungry, feed him; if he is thirsty, give him a drink; for in so doing, you will heap coals of fire on his head.' Do not be overcome by evil, but overcome evil with good. (Rom. 12:17–21)

The problem with the church in general, and with pastors specifically, is that we have bought into the narrative of "being nice" to avoid addressing the evils of society. For example, we avoid addressing controversial issues like abortion or same-sex marriage. However, by being silent about issues in life that are contrary to biblical values, we are not truly loving others according to the Bible. Being nice is not in the Bible, but speaking the truth in love is (see Eph. 4:11–15).

In relationship with unbelievers, Christians must show respect for the moral good that we see in our non-Christian neighbors. To bring about reformation, we must navigate the delicate balance between not compromising with evil and affirming the good in society. We have to find common ground without compromising our values. One without the other means losing the ability to change the values of our culture.

I truly believe that our nation was able to end slavery because those who came to know the Lord in the 1857–1858 Prayer Revival were abolitionists, and the leaders of the revival—Jeremiah Lanphier, Charles Finney, and the Methodist circuit riders—were abolitionists. Unfortunately, this Prayer Revival only hit the northern part of the U.S., which led to the Civil War of 1861–1865. But the fruit of reformation was ultimately abolishing slavery in America.

Today, I believe that we can agree with the commonsense liberals that it is wrong for the state to take away parental rights when it comes to transgender issues for our children in elementary school. In February 2022, three San Francisco school board members were recalled for spending less time deliberating on reopening schools than on renaming schools that had ties to so-called "racist" historical figures like Abraham Lincoln and George Washington. It is telling that the majority of the parents who voted them out were

Democrats.[26] Similarly, the "Don't Mess With Our Kids" movement in Latin America united "Mama Bears" from both the left and the right, and that movement is impacting our nation to this day.[27] (Discover more about modern-day reformer movements in Chapter 10 and Appendix B.)

Recently, President Trump and RFK, Jr. were able to agree on peace in the Ukraine, closing the borders, and health care issues with obese children, although they were miles apart on other issues like climate change. This is what it means to "be at peace with all people" (Rom. 12:18) and to "conduct yourselves with wisdom toward outsiders" (Col. 4:5).

So, how do we treat those who are evil around us, "our enemies"? Paul makes it clear that we are to come in the opposite spirit. We are not to repay evil for evil (Rom. 12:17a) but to see the good that is among our enemies (Rom. 12:17b). We must bless and encourage the good that we see. For example, Paul goes into the next chapter, Romans 13, saying that we are to honor and submit to governing authorities. At that time, the citizens of Rome welcomed the teachings of the Christians. Both are shared values among Christians and nonbelievers in Rome. Understanding that we should submit to governing authorities as long as it does not violate our core biblical values, then we can live at peace with all men. This is what it means by the

---

[26] Gregory Krieg. "San Francisco voters oust three school board members in recall vote..." CNN. February 16, 2022. https://www.cnn.com/2022/02/16/politics/san-francisco-school-board-members-recall-election/index.html
[27] James L. Garlow. *Reversed: From Culturally Woke to Biblically Awake*. Well Versed Publishing, 2024, p.15.

instruction, "If it is possible, as much as depends on you, live peaceably with all men" (Rom. 12:18 NKJV).

To live at peace with all people is one of the reasons Jesus came to die for us. He came to bring spiritual inner peace (John 14:27) and peace with others, including our enemies.

> For he himself [Jesus] is our peace, who has made the two groups one and has destroyed the barrier, the dividing wall of hostility, by setting aside in his flesh the law with its commands and regulations. His purpose was to create in himself one new humanity out of the two, thus making peace, and in one body to reconcile both of them to God through the cross, by which he put to death their hostility. He came and preached peace to you who were far away and peace to those who were near. For through him we both have access to the Father by one Spirit. (Eph. 2:14–18 NIV)

We, as Christians, must always strive to live at peace with our nonbelieving neighbors. If conflict occurs, and it inevitably will, it must come from the opposite side and not from those who love Jesus. Keep in mind that this directive from the apostle Paul was written during the first-century church, where believers suffered extraordinary persecution from the Romans. Nevertheless, their commitment to love their enemies by not physically fighting back brought many Roman citizens to submit to Jesus as Lord en masse.

It is obvious that the early church had a supernatural love for their enemies, as many died for their faith. What was the key to them being laid-down lovers for Jesus? The answer is the power of the Holy Spirit. (You can read more about the baptism of the Holy Spirit in chapter 11.)

If you have never received this love before, or you are born again but need a fresh infilling of God's love through the Holy Spirit, pray this simple prayer by faith:

> *"Father, I come before You in the mighty name of Jesus. Forgive me for all my sins and all my selfishness. I give my life 100 percent to Jesus as my Lord and Savior. Fill me with your Holy Spirit; fill me with Your love. I receive Your love by faith! In Jesus' name, I pray. Amen."*

Chapter 3:

FROM PRIDE TO HUMILITY

"If My people who are called by My name will humble
themselves, and pray and seek My face, and turn from
their wicked ways, then I will hear from heaven, and
will forgive their sin and heal their land"
(2 Chron. 7:14).

I remember the first time I met Dr. C. Peter Wagner.
The year was 1984, and I was getting ready to enroll
in Fuller Seminary after just having moved cross-country to
Pasadena, California. Since Peter was a professor at Fuller's
School of World Mission, I called his office to see if I could
meet him.

To my surprise, Peter invited me to a lunch meeting with
him and his wife, Doris. He took the initiative to order me a
sandwich from a little shop right across from his office. When
Peter asked me what I wanted to drink, I said I wanted a Diet
Coke, and he pulled one out in a jiffy. I had no idea that this
would begin a relationship that would span more than three

decades. From my first interactions with Peter, his humility and servant's heart blew me away.

In addition to his tenure at Fuller Seminary, Peter Wagner was also a missionary, missiologist, theologian, writer, teacher, and church growth specialist. More personally, he became my mentor, my spiritual father, and my apostle. I deeply admired the way Peter always demonstrated his love for his spiritual sons and daughters by championing us in our callings. He would eventually serve on the Board of Harvest International Ministry and founded Wagner University, where I now have the privilege of being the International Chancellor.

Peter's love for learning was central to who he was, and he was passionate about writing his own books for most of his life. He wrote more than 77, almost a book for every year he was alive. His writings covered an immense range of topics: spiritual gifts, church growth, prayer and spiritual warfare, revival and reformation, workplace ministry, apostles and prophets, kingdom wealth, and even jokes.

Out of all Peter's contributions as an author, one of the books that impacted me the most was his book on humility. Following its release in 2002, I remember watching as Peter held up his book in front of a church and said, "I just wrote a new book, and I'm very proud about it. It's called *Humility*."

Peter's book focuses on the essential role of humility in fulfilling the Great Commandment. By clothing ourselves in humility with God, we can extend that same attitude to our interactions with others. Humility, therefore, is one of the keys to inward transformation, and it is a crucial ingredient in living a life that also brings transformation to society.[28]

HUMILITY PRECEDES REVIVAL AND REFORMATION

In my perspective today, I believe humility is central to what the Spirit of God is saying to the church. The verse that began this chapter, 2 Chronicles 7:14 (NKJV), sets the tone for this season: "If My people who are called by My name will *humble* themselves, and pray and seek My face, and turn from their wicked ways, then I will hear from heaven, and will forgive their sin and heal their land." If we want to see our nation transformed (the healing of our land), it begins with us, as God's people, humbling ourselves under the mighty hand of God. The clarion call in this hour is sobering but necessary. God wants us to humble ourselves and repent of our sins, for judgment begins in the house of God (1 Pet. 4:17). This is the beginning of historic revival—when the church turns back to God and is revived by the Holy Spirit.

Intercessors For America released a recent article with prayer points attuned to this current season, which will be marked by greater shaking and greater revival. One of the key emphases is on humility:

Humility is a precursor to seeking His forgiveness and restoration. It implies an admission of guilt and a

---

[28] C. Peter Wagner. *Humility*. Ventura, CA: Gospel Light, 2002.

confession of sin in holy fear of the chastisement we deserve. *Humility also means intentional dependence on God and obedience to His precepts and purposes for us.* It is the heart condition necessary to pray and seek His face with a pure heart and the right motive.[29]

I couldn't agree more. If humility precedes personal and social transformation, we have every reason to seek the cultivation of humble hearts that are aligned with God's heart. This does not come easy, however. Even for believers who have been walking with God for years, humility requires a continual reliance on the Holy Spirit and a willingness to lay down our own agendas for God's rule and reign to be ushered in.

UPROOTING PRIDE

The greatest obstacle to walking in humility—and the most odious sin in one's life—is the sin of pride. In Proverbs 8:13, God explicitly states that He hates pride, arrogance, and the evil way (see also Prov. 6:16–17). Scripture states, "Everyone who is proud in heart is an abomination to the Lord; assuredly, he will not be unpunished" (Prov. 16:5 NASB1995). The language surrounding pride is always severe, for pride is the polar opposite of humility.

To take it one step further, pride is the sin of satan. C.S. Lewis famously wrote, "It was through Pride that the devil

---

[29] "Fanning the Flames of Revival." Intercessors for America. February 2023. https://ifapray.org/wp-content/uploads/2023/02/Fanning-the-Flames-of-Revival-pg.pdf

became the devil."[30] The Bible shows that pride is what caused satan to fall (see Isa. 14:1–15). Pride is so satanic and pervasive that all other sins seem to pale in comparison. C.S. Lewis expounds on this theme in his classic *Mere Christianity*:

> There is one vice of which no man in the world is free; which everyone in the world loathes when he sees it in someone else; and of which hardly any people, except Christians, ever imagine that they are guilty themselves ... Pride leads to every other vice: it is the complete anti-God state of mind.[31]

We can reach the verdict that pride is completely anti-God because it is demonstrably *anti*-Christ. In other words, the spirit of pride is the inverse of who Jesus Christ is. If we want to see revival and reformation from Jesus, we must come in the opposite spirit of satan's pride, with humility and Christlike character.

JESUS IS HUMILITY INCARNATE

My dear friend Bill Johnson has often said, "Jesus Christ is perfect theology."[32] All throughout the Gospels and the New Testament, we see the recurring theme of Christ's supreme humility. The apostle Paul writes in Philippians 2:4–5 (AMPC), "Let each of you esteem and look upon and be

---

[30] C.S. Lewis. *Mere Christianity*. New York: HarperCollins, 2001, p.122.
[31] Ibid., p.120-122.
[32] Bill Johnson. *Jesus Christ is Perfect Theology*. Shippensburg, PA: Destiny Image, 2016.

concerned for not [merely] his own interests, but also each for the interests of others. Let this same attitude and purpose and [humble] mind be in you which was in Christ Jesus: [Let Him be your example in humility.]"

Jesus is the ultimate role model of humility. Philippians 2:7–11 (AMPC) continues the description of what Christlike humility looks like:

> He stripped Himself [of all privileges and rightful dignity], so as to assume the guise of a servant (slave), in that He became like men and was born a human being. And after He had appeared in human form, *He abased and humbled Himself [still further]* and carried His obedience to the extreme of death, even the death of the cross! *Therefore [because He stooped so low]* God has highly exalted Him and has freely bestowed on Him the name that is above every name, that in (at) the name of Jesus every knee should (must) bow, in heaven and on earth and under the earth, and every tongue [frankly and openly] confess and acknowledge that Jesus Christ is Lord, to the glory of God the Father.

Let's pause for a moment and not bypass these familiar truths as we consider this: Jesus, the King of all kings, humbled Himself to be born in a human body in a "barn." Jesus did not arrive on earth as an adult. He was born as a helpless, dependent baby. The highest place of honor and exaltation belongs to Jesus because His humility is equally unmatched. We, who are self-sufficient, should not only come to Christ as little children, humble and dependent, but we must maintain that mentality throughout our lives. John 15:5 declares that apart from Jesus, we can do nothing. And in the Greek, "nothing" means *nothing*! As members of the Body of Christ, we must also remember that we need one another (1 Cor. 12:12–27).

From Jesus' first cry in Bethlehem to His last cry at Calvary, He has given us the gift of His unconditional love (John 3:16). Jesus did not come to be served but to serve (Mark 10:45). He came to a manger—not to a throne. He lived as a servant—not as a ruler. He gave everything—not just a little! His destiny was the cross. His determination was His love for us. His reason was to save you and me. *The King* lived as a humble, servant-hearted lover of God and of people! That is why the Word says we are to be "imitators of God" (Eph. 5:1).

But why did Jesus come in such manifest humility? The key is that satan, Adam, and Eve all fell because of pride. Pride ruled the world. It was the primary stronghold at work in every empire, geopolitical nation, and people group. Jesus came in the opposite spirit. When we move in pride, we are reinforcing the works of darkness, but when we walk in humility, we are reinforcing the work of God.

GOD VALUES HUMILITY

Of all the attributes with which Jesus could characterize himself, He chooses humility. Jesus says in Matthew 11:28–30 (NASB1995), "Come to Me, all who are weary and heavy-laden, and I will give you rest. Take My yoke upon you and learn from Me, *for I am gentle and humble in heart*, and you will find rest for your souls. For My yoke is easy and My burden is light."

As the Creator of all things, God knows what we need to live an abundant life—the kind of life that He desires for us. When we operate in pride, it causes us to be burdened and weary. Humility, on the other hand, sets us free and gives rest to our souls. By coming to Jesus and learning from Him, we will become more like Him as we depend on His strength. Consequently, we will carry an easier yoke and a lighter burden.

Humility is a pathway to becoming more Christlike. It is also a conduit for God's grace and favor in our lives. James 4:6 promises, "But He gives a greater grace. Therefore it says, 'God is opposed to the proud, but gives grace to the humble.'" Likewise, 1 Peter 5:5 offers this exhortation: "...all of you, clothe yourselves with humility toward one another, because God is opposed to the proud, but He gives grace to the humble." These two passages echo one of the Proverbs: "Surely He scorns the scornful, but gives grace to the humble" (Prov. 3:34 NKJV). Another version of that same verse reads, "Toward the scorners he is scornful, but to the humble he gives *favor*" (ESV).

I don't know about you, but I need God's grace. I need His favor on my life. I can easily say that I would not be who I am today if it was not for the grace of God (1 Cor. 15:10). If humility ensures that I will receive more grace from God the Father, then you can sign me up any day for "Humility 101" in the kingdom. This may seem basic and foundational, but it is a necessary part of not only beginning well but "running the race with endurance" and finishing well.

How many of you want intimacy with God? How many of you want God's presence to dwell with you? Choose humility. In Isaiah 57:15 (NIV), the Lord says, "I live ... with the one who is contrite and lowly in spirit, to revive the spirit of the lowly and to revive the heart of the contrite." Several chapters later, in Isaiah 66:2 (BSB), He says, "This is the one I will esteem: he who is humble and contrite in spirit, who trembles at My word." Throughout my walk with Jesus, I have had a desire to cultivate friendship with Him. Because He says, "I esteem the humble," humility becomes my prerogative.

God values humble hearts so much that He chooses to reward the humble with many blessings. Proverbs 15:33, 18:12, and 29:23 all declare that humility comes before receiving honor. Proverbs 22:4 expands on that truth by saying, "The reward of humility and the fear of the Lord are riches, honor, and life." Notice how these rewards— wealth, honor, and abundant life—are often things that the world seeks after. Those who are prideful almost always are characterized by their lust for riches, fame, and long life. But in God's kingdom, He rewards the humble with the very thing that the world pursues but can never be satisfied by.

Just as Jesus chose humility and was highly exalted by the Father, we see a similar promise that is stunning: "Therefore humble yourselves under the mighty hand of God, so that He may exalt you at the proper time" (1 Pet. 5:6). The mandate to choose humility goes hand in hand with our closeness to God. If we submit ourselves under His mighty hand, we will take refuge under the shadow of His wings (Ps. 91:4), where there is no pride. As a direct result, God will be the One to set us on high (Ps. 91:14), exalting us in His timing.

Jesus describes this same dynamic in the Gospels, "Whoever exalts himself shall be humbled, and whoever humbles himself shall be exalted" (Matt. 23:12). Make no mistake: Exalting yourself in pride will always precipitate a fall (Prov. 16:18). But humbling yourself will lead to divine promotion (James 4:10). This principle applies not just to individuals but also to the corporate church. I believe that revival and reformation will come to those who humbly and sincerely cry out in prayer for God to move.

Let's pray this prayer together:

> "Heavenly Father, thank You for sending Your Son, Jesus, to model what humility truly looks like. Today I repent of all my pride. I choose to humble myself before You. By Your grace, empower me to live the life of a servant-leader. I believe as I humble myself under Your mighty hand, You will lift me up in due season (1 Pet. 5:6). In Jesus' name I pray, amen!"

ESSAY:
HOW TO DEVELOP HUMILITY

1. Humility is a choice.

A humble heart is not just descriptive, as in the observation, "That man is humble." The biblical call to humility is pre-scriptive. In other words, it is a command, which means we can choose to obey or disobey. You have to choose to walk humbly with God.

Looking again at 1 Peter 5:5, we see the instruction to "clothe yourselves with humility toward one another." Clothing yourself is a conscious decision (which I hope you make every day!) If we can decide what type of clothes we will put on each morning, we have just as much of a decision to make whether we will choose to remain hum-ble or operate in pride.[33] James 4:10 urges us to make that choice: "Humble yourselves in the presence of the Lord, and He will exalt you."

2. Repent of pride and walk in the fear of the Lord.

We discussed earlier how pride is the exact opposite of God's nature. Pride is a grievous sin that we must quickly address, repent of, and turn from whenever we notice it creeping into

---

[33] C. Peter Wagner. *Humility*. Ventura, CA: Gospel Light, 2002, p.10.

our lives. This requires a continual spirit of humility and often involves accountability in the context of discipleship.

In tandem with repentance, walking in the fear of the Lord will keep us away from pride and keep us humble before God. A healthy understanding of the fear of the Lord is to have the right view of God and of ourselves in relation to Him. It is to live in holy awe of who Jesus is. To dig deeper, the fear of the Lord is to hate what Jesus hates. Proverbs 8:13 (NASB1995) says, "The fear of the LORD is to hate evil; pride and arrogance and the evil way and the perverted mouth, I hate." At the same time, the fear of the Lord is to love what He loves. Scripture lays this out for us in Micah 6:8 (NKJV), which reads, "He has shown you, O man, what is good; and what does the LORD require of you but to do justly, to love mercy, and to walk humbly with your God?"

3: Choose to be a servant.

In Jesus' kingdom, humility is the fast track toward greatness. Choosing to be a servant is the highest call of a follower of Jesus. In Matthew 20:25–28 (NIV), we read:

> Jesus called them together and said, 'You know that the rulers of the Gentiles lord it over them, and their high officials exercise authority over them. Not so with you. Instead, whoever wants to become great among you *must be your servant*, and whoever wants to be first *must be your slave*—just as the Son of Man did not come to be served, but *to serve*, and *to give his life* as a ransom for many.'

Jesus was the perfect servant-leader. Before laying down His life for our redemption, Jesus washed the feet of His disciples (John 13)—a task that only the lowest servant or slave was in charge of doing.[34] Also consider what Matthew 12:18 (NKJV) says: "Behold! My Servant whom I have chosen, My Beloved in whom My soul is well pleased! I will put My Spirit upon Him, and He will declare justice to the Gentiles." Note that Jesus served out of a motivation by the grace and love He received from the Holy Spirit. We, too, have the Holy Spirit that has been shed abroad in our hearts (Rom. 5:5), and we, too, should demonstrate humility through love, serving one another (Gal. 5:13).

This was a major lesson that God taught me from John Dawson back in 1992. John was resigning from the Board of Love LA, which was founded by Jack Hayford and Lloyd Ogilvie (the Senior Pastor of Hollywood Presbyterian Church), Bishop Charles Blake, and Bishop Ken Ulmer. When John Dawson was selected to be the President of YWAM, I was invited to take his place on the Board of Love LA. I felt totally intimidated to be accepted into this position.

When I asked John for his advice, he said, "Just be a servant. Serve the Board and serve the pastors of LA. If you do this, you will be successful." I applied that principle to my time with Love LA, and I have applied it to every position that the Lord has given me in the years since then. Whether at Harvest Rock Church, Harvest International

---

[34] Mike Cosper. "What's The Deal With Footwashing?" Crossway. November 20, 2014. https://www.crossway.org/articles/whats-the-deal-with-footwashing/

Ministry, Wagner University, or elsewhere, I have sought to be a servant to those whom God has entrusted to my sphere of ministry.

4: Submit to one another.

Humility is developed best within the context of community. Learning to love and serve others also involves "submitting to one another in the fear of God" (Eph. 5:21 NKJV). On the nuclear level, this means being submissively obedient to your parents (Eph. 6:1–2).

This story has been around for a while, but it reveals a lesson that we need to embrace. It is the story about a spirited young boy who kept standing up in the pew during a church service. His mother, exasperated, told him, "Be still and sit down this instant!" After a short pause, the boy finally complied and said, "I may be sitting on the outside, but I am standing on the inside." Because God looks at the heart, humility must be cultivated inwardly so that our outward behavior will follow suit.

Beyond the sphere of your home, I believe humility also means being obedient to spiritual authority. First Peter 5:5 (NKJV) says, "Likewise you younger people, submit yourselves to your elders. Yes, all of you be submissive to one another, and be clothed with humility, for 'God resists the proud, but gives grace to the humble.'" Hebrews 13:17 says, "Obey your leaders and submit to their authority. They keep watch over you as men who must give an account. Obey them so that their work will be a joy, not a burden, for that would be of no advantage to you" (my paraphrase). By leading your life in humility, you will be able to walk out your God-given love for others in right relationship with them.

God wants to raise you up to be a revivalist and reformer. But before you can be in authority, God wants you to learn how to be *under* authority. Our independent and freedom-oriented minds buck the idea, but this is such an important principle that the Bible gives us a clear mandate that we are to submit to one another in the fear of the Lord (Eph. 5:21).

Chapter 4:

FROM LITTLE FAITH TO GOD'S FAITH

For in it the righteousness of God is revealed from faith to
faith; as it is written, "The just shall live by faith."
(Rom. 1:17 NKJV)

So then faith comes by hearing, and hearing by the word of
God. (Rom. 10:17 NKJV)

aith is essential for every follower of Jesus. Scripture makes it clear that *by faith*, we receive God's gift of salvation (Eph. 2:8). If you are reading this book, you have most likely received the grace of God and salvation by faith. What you might not know is that faith is also a gift of God. It is a grace given by the Holy Spirit.

Paul uses the terminology of faith as a gift from God. Romans 12:3 (NLT) says, "Measuring yourselves by the faith God has given us." In 1 Corinthians 12:7–9, Paul writes, "But to each one is *given* the manifestation of the Spirit for the common good. For to one is given the word of wisdom through the Spirit, and to another the word of knowledge according to the same Spirit; to another faith by the same Spirit..." Craig Keener, a dear friend and brilliant New Testament scholar, explains in his commentary on 1 Corinthians 12: "'Faith' as a distinct gift probably refers, as some church fathers opined, to extraordinary, mountain-moving faith." And it is going to take extraordinary, mountain-moving faith to bring about the transformation of nations.

Jesus talks about this mountain-moving faith in Mark 11:22, and it is interesting that He begins with "Have faith in God." This verse can be translated from the Greek as "Have faith *of* God." This makes sense since Paul teaches that faith is a gift of the Holy Spirit, and it is God who gives us a measure of faith.

Charles Price's healing ministry was revolutionized when he received the revelation that faith is a grace from God. He goes on to say in *The Real Faith*:

> The revelation has answered my questions. It has solved my problems. It has deepened my love for my Lord and strengthened my surrender of heart and life to Him. It has revolutionized my healing ministry, for it has revealed to me the helplessness of self; and the need of the presence, the love, the grace, and the faith, of Jesus.[35]

Many times, this grace or gift of faith comes from the revelation of God's Word. Faith comes by hearing, and more specifically, hearing the *rhema* (revelatory) word of God.

---

[35] Charles S. Price. *The Real Faith.* Jawbone Digital. Kindle Edition, p.3.

THE GRACE OF FAITH COMES FROM THE RHEMA WORD OF GOD

So, what does mountain-moving faith look like? I want to share a personal story illustrating how the Lord gave me His faith to see a major breakthrough in my life. This life of faith has been a constant reality in my journey with Jesus—from the first day I gave my life to Him until today.

In 51 years of walking with God, I have only heard the audible voice of God once. It was in 1979, when God spoke to me about who I was to marry. Before you jump to any conclusions, let me be clear that I do not consider hearing God's audible voice as a sign of spirituality. Rather, it was almost like God had to resort to speaking to me in an audible voice because I was so determined to do something other than His perfect will for my life. Though they've also come in other forms, most of my *rhemas* have been Scripture that pops off the pages of the Bible.

After getting radically saved and delivered, I made a vow of celibacy that I was not going to get married. Because of my immoral background, I felt that I had to make this vow in order to walk in moral purity and holiness. The Lord knew that He had to do something dramatic to get my attention so I would course-correct.

One day, as I was driving home from my friend's house, all of a sudden, I heard these words resounding in my ears: "You will marry Sue Roxas!" My initial reaction shocked even me. I pounded my hand on the steering wheel and said an emphatic "no!" to the Lord. After all, I had made a vow of celibacy to Him. Even so, He began to change my heart.

But I knew the bigger obstacle was that my father would never bless me marrying anyone who was not Korean.

A few days later, I was having lunch with my prophet friend, James Golden. He stopped eating whatever was on his plate and said, "Oh, my goodness. Jesus just spoke to me that you are going to marry Sue Roxas!" (Over the years, I've had many *rhema* prophetic words from trusted prophets.) The next day, I was waiting for a meeting with Jim Wilson, a friend I was discipling. I was parked in front of University Blvd., a busy street with hundreds of cars passing by. I prayed a simple prayer: "Lord, if it is Your will that I marry Sue, please confirm this." As soon as I finished praying, Sue drove by and turned her head toward me, and we made eye contact. Later, she asked me what I was doing parked facing University Blvd. You cannot make this up! God will supernaturally confirm the word with circumstances that are graces from Him.

Over the course of several days, God had provided five major confirmations, one of which was a minor detail (just joking), when the Holy Spirit also spoke a *rhema* to Sue about us getting married! But the last confirmation would take a miracle because I believed that any Christian should submit a marriage proposal for their parents to bless, especially if they are also believers. That was part of my way of honoring my parents as the Bible teaches. What made it difficult for me was the fact that my parents were traditional Koreans, and I knew my dad, who was at best a nationalist and, at worst, a racist, would not give his approval.

So, I mustered up the courage to ask my father and mother to sit down so I could tell them something important.

Seated across from my parents at their kitchen table, I confidently told them that I wanted to marry Sue, who is Filipina. My father looked at me sternly and said, "I am not blessing this. This is not of the Lord. She is not Korean." His ugly racism manifested itself in front of my eyes.

Even though I expected that response, I was still disappointed. I quickly replied, "Dad, the only biblical basis is whether she is a believer or not, so we can be equally yoked. And Sue is not an unbeliever. She loves Jesus."

"It doesn't matter," he retorted. "God is speaking through me now. I won't bless this."

I would not let the conversation end there, so I quickly thought on my feet. "Dad, you're a pastor," I continued. "You haven't even prayed about it."

"I don't need to pray about it," he snapped back. "I already know this is not God's will."

Thus went our crazy debate for some while. After reaching the end of our heated dialogue, I offered my final plea: "Dad, all I can do is ask if you and Mom will pray."

My dad said, "Not only are we going to pray, but we are going to pray and fast over the weekend." Now, Koreans are known for their fervent intercession. So, when my dad told me that he was going to pray and fast, I *really* knew he was going to pray and fast. My parents then left for a three-day retreat to a large vacation home they had in West Virginia to seek the Lord on the matter. They often used this property as a house of prayer and retreat center for the church, but that fateful weekend, it was personal.

But Sue and I also committed ourselves to praying. That was the natural thing to do—especially since our future together was on the line! We determined that God had spoken to both of us, so we thought, *Let's just believe that this is of Him and He is going to bless our marriage.* This was our moment to learn in real time that "faith comes by hearing, and hearing by the [*rhema*] of God" (Rom. 10:17). I knew without a doubt that God spoke to me that marrying Sue was His will. The *rhema* sparked faith within me, and I held onto faith as I prayed that God was going to change my dad's heart.

I'll never forget when my parents called me for dinner as soon as they got back from their retreat. To be honest, I was really scared. I was not sure how things were going to pan out. My dad was so stubborn and rooted in his traditional Korean ways that I was afraid he would say, "I prayed and fasted about it. I did what you asked me to do. And the word is still 'no.'" As I sat at the dinner table, the worst-case scenario replayed in my mind. I couldn't eat a thing during the meal.

Finally, my dad released the verdict: "We prayed about it. God spoke to us, and He said this is of the Lord. So, we are giving our blessing." Thank You, Jesus! You gave my dad a *rhema* to have faith for this marriage! It's all grace! It's all about Jesus and His faith that pours abundantly into our hearts.

I wanted to shout "hallelujah!" and dance around my parents' dining room! It was one of the biggest miracles I had witnessed up to that point in my life. And it has been one big journey of faith ever since. That helped set the stage for what God was planning to do in time to come. I had no idea in 1979 that God would call us to move to Los Angeles a few years later—a destination 3,000 miles away from home where we knew no one—all based on a prophetic dream.

PUTTING IT ALL TOGETHER: WHAT IS FAITH?

During the revival that broke out in Toronto and in our church in 1994, we saw amazing miracles. For example, blind eyes were opened, an amputated finger grew out with a new fingernail, and people were healed of incurable diseases like multiple sclerosis (MS) because God's manifest presence was so thick and tangible. But I would go to other places, having full faith and being full of the Holy Spirit, to do a healing service, and I would come home discouraged because only a few people got healed. I would feel a sense of shame for the lack of results, but the Lord told me that it was not me but the unbelief of the people in the meeting. This is not to condemn anyone. Yet I think we would all agree that faith is absolutely indispensable for seeing everything from a personal breakthrough to taking our cities for God.

So, how can we grow in faith? It is at this point that I want to say that we all have been given a measure of faith (Rom. 12:3). At the same time, I also believe that faith, like a muscle, can be developed and that we need to grow from faith to greater faith. Here are three truths that have helped me to personally grow in faith.

1. Faith is a present reality.

Faith is so important that the Bible gives us a definition of it. The eleventh chapter of Hebrews begins with this statement: "Faith shows the reality of what we hope for; it is the evidence of things we cannot see" (Heb. 11:1 NLT).

Hope is very important in relation to faith. It is one of the "big three" that Paul highlights in his famous chapter on love. In 1 Corinthians 13:13 (NLT), he writes, "Three things will last forever—faith, hope, and love—and the greatest of these is love." Hope is in the future. Hope is the confident expectation of good from a good and loving heavenly Father. But faith is having the reality of what you hope for *now*. It is the "evidence" or "conviction" (NKJV) that you have what you hope for. You have it now!

2. Faith comes by hearing a rhema word.

"So then faith comes by hearing, and hearing by the [rhema] of God." (Rom. 10:17 NKJV)

In the New Testament, there are two Greek words that are translated as "word" in our English Bibles: *logos* and *rhema*. The Greek word *rhema* is used when Jesus said, "It is written, 'Man shall not live by bread alone, but by every word that proceeds from the mouth of God'" (Matt. 4:4 NKJV). *Logos* is the written word ("It is written..."). The *rhema* is the prophetic word that "proceeds from the mouth of God" that speaks to our hearts. This *rhema* comes to a person in so many different ways.

I mentioned earlier how God gave me an audible word that I was going to marry Sue. But that is very rare. Most *rhema* words come simply by reading the Bible or through the small, still voice of the Holy Spirit (John 10:27). They can also come through dreams, visions, open doors, closed doors, godly counsel, and so on. A great book on how God speaks to us is *Hearing God's Voice Today*, by my good friend James Goll.

Of course, it is a given that every "word" we hear from God has to be based on God's Word, the Bible. The Bible is the most important source for the *rhema* of God. This may sound mundane, but often, when I need a breakthrough, I simply read the promises of God pertaining to what I am contending for. I read until the written word becomes the prophetic *rhema* word I need for my breakthrough.

For example, years ago, I had a major case of TMJ, a type of arthritis in the jaw. I meditated on two verses for over one year: Isaiah 53:5 (NKJV), which says, "And by His stripes we are healed," and Mark 11:24 (NKJV), which says, "Therefore I say to you, whatever things you ask when you pray, believe that you receive them, and you will have them." In fact, I quoted these two verses every time I saw my face in the mirror. This was a personal accountability commitment that I made to constantly meditate on God's Word until it became *rhema* to me. It was about a year and a half later when I knew I had the healing. It was a done deal in my mind and in my heart. Sure enough, I woke up after a night of sleep, yawned, and my mouth opened with full extension and no pain! Thank You, Jesus! I have been healed of TMJ ever since.

In 2020, when my attorney Mat Staver counseled me to sue Governor Gavin Newsom for the discrimination against the church during the lockdown, philosophically, I was in total agreement with Mat. For instance, Gov. Newsom said that abortion clinics, marijuana dispensaries, liquor stores, a strip club in San Diego, and other things were essential, but not the local church. Even with my mental agreement with Mat, I needed a *rhema* of God—first of all, just to sue Gov. Newsom. You can't just sue the governor without hearing from God!

At that time, I was reading a book that quoted Joshua 1:9, and that verse became *rhema* to me: "Have I not commanded you? Be strong and of good courage; do not be afraid, nor be dismayed, for the LORD your God is with you wherever you go" (NKJV). That word gave me the faith and confidence to persevere, even though we initially lost the case in the lower courts. But by God's grace, our case went all the way to the Supreme Court, and we won 6-3 on February 5, 2021, including a $1.3 million settlement from the state of California to pay for our legal bills. All glory belongs to Jesus, and of course, we had a great attorney representing us!

3. Rhema can come from hearing or reading a testimony.

"For the testimony of Jesus is the spirit of prophecy..." (Revelation 19:10b)

"But he who prophesies speaks edification and exhortation and comfort to men." (1 Cor. 14:3 NKJV)

A testimony is any account of a breakthrough that a person had in the past that brings faith for the present. For example, reading or hearing about past revival could give you faith for a revival today. That is why I love reading church history and biographies—it builds faith for now and the future. Prophecy is intended to bring faith; that is, it edifies and encourages your faith. In that light, hearing or reading a testimony of someone else's healing will give you faith for your similar sickness or pain.

One of the most powerful healings that I have ever witnessed was when I prayed for a non-Christian named Sharon Trainer, who had an incurable disease called reflexive sympathetic dystrophy syndrome (RSD). RSD causes constant excruciating pain in either one's feet or hands. Sharon came to the church meeting because she had read a flyer advertising a healing service that was posted on the door of a local grocery store. She had been treated by some of the top doctors and hospitals in the city of Philadelphia for almost 20 years with no solution. She was on a morphine drip just to manage her pain.

When I prayed for Sharon, God gave me a word of knowledge that she had been sexually molested as a child and that trauma had opened the door to her problems. I prayed for her by rebuking that spirit, and she fell out under the power of the Holy Spirit, known also as being "slain" or "resting" in the Spirit. As she lay there on the floor, Sharon realized she had no more pain in her feet. It got somewhat humorous because she was the last one to get off the floor and leave. She didn't want to move because she was afraid that she would, in her words, "jinx" the healing. Finally, she drove home and went to bed.

The next morning, Sharon woke up thinking that the healing had simply been a vivid dream during the night. But when she got out of bed, she put her feet on the floor and noticed that she still had no pain. It then dawned upon her that she was totally healed. She got up and ran around her house, waking everyone up by shouting, "I'm healed! I'm healed!" Sharon called the pastor of the church where she got healed. Pastor Jack came to her house right away and led the whole family to the Lord.

Over the years, I have shared this testimony in England, Bakersfield, California, and Honolulu, Hawaii. Each time

I have shared this testimony, someone who heard the testimony in each place got healed of this incurable disease. Glory to Jesus, who is our great Healer and Physician!

Rhema comes from rehearsing past victories and breakthroughs. When David, the young shepherd, volunteered to take on the giant Goliath, he said, "Is there not a cause?" (1 Samuel 17:29 NKJV). Essentially, David was saying, "I have a history where God gave me past victories, and He will give me victory over Goliath."

> Moreover David said, 'The LORD, who delivered me from the paw of the lion and from the paw of the bear, He will deliver me from the hand of this Philistine.' And Saul said to David, 'Go, and the LORD be with you!' (1 Sam. 17:37 NKJV)

I recall when our church needed $13 million to purchase the Ambassador Auditorium in 2004, and we had nothing in our bank account. We had spent all of our savings by that time, leading the way to do seven major events. They were mostly stadium events except for TheCall D.C. and TheCall New York, which took place on the D.C. Mall and Flushing Meadow Park, respectively. God had provided the $10 million we needed from 2000 to 2003 for these kingdom prayer events. Because of our history with God, I knew He would faithfully provide the money we needed to purchase this iconic performance arts building in the spring of 2004. And sure enough, Jehovah Jireh came through, just in the nick of time. This leads us to the most important truth about faith.

4. Faith is all about an intimate relationship with God the Father.

Faith springs out of a relationship with a loving and faithful heavenly Father. The Bible doesn't say to "have faith in faith" but to "have faith in *God*" (Mark 11:22). The writer of Hebrews says that "faith toward God" is part of the foundational teachings of Christ (Heb. 6:1). Abraham, who is known as the father of our faith (Rom. 4:16), was known more importantly as a friend of God. The Bible says, "… Abraham believed God, and it was accounted to him for righteousness. And he was called the friend of God" (James 2:23 NKJV).

Jesus said that if you have children and they ask for bread, you are not going to give them a stone. "So if you sinful people know how to give good gifts to your children, how much more will your heavenly Father give good gifts to those who ask him" (Matt. 7:11 NLT). We see how generous our heavenly Father is by this statement in Luke 12:32 (NKJV): "Do not fear, little flock, for it is your Father's good pleasure to give you the kingdom." By contrast, Herod Antipas, a worldly king, promised his stepdaughter that he would give her up to half of his kingdom (Mark 6:23). But God the Father is pleased to give the *whole* kingdom to us, His sons and daughters! This is a major promise that I hold before the Lord for the transformation of society. He wants His kingdom rule to come through us—that is, His "righteousness and peace and joy in the Holy Spirit" (Rom. 14:17).

With the two previous verses on God's kingdom, I want to focus our faith on seeing nations transformed.

FAITH TO TRANSFORM NATIONS

First, we must deal with unbelief when it comes to discipling a whole nation. The Bible teaches us that the stories of the Old Covenant are to help us learn from the mistakes of the past (see Hebrews 3–4). One of the most important truths is how unbelief prevented the nation of Israel from conquering the land of Canaan in Numbers 13.

> But the men who had gone up with him said, 'We are not able to go up against the people, for they are stronger than we.' And they gave the children of Israel a bad report of the land which they had spied out, saying, 'The land through which we have gone as spies is a land that devours its inhabitants, and all the people whom we saw in it are men of great stature. There we saw the giants (the descendants of Anak came from the giants); and we were like grasshoppers in our own sight, and so we were in their sight.' (Num. 13:31–33 NKJV)

> So all the congregation lifted up their voices and cried, and the people wept that night. And all the children of Israel complained against Moses and Aaron, and the whole congregation said to them, 'If only we had died in the land of Egypt! Or if only we had died in this wilderness! Why has the LORD brought us to this land to fall by the sword, that our wives and children should become victims? Would it not be better for us to return to

Egypt?' So they said to one another, 'Let us select a leader and return to Egypt.' (Num. 14:1–4 NKJV)

Keep in mind that God had delivered the nation of Israel by a mighty hand, including dividing the Red Sea, and yet their unbelief prevented them from possessing the Promised Land. Only Joshua and Caleb were allowed to enter the land with a new generation of Israelites.

Even Jesus could not do many miracles in His hometown of Nazareth because of their unbelief. Matthew 13:58 (NKJV) tells us, "Now He did not do many mighty works there because of their unbelief." This verse stuns me. We know that Jesus is God, and Jesus had perfect faith. Yet, in this instance, Jesus could not heal the sick.

The context of this verse is that Jesus had returned to Nazareth, and as He did in other towns and villages, He went into the synagogue to teach God's Word. Initially, the people were amazed at His wisdom. They had also heard about the miracles that Jesus did in other villages. But instead of wondering if Jesus was the coming Messiah, which would have begun their journey of faith, they began to rationalize and reduce Jesus to their familiarity.

'Is this not the carpenter's son? Is not His mother called Mary? And His brothers James, Joses, Simon, and Judas? And His sisters, are they not all with us? Where then did this Man get all these things?' So they were offended at Him. (Matt. 13:55–57 NKJV)

Essentially, they were saying, "We have known Jesus since he was a little boy. He is the son of Joseph. We know his family. He is just a carpenter. Who does he think he is?"

The Bible says that His words are Spirit and life (John 6:63). In Luke's version of His rejection in Nazareth, initially, the people were stirred in their spirit. "So all bore witness to Him, and marveled at the gracious words which proceeded out of His mouth." (Luke 4:22 NKJV). But they moved into familiarization, rationalization, and unbelief. "Wait a minute," they said to one another, "isn't this Joseph's son?" Not only did they reject Jesus as the Messiah, but they saw Him as a heretic and tried to push Him off a cliff when He walked past them (see Luke 4:28–30).

Unbelief, according to Scripture, is *sin*. Hebrews 3:12 offers this exhortation: "Beware, brethren, lest there be in any of you an evil heart of unbelief in departing from the living God." Billy Graham says:

> Unbelief is a sin because it is an insult to the truthfulness of God. 'He that believeth on the Son of God hath the witness in himself. He that believeth not God hath made him a liar because he believeth not the record that God gave of his Son' (1 John 5:10). It is unbelief that shuts the door to heaven and opens it to hell. It is unbelief that rejects the Word of God and refuses Christ as Savior. It is unbelief that causes men to turn a deaf ear to the gospel and to deny the miracles of Christ.[36]

---

[36] Billy Graham. *Peace with God: The Secret Happiness.* Thomas Nelson. Kindle Edition, p.56.

Today let's humble ourselves to repent and step out in faith. God has given us the authority to take the territory He has promised us. Let's ask God for wisdom and faith to transform our land.

Pray with me:

> *"Father, we come before You with repentance and humility. Forgive us for our unbelief. You have given us authority to tread upon serpents and over all the power of the enemy. We bind satan and his cohorts in Jesus' mighty name. We pray for revival and reformation for our nation and that our nation will be saved! In Jesus' name, amen."*

Chapter 5:

FROM KNOWLEDGE TO WISDOM

That the God of our Lord Jesus Christ, the Father of
glory, may give to you a spirit of wisdom and of revelation
in the knowledge of Him. (Eph. 1:17)

The Spirit of the Lord shall rest upon Him, the Spirit
of wisdom and understanding, the Spirit of counsel and
might, the Spirit of knowledge and of the fear of the Lord.
(Isa. 11:2 NKJV)

J flipped open my laptop one morning to catch up on a
litany of unread emails when my iPhone buzzed with
an incoming text message from my friend Ed Silvoso: "I need
to meet with you. It's urgent."

It was November 2017, and I had just returned home
from a round-the-world trip to visit our international churches
in Harvest International Ministry (HIM). My schedule only
allowed me to be in town for a week, with just enough time
to do my laundry and see my grandkids before leaving to cir-
cumnavigate the globe on another jam-packed ministry trip.

I looked back at the text from Ed. "I need to see you face to face," he insisted. Knowing Ed was writing from San Jose, California, I texted him back with a pragmatic request, "Can we just talk over FaceTime or Zoom?"

Ed's reply appeared in my notifications soon afterward: "This is so personal. I need to see you face to face, and you don't have to pay for me to fly out. I will get my own transportation. Just tell me where to meet."

Before sending another text, I went downstairs to find Sue in the kitchen and told her about the messages. "This is not like Ed," she began saying. "He's not the type of person who's going to fly out here just to give us any old word. You need to meet with him." I agreed with Sue's discernment that this was an important meeting.

Knowing Ed was from Argentina, a country that loves steak, I arranged to meet him at a prime steakhouse in our area. Later that week, I made the short drive over to the restaurant and gave my friend a hug as he walked through the door. Ed and I were both part of Peter Wagner's "Eagles Vision Apostolic Team" (EVAT), and we spent the first hour just trying to catch up because we've known each other for years.

Finally, I couldn't contain my impatience any longer. I popped the question, "Ed, what would cause you to come fly down here at a moment's notice? What is the word that you have for me?"

Ed, in turn, proceeded to ask me several questions. First, he asked, "Have you seen the fulfillment of the vision that God gave you when you were in Maryland?" Every now and then, I would share about the dream I had in 1982 that led me to come to Los Angeles for a great harvest, and he knew it was part of my faith journey.

I replied, "You know, Ed, I could rationalize it and say 'yes.' Because we've seen it globally through HIM, as the harvest is coming in—in the Philippines, in Kenya, in India. And we've had revival, as you know, when our church was birthed in 1994, and we went into protracted meetings in 1995, and we've seen thousands of people renewed and refreshed. But have we seen revival as far as a great harvest like the Jesus People days? The answer is 'no.'"

Ed nodded and said, "You are going to see it." He went on to ask the second question: "Who is the spiritual father in Northern California?"

"There are a number of them, but I would say Bill Johnson."

Ed agreed with me and then asked me the third question: "Who is the spiritual father in Southern California?"

I said, "Jack Hayford."

"Jack used to be," Ed said, "but he has retired." (Jack was my pastor, and since then, he went home to be with the Lord on January 8 at the age of 88. It was an honor for me to know Pastor Jack and participate in his memorial service in February 2023.)

After thinking for a moment, I tried again: "In that case, I would say the late John Wimber."

"No, he is dead."

Finally, I said, "I don't know."

Ed looked me in the eyes and said, "You are. And the word I have for you is if you turn your heart back to California, God is going to give you apostolic strategy to see revival and transformation in California."

Honestly, the word went over my head, just like when Cindy Jacobs had prophesied to me to start HIM over two decades earlier. In the moment, I felt kind of embarrassed that Ed would even say that about me. I wanted to be frank with my friend, so I spoke my mind: "It doesn't make sense because I am focusing on international ministry, traveling around the world. And I feel like the world is my parish now that I am no longer a senior pastor." (The year prior, I had turned Harvest Rock Church over to my son Gabe and my daughter-in-law Monica to lead.)

"I am not telling you it will make sense," Ed responded. "I am just telling you what the Lord told me to share with you."

As I acknowledged the word, I began to pray into it in the days that followed. I took the phrase "apostolic strategy" to also mean "apostolic wisdom" because I recognized that it was not man's strategy but God's wisdom that Ed was talking to me about.

The next thing I knew, a year went by, and my son resigned from his pastoral position in December 2018 as God was redirecting his vocational journey. By January 2019, Sue and I were back at the helm of Harvest Rock Church as senior pastors.

Another year later, the COVID lockdown took everyone by surprise in the spring of 2020. I had six international trips planned that were immediately canceled due to the pandemic. I couldn't travel anywhere even if I wanted to. Thus, I was forced to focus on the only sphere of ministry that was left: *California.*

It was during this time that I experienced a supernatural grace, an insatiable desire to know God, to know His ways, and to get into the Word like never before. On a practical note, I was preaching every week and often spent over 20 hours in sermon preparation besides my regular time in prayer and Scripture. As I got into His Word, I felt that wisdom was growing in me. By immersing myself afresh in the Word and seeking the Holy Spirit, I was put onto the fast track of the Lord's wisdom. In retrospect, I can say that I probably grew more in wisdom between 2019 and 2024 (as of the writing of this book) than the previous 45 years of walking with the Lord.

The Word of God exploded in my life, and it was the spirit of wisdom and revelation (Eph. 1:17) giving me insight into Scripture that I didn't have before. This is another important key to transforming the world. We have to move out of humanism, or man's wisdom, into God's supernatural wisdom that He has given to us through the mind of Christ (1 Cor. 2:16).

GREEK THINKING VS. HEBRAIC THINKING

Sometimes paradigm shifts are needed in areas with deep roots, beyond easy recognition at first glance. The Greek philosophy of Platonic thinking, or dualism, is one such problem that has significantly influenced the church. This is not a new phenomenon. Rather, it has had a slow but steady influence over the past two millennia.

Some 400 years before Christ, the Greek philosopher Plato made waves in the ancient world as a thought leader, following in the footsteps of Socrates and going on to mentor Aristotle. Before I give the concerns that I have on Platonic thinking, let me say that *truth is truth*, and these Greek philosophers discovered a measure of truth, logic, and rational thinking that have tremendously benefited the Western world. For example, Greek thinking brought balance and rationale to certain aspects of religious extremism. Specifically, the Islamic world was virtually untouched by Greek thinking, and as a result, you have the extremism of Sharia law and Jihadism that have provoked terrorism, including the genocide of 1,200 women and children that were heinously murdered on October 7, 2023, in Israel near the Gaza strip.

The Greeks also contributed to the foundation of a democratic form of government that helped shape our nation. Our founding fathers took the essence of democracy and brilliantly built a constitutional republic with the division of power between Congress, the executive branch, and the judicial branch of government. In a constitutional republic, the people vote for leaders who make laws. However, the leaders cannot make just any laws they please because the Constitution severely restricts their law-making power, thus avoiding totalitarian leaders.

But here is one of my concerns on Platonic thinking. One of the underlying tenets of Plato's teaching was dualism. This mindset proposed that the world should be understood in two separate categories: the natural world and the spirit world—the upper and the lower. Dualism divides reality into the realm of the tangible (physical matter) and the intangible (ideas and ideals). The value attributed to each carries a strong bias: The material world is evil, and only the spirit world is good. The two worlds are not just different; they are intrinsically disconnected from one another.[37]

This Greek way of thinking may seem appealing and even "Christian." In fact, that mindset comes naturally to many Christians today because of the influence of Augustine of Hippo (modern-day Algeria, AD 396–430) and Thomas Aquinas (1225–1274). These two theologians helped shape the rhetoric used throughout much of church history. The problem is that Platonic Greek thinking is ultimately incompatible with Hebraic thinking based on Scripture.[38]

Dualism is a false dichotomy. In Genesis 1, God emphatically called the material world that He made *good*. On each day of creation, He declared that "it was good." According to the Hebraic worldview, humans are wholistic beings. Therefore, we are both spiritual and earthly. We are living souls, and we live in physical bodies formed from the dust of the earth. God created us to experience heaven on earth. The two aspects of creation, spiritual and physical, are meant to be in harmony, not division.

This is especially important because of our understanding of who Jesus is. Jesus is 100 percent God and 100 percent man. John 1:14 (NIV) tells us, "The Word became flesh and made His dwelling among us." Jesus became a human being with a physical body. He did not just come as a ghostly apparition or a purely spiritual being. He came in the flesh, died a physical death, and was raised to life. He did this to redeem us wholly—spirit, soul, and body.

---

[37] Wagner, C. Peter. *This Changes Everything*. Baker Publishing Group. Kindle Edition, p.129-130.
[38] Ibid.

Similar to the dichotomy we saw during the Jesus People days, Platonic thinking has deceived the church to this day. "The gospel and all things spiritual are good," some Christians will say. "But the world and government and school systems and man-made structures? Forget about them! We're just hanging on for the rapture."

Out of the error of dualism has come the separation of sacred and secular—clergy and laity—church and state. That is fundamentally unbiblical. All believers are kings and priests (see Rev. 1:6, 5:10; 1 Pet. 2:9; Ex. 19:6). Everything that we are involved in is sacred. There is no separation between sacred and secular when our whole lives are consecrated to God. Making this paradigm shift will help us understand our call to influence and transform society for God's glory.

THE FOUNDATIONS OF WISDOM

As I have shared in my stories above, the Word of God is essential to walking in wisdom. The book of Proverbs, an entire book of the Bible dedicated to wisdom, provides a wonderful starting point for any discussion on godly wisdom. The first two chapters of Proverbs begin this way:

> These are the proverbs of Solomon, David's son, king of Israel. Their purpose is *to teach people wisdom* and discipline, to help them understand the insights of the wise. Their purpose is to teach people to live disciplined and successful lives, to help them do what is right, just, and fair ... *Fear of the Lord* is the foundation of true knowledge,

but fools despise wisdom and discipline." (Prov. 1:1–3, 7 NLT)

Though I entitled this chapter "From Knowledge to Wisdom," I am not against knowledge, per se. However, I do believe that knowledge without wisdom will lead to a nation going backward and not forward into reformation. For example, the scientists at the CDC and NIH had more PhDs and MDs than some nations have, but they had no wisdom by recommending locking down our nation during COVID-19. True wisdom comes from the knowledge of God, and *that* is the knowledge that we need.

> *My son,* if you *receive my words, and treasure my commands within you,* so that you *incline your ear to wisdom,* and apply your heart to understanding … Then you will understand the *fear of the Lord* and find the knowledge of God. (Prov. 2:1–2, 5 NKJV)

There are two important lessons that stand out from these verses. Let's explore them.

1. You will come into wisdom by embracing the fear of the Lord.

Walking in the fear of the Lord can be described as having a holy awe of God. To fear the Lord in a biblical sense is to have the right view of God, the right view of yourself, and the right view of sin. Those who fear God acknowledge His supreme value and preeminence; therefore, they are humble. They have received His lavish love and forgiveness, so they would never want to do anything to grieve His heart. Instead, they will be doers of the Word, operating in God's wisdom and desiring to "do what is right, just, and fair" (Prov. 1:3 NLT). As John Bevere writes in his amazing book *The Awe of God*, the fear of the Lord makes us want to come *closer* to God, not further away.[39] He goes on to say that the fear of the Lord is to love what God loves and to hate what He hates. "The fear of the LORD *is* to hate evil; pride and arrogance and the evil way and the perverse mouth I hate" (Prov. 8:13 NKJV).

2. Another key to coming into wisdom is meditating on God's Word.

In my reading, these passages in Proverbs 2 are not only referring to the written word (*logos*) but also to the revelatory word (*rhema*). When it says, "Incline your ear to wisdom" (Prov. 2:2 NKJV), I believe we can understand this in the New Covenant context of listening to the voice of the Holy Spirit.

In the Gospel of John, Jesus told the 12 disciples, "But the Helper, the Holy Spirit, whom the Father will send in My name, He will teach you all things, and bring to your remembrance all that I said to you" (John 14:26 NKJV). Over three years, Jesus had taught them about the kingdom of God, day in and day out. Even so, He recognized that there was still so much more that needed to be taught: "I have many more things to say to you, but you cannot bear them at the present

---

[39] John Bevere, *The Awe of God*. Thomas Nelson, 2023. Ebook, p.12-13.

time" (John 16:12). That is why Jesus elaborated on the Holy Spirit's role as their teacher:

> But when He, the Spirit of truth, comes, *He will guide you into all the truth*; for He will not speak on His own initiative, but whatever He hears, He will speak; and *He will disclose to you what is to come.* He will glorify Me, for He will take of Mine and will disclose it to you. All things that the Father has are Mine; therefore I said that He takes of Mine and will disclose it to you. (John 16:13–15 NASB1995)

In this passage, the emphasis is that Jesus is still teaching us His Word, but He now does so through the Holy Spirit. Notice how the Spirit reminds us of what Jesus said (John 14:26) *and* tells us what is coming in the days ahead (John 16:13). Thus, our relationship with the Holy Spirit will keep us grounded, meditating on the *logos* Word of God, while letting Him speak prophetic *rhema* to us about the future. The Holy Spirit is eager to teach us today if we will only lend our ears to listen. "He who has ears to hear, let him hear" (Matt. 11:15).

GOD'S WISDOM CREATED THE WORLD

Wisdom is not just a nice "add-on" in our walk with God. It is central to God's identity and nature, and we, as born-again believers, now partake of His divine nature (2 Pet. 1:4). God is the Creator of all things, and the Bible reveals it was His *wisdom* that created the world as we know it. This truth is apparent all throughout Scripture:

> The Lord *by wisdom* founded the earth, by understanding He established the heavens. (Prov. 3:19 NKJV)

> It is He who made the earth by His power, who established the world *by His wisdom*, and by His understanding He stretched out the heavens. (Jer. 51:15)

> O Lord, how many are Your works! *In wisdom* You have made them all; the earth is full of Your possessions. (Ps. 104:24 NASB1995)

In Proverbs 8, wisdom is personified as we get an "insider's look" at how God created the world. I have highlighted three takeaways from the verses below. Remember that Wisdom is the voice that is speaking here.

1. Wisdom existed with God before creation.

> The Lord possessed me at the beginning of His way, before His works of old. From everlasting I was established, from the beginning, from the earliest times of the earth. When there were no depths I was brought forth, when there were no springs abounding with water. Before the mountains were settled, before the hills I was brought forth; while He had not yet made the earth and

102

the fields, nor the first dust of the world. (Prov. 8:22–26 NASB1995)

2. Wisdom was present during creation.

When He established the heavens, I was there, when He inscribed a circle on the face of the deep, when He made firm the skies above, when the springs of the deep became fixed, when He set for the sea its boundary so that the water would not transgress His command, when He marked out the foundations of the earth. (Prov. 8:27–29 NASB1995)

3. Wisdom played an active role in creation.

Then I was beside Him, *as a master workman*; and I was daily His delight, rejoicing always before Him, rejoicing in the world, His earth, and having my delight in the sons of men. (Prov. 8:30–31)

Verse 30 tells us that wisdom was beside God the Father "as a master workman." Other Bible translations phrase this as "a master craftsman" (AMP), "the architect at his side," (NLT) or "his master artist" (TPT).

Overall, these three descriptions should sound familiar to anyone who has read the New Testament: Wisdom (1) existed with God before creation, (2) was present during the act of creation, and (3) had an active role in creating all things. That sounds a lot like the description of *the Word* in the Gospel of John.

In the beginning the Word *already existed*. The Word was with God, and *the Word was God*. He existed in the beginning with God. God *created everything through him*, and nothing was created except through him. The Word gave life to everything that was created, and his life brought light to everyone. (John 1:1–4 NLT)

John the Beloved begins his Gospel with the radical statement that Jesus was the Word of God from eternity. This language is intentional because it explicitly shows Christ's divinity and His role in creating all things, which only God can do. First Corinthians 1:30 (NASB1995) affirms this connection and explicitly states that Jesus *is* divine wisdom: "But by His doing you are in *Christ Jesus, who became to us wisdom* from God, and righteousness and sanctification, and redemption." The New Living Translation puts it this way: "For our benefit God made [Jesus] to be wisdom itself."

In that light, we can see that walking in wisdom is having the mind of Christ (1 Cor. 2:16). To be wise is to be like Jesus, to think like He does. Wisdom is being full of Him, full of His Holy Spirit. When the prophet Isaiah describes seven attributes of the Holy Spirit that would characterize the Messiah, one of these is the Spirit of wisdom, and another, unsurprisingly, is the fear of the Lord.

The Spirit of the Lord shall rest upon Him, *the Spirit of wisdom* and understanding, the Spirit of counsel and might, the Spirit of knowledge and of *the fear of the Lord*. (Isa. 11:2 NKJV)

If we want to grow in wisdom, we must cultivate a living, dynamic relationship with Jesus. The apostle Paul prayed this for the church in Ephesus, "that the God of our Lord Jesus Christ, the Father of glory, may give to you a spirit of wisdom and of revelation in the knowledge of Him" (Eph. 1:17). Wisdom starts and ends with knowing God, whose wisdom is infinite.

Just as God's wisdom is creative and active in nature, we are meant to play an active role in revealing His wisdom on the earth today. God's purpose was that *through the church,* "the manifold wisdom of God might be made known" (Eph. 3:10 NKJV). Because we were made in His image, we are called to reflect the wisdom of God the Father in society, much like the moon reflects the light of the sun. That wisdom will be seen through the transformative work of the *Ekklesia*—God's called-out ones—as we advance His kingdom in our mountains of culture.

SOLOMON'S KINGDOM: A PROTOTYPE OF TRANSFORMATION

Why is wisdom so crucial? The Word of God reveals that wisdom is a key to transform society. Of all the kings of Israel in the Old Testament, the kingdom of Solomon provides a prototype of how wisdom results in a transformed nation.

Solomon was one of the sons of King David, an archetype for the coming Messiah. Besides being a prolific musician and worshiper after God's heart, David made a name for himself as a warrior king. From battling wild animals as a shepherd boy to killing the giant Goliath, rallying his mighty men in

the Cave of Adullam to leading the vast armies of Israel—
David was a fighter, often going from one battle to the next.
If David established a kingdom of victorious military might,
Solomon (whose name means "peaceful") established a king-
dom of peace and extreme blessings. How did this drastic
change take place?

Shortly after beginning to reign, King Solomon had a dramatic dream encounter where the Lord basically offered him
carte blanche. The Bible says, "In Gibeon the Lord appeared to
Solomon in a dream at night; and God said, 'Ask what you
wish Me to give you'" (1 Kings 3:5). Solomon's reply was
revealing, as he had a true heart of humility and hunger to
know God:

> Now, O Lord my God, You have made Your ser-
> vant king in place of my father David, yet I am but
> a little child; I do not know how to go out or come
> in. Your servant is in the midst of Your people
> which You have chosen, a great people who are
> too many to be numbered or counted. *So give Your
> servant an understanding heart* to judge Your people to
> discern between good and evil. For who is able to
> judge this great people of Yours? (1 Kings 3:7–9
> NASB1995)

The Hebrew phrase in verse 9, here translated as "an
understanding heart," is literally "a *hearing* heart." Solomon
knew that God was the source of wisdom, and he refused to
rely on his own human understanding as he began undertak-
ing the monumental responsibility of governing a nation. In

short, Solomon knew he needed to hear from God in order to walk in wisdom, and God was more than willing to fulfill this request.

> The Lord was pleased that Solomon had asked for this. So God said to him, 'Since you have asked for ... *discernment* [literally, *hearing*] in administering justice, I will do what you have asked. I will give you *a wise and discerning heart*, so that there will never have been anyone like you, nor will there ever be.' (1 Kings 3:10–12 NIV)

Not only did Solomon receive a divine infusion of wisdom, but God also gave him what he did not ask for: wealth, honor, and long life (1 Kings 3:13–14). You see, wisdom—a heart attuned to the voice of God—set Solomon up to prosper in unprecedented ways. King Solomon ruled with such justice and righteousness that the nation of Israel became a hub of abundance, well-being, and success. The nation prospered so radically that gold and silver became as common as stones in Jerusalem (2 Chron. 1:15)! Because of God's boundless wisdom, Solomon's fame quickly spread to the surrounding nations (1 Kings 4:29–34), to the extent that royal dignitaries eagerly wanted to come and witness the fruit of Solomon's wisdom for themselves (1 Kings 10:1–13).

The transformation of Israel was so complete that Solomon made this astonishing observation: "But now the LORD my God has given me rest on every side; there is neither adversary nor evil occurrence" (1 Kings 5:4 NKJV).

Let's unpack this statement to better understand what had taken place in Solomon's kingdom.

1. "The LORD my God has given me rest on every side..."

First, the nation was at rest from war. Therefore, Solomon did not have to follow in his father's footsteps as a military commander, constantly defending the nation from belligerent intruders. A truly wise and strong leader will not only win wars but prevent them from happening in the first place. Solomon's kingdom thrived on the godly wisdom of being a peacemaker (see Matt. 5:9).

2. "There is no evil occurrence..."

Next, we know that society was transformed because there was no evil or injustice taking place. Wisdom is again connected with the fear of the Lord, for Solomon would go on to write, "The fear of the Lord is to *hate evil...*" (Prov. 8:13). Ruling a nation in divine wisdom meant inculcating society with the values of God's kingdom, leading to righteousness (right living) and justice, and eliminating evil influences from the cultural landscape.

Imagine living in a nation with virtually no crime, and you'll get the picture. We have seen echoes of this reality throughout revival history, for example, during the Welsh Revival (1904–1905). Historians tell us that courts and jails throughout Wales were empty, leaving the police force with nothing to do other than go to church![40]

[40] R.T. Kendall. *The Presence of God: Discovering God's Ways Through Intimacy With Him.* Charisma House, 2017. Ebook, p.141.

3. "There is no adversary..."

To go one step further, we must realize that the Hebrew word for "adversary" is actually the word *satan*. In other words, we know that satan was still in existence, but there was no room for him to have a legal right to attack. He could not wreak havoc in Israel because there was righteousness throughout the entire land. That is the level of transformation I am praying over my nation, and I believe God wants to see that take place across the globe as we "disciple nations" with His kingdom values.

WISDOM HAS BUILT HER HOUSE

In sum, the wisdom of God is essential to transform our world. Without His divine wisdom, no family, business, church, or nation can be built well. Proverbs 9, written by King Solomon, makes this clear:

> *Wisdom has built her house; she has set up its seven pillars.* She has prepared her meat and mixed her wine; she has also set her table. She has sent out her servants, and she calls from the highest point of the city, 'Let all who are simple come to my house!' To those who have no sense she says, 'Come, eat my food and drink the wine I have mixed. Leave your simple ways and you will live; walk in the way of insight.' (Prov. 9:1–6 NIV)

Just as King Solomon needed wisdom to build an awe-inspiring temple, palace, and nation (1 Kings 10:4–5), we likewise need to look to God as our constant source of wisdom to build well. Each of our lives and ministries are pieces of God's macro puzzle. Our choices to build wisely are part of the bigger picture of turning our nation back to God and transforming it into a godly "sheep nation" (see Matt. 25:31–33). In his first letter to the Corinthian church, the apostle Paul wrote:

> For we are God's fellow workers; *you are … God's building.* According to the grace of God which was given to me, *like a wise master builder* I laid a foundation, and another is building on it. But each man must be careful how he builds on it. For no man can lay a foundation other than the one which is laid, which is Jesus Christ. (1 Cor. 3:9–11)

At the end of the day, Jesus Himself is building His church, which includes you and me (Matt. 16:18). We need to tune into His voice and know His wisdom intimately to be effective collaborators, building His kingdom together. Let's agree in prayer:

> *"Heavenly Father, Your Word says that if I lack wisdom, I can confidently ask and expect You to answer my prayer generously (James 1:5–6). So, by faith, I ask You to fill me with Your divine wisdom. Jesus, give me a hearing heart that I would know Your voice intimately. Holy Spirit, help me to build Your kingdom in my sphere of influence—all for Your glory and in Jesus' mighty name!"*

Chapter 6:

FROM THE GOSPEL OF SALVATION TO THE GOSPEL OF THE KINGDOM

This gospel of the kingdom shall be preached in the whole world as a testimony to all the nations, and then the end will come. (Matt. 24:14)

Your kingdom come. Your will be done, on earth as it is in heaven. (Matt. 6:10)

The gospel, in general, means good news. Specifically for Christians, it is the good news that Jesus died for our sins, He was buried, and He rose again on the third day, as enumerated here:

> Moreover, brethren, I declare to you the gospel which I preached to you, which also you received and in which you stand, by which also you are saved, if you hold fast that word which I preached to you—unless you believed in vain. For I delivered

to you first of all that which I also received: that Christ died for our sins according to the Scriptures, and that He was buried, and that He rose again the third day according to the Scriptures. (1 Cor. 15:1–4 NKJV)

Just as I wrote this paragraph, I suddenly saw a silver sparkle on the floor next to the dresser in my hotel room. I leaned down to get a closer look, and it was a tiny cross earring that someone who had stayed at the hotel before me may have lost. God used this as a small but significant confirmation that I had to begin with the good news of Jesus' sacrificial death on the cross. Billy Graham once said, if given the chance to start over, "I would preach more on the cross and the blood of Christ. That's where the power is."[41]

Paul begins his famous chapter on Christ's resurrection stating that Jesus "died for our sins according to the Scriptures" (1 Cor. 15:3). I wonder if Paul was thinking of Isaiah 53, the famous passage of the suffering Messiah and His sacrificial death on the cross. When we understand what Jesus did for us on the cross, we will understand why we call the gospel the good news!

The question is, why did Jesus have to die in order to forgive and save humanity from sin and eternal death? Theologians have tried for many decades to explain the

---

[41] Greg Laurie. "Billy Graham and His Last Crusade?" Harvest Ministries. November 19, 2010. https://harvest.org/resources/gregs-blog/post/billy-graham-and-his-last-crusade/

atonement, and volumes of books have been written about it. Still, let me humbly give my take on why Jesus died for us.

God said to Adam in Genesis 2:16–17 (NKJV), "Of every tree of the garden you may freely eat; but of the tree of the knowledge of good and evil you shall not eat, for in the day that you eat of it you shall surely die." The greatest tragedy in human history is that Adam and Eve disobeyed and rebelled against God when they ate the forbidden fruit. As a result, sin, death, and every evil entered into this world, and satan became the ruler of this world.

God desires to forgive and show mercy, but He is also a just God and cannot lie. The only answer is a substitution. The only solution was for an innocent party to volunteer to die physically and spiritually as a substitute for the world's sins. But who is qualified? It would have to be someone who is innocent himself. It would have to be someone who really loved us because he certainly would not owe it to us—he would willingly die. It would be someone of such importance that his death and suffering would have an impact on the whole world for all of history.

The only person qualified is God Himself, and that is exactly what happened. The God who created the universe came for the purpose of being executed in your place so that you might have life. Jesus, God the Son, died an excruciating death but also died of a broken heart. As He took our sins, He was separated from the oneness and intimacy with God the Father. He who knew no sin became sin for us (2 Cor. 5:21). And whoever repents of one's sins and believes in what Jesus did for them on the cross will become born again. God's Spirit will come inside the believer and give them a new life.

THE DIVINE EXCHANGE

Over the years, I have given a series of sermons at my home church called "The Great Exchange" or "The Divine Exchange," and it is based on the following passage from Isaiah:

> Surely He has borne our griefs and carried our sorrows; yet we esteemed Him stricken, smitten by God, and afflicted. But He was wounded for our transgressions, He was bruised for our iniquities; the chastisement for our peace was upon Him, and by His stripes we are healed. All we like sheep have gone astray; we have turned, everyone, to his own way; and the LORD has laid on Him the iniquity of us all ... Yet it pleased the LORD to bruise Him; He has put Him to grief. When You make His soul an offering for sin... (Isa. 53:4–6, 10 NKJV)

Before we can appreciate the magnificent Good News of what Jesus did for us on the cross, we have to look more closely at the bad news of humanity's sin. This is just like a jeweler who doesn't show off a brilliant diamond with a white backdrop, but shows the diamond with a black velvet backdrop for the purpose of contrast. In order to appreciate the beauty of the gospel—how God, in His mercy, saved us from our sin—we need to look at sin for what it is.

Isaiah intentionally describes humanity like "sheep gone astray." The Bible has over a dozen descriptions of sin, like "missing the mark" and "falling short of God's glory," but Isaiah uses the description of selfishness and iniquity: "*we have turned, everyone to his own way"* and *"the iniquity of us all"* (Isa. 53:6 NKJV).

Sin is essentially selfishness. We have turned our backs to God and have become our own god, doing what pleases us supremely. The Hebrew word that sums this up is the word *awon*, and it is translated here as iniquity. Perhaps the closest word in the English language is the word *rebellion*, not against man but against God. In Hebrew, iniquity also implies the punishment that comes as the consequences of sin. For example, when God declares the punishment for Cain's murder of his brother Abel, Cain cries out, "My punishment is too great to endure!" (Gen. 4:13). The word *punishment* in Hebrew is the same word for iniquity, *awon*. One can translate this as "the punishment for my iniquity."

Now that we've covered the bad news, let's take a look at the good news of the divine exchange.

Divine Exchange #1

The first divine exchange took place when Jesus "became sin" with our sins so that we could be righteous with His righteousness. The Bible says, "And the LORD has laid on Him the iniquity of us all" (Isa. 53:6). Not only was Jesus identified with our sin, but He also endured all the evil consequences of our rebellion. Like the scapegoat that carried away the sins of Israel and was never to return to Israel, so, too, Jesus took away our sins and the consequences of our sins, never to return to our lives again.

Paul says it this way, "For He made Him who knew no sin *to be* sin for us, that we might become the righteousness of

God in Him" (2 Cor. 5:21 NKJV). In essence, Jesus was made sin with our sinfulness so that we might be made righteous with His righteousness and holiness. The truth about the cross is that a divine exchange took place. Jesus took the sins and the evil consequences upon Himself so that you might be forgiven and totally delivered from the consequences of sin. That is why it is called the good news. Yet there is more (insert TV commercial voice here)!

Divine Exchange #2

Interwoven with taking on our sin, the second divine exchange took place when Christ took our sickness so that we might be healed and walk in divine health. Scripture says in Isaiah 53:4–5, "Surely, He has borne our griefs [literally, *our sickness*] and carried our sorrows [literally, *our pains*]; yet we esteemed Him stricken, smitten by God, and afflicted. But He was wounded for our transgressions, He was bruised for our iniquities; the chastisement for our peace was upon Him, and by His stripes we are healed." Jesus took our sickness, diseases, and physical pains that "by His stripes"—by His wounds—we might be healed.

The physical application of the divine exchange is confirmed in the New Testament. Matthew comments on Isaiah 53:4 in Matthew 8:16–17 (NKJV) by saying, "When evening had come, they brought to Him many who were demon-possessed. And He cast out the spirits with a word, and healed all who were sick, that it might be fulfilled which was spoken by Isaiah the prophet, saying: 'He Himself took our infirmities and bore our sicknesses.'" The context is clear that this passage is referring to physical sickness and not emotional griefs and sorrows. In short, Jesus was wounded that we might be healed physically!

Divine Exchange #3

Finally, the third exchange is seen in Isaiah 53:10b (NKJV): "When You make His soul an offering for sin." The context for this statement is the Mosaic ordinances for various sin offerings. A person would bring an animal—whether a goat, sheep, or bull, depending on what they could afford—and bring the sacrificial animal to the priest. The priest would lay hands on the head of the animal and transfer the sins of the person to the animal, and then sacrifice the animal before the Lord. The person's sin, having been transferred over, would be declared forgiven and the animal sacrificed.

On the cross, Jesus became the Lamb of God who took away the sins of humanity and died for all humanity. The writer of Hebrews says, "But we see Jesus, who was made a little lower than the angels, for the suffering of death crowned with glory and honor, that He, by the grace of God, *might taste death for everyone*" (Heb. 2:9 NKJV). Jesus died our death so that we might receive His life. Paul says, "For *the death* that He died, He died to sin once for all; but *the life* that He lives, He lives to God" (Rom. 6:10 NKJV), so that everyone who believes in Him will not perish but have everlasting life (John 3:16b).

There are many more divine exchanges that took place on the cross. Jesus became a curse for us to set us free from all curses so that we might enter into a blessed life (Gal. 3:13). In 2 Corinthians 8:9, we also read, "For you know the grace of our Lord Jesus Christ, that though He was rich, yet for your sake He became poor, so that you through His poverty might become rich." This latter verse deserves more attention, and I devote a whole chapter to this divine exchange later on in this book.

Next, let's look at why the good news is called the gospel of *the kingdom*.

THE KINGDOM

The gospel of the kingdom is called good news because the divine exchange, or what the writer of Hebrews calls our "great salvation" (Heb. 2:3), cannot be realized unless one enters the kingdom of God. So, how does one enter the kingdom? Jesus said to Nicodemus in John 3:5 (NKJV), "Most assuredly, I say to you, unless one is born of water and the Spirit, he cannot enter the kingdom of God." By water, Jesus meant water baptism, which is the outward washing of an inner repentance that Jesus required and preached in Matthew 4:17—"Repent, for the kingdom of heaven is at hand."

John the Baptist, in Mark 1:4–5 (NKJV), gives a fuller account of the demands of the kingdom: "John came baptizing in the wilderness and preaching a baptism of repentance for the remission of sins. Then all the land of Judea, and those from Jerusalem, went out to him and were all baptized by him in the Jordan River, confessing their sins." What Jesus and John preached is that one cannot enter into the kingdom without first repenting of one's sins, and then Jesus adds that one must also *believe* in the gospel. We see this in Mark 1:14–15 (NKJV):

> Now after John was put in prison, Jesus came to Galilee, preaching the gospel of the kingdom of God, and saying, 'The time is fulfilled, and the kingdom of God is at hand. *Repent*, and *believe* in the gospel.'

In today's Christianity, "to believe in Jesus" has been watered down to easy believism. To believe in the gospel is not just to give mental assent to the truth of Jesus' death and resurrection. The emphasis is to accept Jesus as your *Savior*. It is arresting to note that the Bible never says the words "the gospel of salvation." To believe in the New Testament sense is to totally surrender oneself to the rule and reign of God. The Bible's emphasis is that Jesus is *Lord*.

The title *Lord* appears over 7,000 times in the Bible, whereas the word *Savior* shows up 37 times. Of course, Jesus is our Savior, but the emphasis is first on His Lordship, and *then* He becomes your Savior. Romans 10:9 says, "If you confess with your mouth Jesus as Lord, and believe in your heart that God raised Him from the dead, you will be saved." To believe in Jesus means to obey Him and His commands. That is why the words *believe* and *obey* are used interchangeably in John 3:36:

> "He who *believes* [*pisteuo*] in the Son has eternal life; but he who does not *obey* [*apeitheo*] the Son will not see life, but the wrath of God remains on him."

When I came to Christ during the Jesus People days, the Lordship of Jesus was emphasized and proclaimed. This meant we preached against the notion of "Come to Jesus as your Savior and later make Him Lord." Instead, the message was, "Come to Jesus as Lord, and He will *become* your Savior." I believe that we have lost the message of the gospel of the kingdom and have resorted to the gospel of salvation. As a result, many who profess to know Jesus have never been truly saved.

After I became a pastor during the Jesus movement, a young man came into the counseling room and asked that I pray for him to be baptized in the Holy Spirit and speak in tongues. After giving a brief teaching on the doctrine of the baptism of the Holy Spirit, I prayed for him, but nothing happened. Then I backed up and asked this young man to tell me how he came to know Jesus.

He began by saying, "One day, I went to a Baptist church," which I could relate to as the son of a Baptist pastor. "The pastor preached the gospel and said, 'If you want to give your life to Jesus, raise your hand.' So, I raised my hand, and then he asked those who raised their hand to pray this prayer. I prayed the prayer. And then he basically said, 'Congratulations to all those who prayed this prayer. You're born again.'"

I thought, *So far so good.* "What was your life like before?" I asked. "And tell me how you've been changed."

At that point, the young man looked down, almost embarrassed. He said, "My life before? I was an alcoholic. I did drugs, but my primary problem was alcoholism."

"What did that look like?"

"I got drunk every night," he confessed. "I'd buy a case of beer every day and drink the whole case."

The first thought that came to mind was, *Wow. That's a lot of liquid. He must run to the bathroom every hour!* (I didn't say that out loud, of course.)

"OK," I replied. "Was there anything else? Were you living in immorality?"

"Yes," he told me. "I was sleeping with my girlfriend. But I was also sleeping with both guys and girls. I was bisexual."

I acknowledged his transparency and asked, "So, tell me, what happened after you gave your life to Jesus Christ?"

At this point, the young man shifted his gaze again, looking at the floor in embarrassment.

"Has anything changed?" I asked.

"Not really."

"Are you still getting drunk?"

"Yes," he admitted. "I'm still drinking a case of beer a day."

Then I said, "Well, what about your moral life?"

"I'm still practicing bisexuality," he told me.

I was in shock! While I appreciated his honesty, I was really stunned that there was zero change in his life after praying "the sinner's prayer."

That is when I gave the young man my verdict: "I have some good news and some bad news. Let me give you the bad news: *You're not saved.* You never got converted. Because if anyone becomes a Christian, you are a new person—your old life is passed away—behold, all things are made new, as it says in 2 Corinthians 5:17. But the good news is *you can be saved.*" Then, I shared the gospel with him. "You have to surrender your whole heart to Jesus Christ. You have to repent of these sins. What that means is that you are going to have to *hate* sin. You are going to have to stop drinking. No more buying a case of beer a day. You also have to be celibate until you get married."

In humility, the young man agreed to do that. So, for the first time, he gave his life to Jesus Christ. When I saw his faith in that moment, I prayed that God would fill him with the Holy Spirit, and he started to speak in tongues. This man ended up becoming one of our small group leaders at our church in Maryland before we moved to Southern California. Moreover, he got married, had several children, and got a very successful job. His story became a powerful testimony that I have shared for decades because of the fruit that has grown in his life as a result of true repentance.

This is just a small example of where many people are in the American church today. Many so-called Christians run around thinking that they are saved, but they have truly not entered the kingdom. This is a result of never hearing *the gospel of the kingdom* but only hearing the gospel of salvation and easy believism. This is why we need to understand fully what the kingdom of God, or the kingdom of heaven, means.

DEFINING THE KINGDOM

Jesus and John the Baptist both began their ministry by preaching the gospel of the kingdom. The word *kingdom* appears 157 times in the New Testament. When you compare the word *church* in the four Gospels (Matthew, Mark, Luke, and John)—where it appears only once in Matthew 16:18 and twice in Matthew 18:17—you begin to realize that the kingdom is a very important theological truth in the

Bible. The word *kingdom* means the rule and reign of God, or the realm ruled by God. It means the Lordship or Kingship of God. One of the most important passages of God's kingdom is found in the Old Testament in the book of Isaiah. It gives us a basic theology of the kingdom.

> For unto us a Child is born, unto us a Son is given; and the government will be upon His shoulder. And His name will be called Wonderful, Counselor, Mighty God, Everlasting Father, Prince of Peace. Of the increase of His government and peace there will be no end, upon the throne of David and over His kingdom, to order it and establish it with judgment and justice from that time forward, even forever. The zeal of the LORD of hosts will perform this. (Isa. 9:6–7 NKJV)

This prophecy delineates seven characteristics of the kingdom:

1. Jesus the Messiah will inaugurate the kingdom age by His birth and life. "For unto us a Child is born, unto us a Son is given…" (Isa. 9:6a NKJV).

2. The government or the kingdom will rest upon His shoulders. "And the government will be upon His shoulder" (Isa. 9:6b KNJV). He is the head, the King, and He will shoulder the responsibility of seeing His kingdom established on earth as it is in heaven.

3. His kingdom will start off small, but it will increase until it covers the whole earth. "Of the

increase of His government…" (Isa. 9:7a NKJV). He is the small rock that came out of nowhere and crushed the statue in Daniel 2:35b: "But the stone that struck the statue became a great mountain and filled the entire earth." Jesus was born in a manger and began His ministry with the words, "Repent, for the kingdom of heaven is at hand" (Matt. 4:17). His kingdom has been advancing and expanding throughout the earth ever since, and will continue until, "…the kingdom of the world has become the kingdom of the Lord and of His Christ, and He will reign forever and ever" (Rev. 11:15).

4. His kingdom is eternal. "Of the increase of His government and peace there will be no end" (Isa. 9:7a NKJV). The psalmist says, "Your kingdom is an everlasting kingdom, and Your dominion endures throughout all generations" (Ps. 145:13).

5. Jesus is the Messiah that was prophesied to King David by the prophet Nathan in 2 Samuel 7:12–16 (NKJV):

> When your days are fulfilled and you rest with your fathers, I will set up your seed after you, who will come from your body, and I will establish his kingdom. He shall build a house for My name, and I will establish the throne of his kingdom forever. I will be his Father, and he shall be My son. If he commits iniquity, I will chasten him with the rod of men and with the blows of

the sons of men. But My mercy shall not depart from him, as I took it from Saul, whom I removed from before you. And your house and your kingdom shall be established forever before you. Your throne shall be established forever.

6. His kingdom will be established with peace, righteousness, and justice. "Of the increase of *His* government and peace ... to order it and establish it with judgment and justice from that time forward, even forever..." (Isa. 9:7 NKJV). The apostle Paul sums it up in Romans 14:17: "For the kingdom of God is not eating and drinking, but righteousness and peace and joy in the Holy Spirit."

7. **To sum it up: We enter the kingdom of His righteousness, peace, and joy through repentance and total surrender to the Lordship of Jesus.**

If you have never totally made Jesus the Lord of your life, or you want to make sure that you are truly saved, pray this prayer with me and mean it with all your heart:

> *"Heavenly Father, I thank You for sending Jesus, who died for my sins and rose again. I want to make a quality decision to repent from all my sins and surrender my life 100 percent to Your loving Lordship. By Your grace, I will love You with all my heart, radically and immediately obey You, and trust You all the days of my life. In Jesus' name, amen."*

A SPIRITUAL KINGDOM, NOT A PHYSICAL ONE

"Jesus answered, 'My kingdom is not of this world. If My kingdom were of this world, My servants would fight, so that I should not be delivered to the Jews; but now My kingdom is not from here.'" (John 18:36 NKJV)

The Jewish people, including Jesus' disciples, expected the Messiah to establish a geopolitical, physical kingdom where he would establish his throne after vanquishing the pagan thrones of God's enemies. Specifically, during the time of Jesus, they wanted to see the Messiah throw Caesar off his throne and overcome the hated Roman Empire, replacing Caesar with Jesus the Messiah.

Even though Jesus taught about His kingdom for three years and another 40 days after His resurrection, His disciples still asked for a physical kingdom to be established. "Therefore, when they had come together, they asked Him, saying, 'Lord, will You at this time restore the kingdom to Israel?'" (Acts 1:6 NKJV). Jesus gives a cryptic answer by saying, "It is not for you to know times or seasons which the Father has put in His own authority" (Acts 1:7 NKJV). It sounds similar to His answer about His second coming in Matthew 24:36: "But about that day and hour no one knows, not even the angels of heaven, nor the Son, but the Father alone." When you put these two together, it seems to me that Jesus will establish His perfect kingdom on earth when He comes back at His second coming.

I know that some scholars have concluded that because Matthew was writing to a Jewish audience, he didn't want

to bring dishonor to God's name, so Jesus used the syn-
onym of *heaven* rather than *God* throughout Matthew's
gospel. Regardless of whether that is correct or not, both
God and heaven have to do with the spiritual realm and
reality. God is first a Spirit, and those who worship Him
must worship Him in Spirit and in truth. Heaven is an
unseen realm of the spirit world. The Jews believed in
three different heavens: (1) the atmosphere and the galaxy,
(2) the second heaven where satan and his cohorts dwell,
(3) the third heaven where God refers to as His throne in
Isaiah 66:1 (NKJV): "Thus says the LORD: 'Heaven *is* My
throne, and earth *is* My footstool.'"

My understanding is that God's kingdom was over the
universe, but God, in His sovereignty, wanted man to co-
rule with Him over earth (Gen. 1:28). However, when man
sinned, satan the usurper took the kingdoms of this world
and became the god of this age (2 Cor. 4:4), the ruler of this
world (John 14:30), and the prince of the power of the air
(Eph. 2:2).

So, there seem to be three stages of the coming of the
kingdom.

1. The Old Covenant period, which we can call the
   preparation of the coming King and His kingdom.

2. The kingdom age, which is marked by the first coming of Jesus and the expansion of His kingdom in the
   "last days" (Acts 2:17ff).

3. The perfecting of the kingdom at Christ's second
   coming (Rev. 11:15).

It is during this present time, the second phase of the kingdom, that God expects us to bring His kingdom to earth as it is in heaven through revival and reformation of society.

HIS KINGDOM RULE AND REIGN IS OVER ALL THE EARTH

As I mentioned before, my mentor and spiritual father was Dr. C. Peter Wagner. One of the truths he taught was that every believer in Jesus should be "kingdom-minded and kingdom-hearted." What he meant by that is that God's rule is not just over our individual lives or the church. We must realize that God's rule and will are to be done over all the earth as it is in heaven. The key here is *over the earth*. What does that look like?

Let me explain by addressing one of the arguments many believe concerning the separation of church and state. The reasoning goes that we as believers should be focused on the church and the family but let the state be focused on institutions of society that it runs, like government, education, and media. But Peter Wagner taught that God's rule should be over every sphere of society, *including* government, education, and media. God is not just King over you, your family, and the church, but He is King over all the institutions and spheres of society.

Jesus taught us to pray that God's kingdom (His rule) and His will be done on earth as it is in heaven. In the opening chapter, we established what heaven looks like: being perfect in God's righteousness and justice. Thus, His will is to see His righteousness and justice over all the earth as a pure reflection of heaven's realities.

Let's use government as an example since people are so divided over Christians' involvement with the government mountain. To bring the kingdom of God to earth is to bring righteousness and justice to the government—that means to make right the areas in our government that sin and this fallen world have broken.

Of course, the road to reformation begins with prayer. But we also have to be doers of the Word. We are called to be Christian activists by voting biblically and even running for local or national offices as the Holy Spirit leads and directs. Others may be called to volunteer as poll watchers or attend their school board to voice their position on relevant issues.

One of the greatest ways to exercise kingdom authority is to speak the truth in love to both the principalities and powers of darkness and nonbelievers, so let's explore the power of truth in the next chapter.

Pray with me:

> *"Father God, I make a fresh consecration to seek first Your kingdom and Your righteousness. Empower me by Your Spirit to do what is right and to walk in radical obedience to You. Kingdom of God, come and invade every area of my life, my city, and my nation—in the mighty name of King Jesus!"*

Chapter 7:

FROM IGNORANCE TO A
BIBLICAL WORLDVIEW

This book of the law shall not depart from your mouth,
but you shall meditate on it day and night, so that you may
be careful to do according to all that is written in it; for
then you will make your way prosperous, and then you will
achieve success. (Josh. 1:8)

When I came to know Jesus Christ in 1973, I had a steep learning curve ahead of me. During my time as a drug pusher and addict, my mind had been seriously messed up by daily drug use, not just smoking pot but taking hard drugs. I was a high school dropout and had fried my brain on acid and PCP (pig tranquilizers). As a result, I could not think clearly. Before I dropped out of school, there were many days I found myself unable to remember how to spell or write. I was a total basket case.

Once I got saved and delivered from drugs, I went back to school for my senior year. (I also got a haircut, which convinced my dad that I was telling the truth about getting

saved!) Classes were back in session, and I was also learning how to do life as a new creation in Christ. That meant
I was actually going to *try* to get good grades. By God's
grace, I did very well in my senior year, pushing my grade
point average up to an impressive 2.0! Looking back, I realize that I got into the University of Maryland by the skin
of my teeth.

During my first year of walking with God, I did not yet
recognize the importance of meditating on God's Word.
However, everything changed once I received the baptism
of the Holy Spirit in 1974. Soon afterward, the Spirit led
me to read Joshua 1:8 (NASB1995), which says, "This book
of the law [the Word of God] shall not depart from your
mouth, but *you shall meditate on it day and night*, so that you
may be careful to do according to all that is written in it; for
then you will make your way prosperous, and then you will
have success."

For me, meditating on God's Word looks like prayerfully reading a select portion of Scripture, chewing on
it, quoting it audibly, going over the same verse and passages throughout the day, asking the Holy Spirit to give
me revelation of the passages, and then visualizing how
it all applies to my life. The word *meditate* can mean many
things depending on the context of the verse. It can mean
hoping to meet with God (Gen. 24:63), to lay thinking
within one's heart (Ps. 77:6), or to speak of, to imagine, or
to keep in mind.[42]

---

[42] *International Standard Bible Encyclopedia, Volume III*. Edited by Geoffrey W. Bromiley. Eerdmans Publishing Company, 1979, p.305.

Personally, I pick either one significant verse or a passage of Scripture that I want to have memorized. First, I speak the Word audibly. Then, I personalize the verse by putting my name or personal pronouns where appropriate. I begin to look at the passage in the morning and go to bed quoting and going over the passage in my mind. I also journal my prayers daily. Often, the Lord will have me type out a verse I have just memorized, and then I use my Bible software to check how accurate I was in recording the verse. By correcting the mistakes, I reinforce the verse in my spirit and my mind. My goal is to be one with God's Word. The Bible says that Jesus and His Word are one (John 1:1). As I am one with the Word, I become more one—or more intimate—with Jesus.

As a young believer, I heard an illustration that I still use to this day about how a cow chews his food. When he chews the grass, he has several stomachs to digest the food. He chews and regurgitates the cud, chews it again, swallows, and then goes through the process several times before his cud is digested and becomes one with the cow. *That* is what mediation is all about.

A key to meditating on the Word is memorizing a passage so that even if you don't have your Bible handy, you can still go over it throughout the day. I used to get 5-by-8 index cards, cut them into four sections, and write a verse in each section. I would then wrap them in a rubber band to pull out throughout the day. But today, with smartphones and Bible apps, you have the ability to pull out your phone to look at the Bible passage you are meditating on. Regardless of the method, I encourage you to set a goal to memorize Scripture.

THE LOST ART OF MEMORIZING SCRIPTURES

When I was a young believer, the Holy Spirit spoke to me that if I would memorize the Scriptures—a chapter of the Bible per week—He would heal my mind. As I sought God daily, each verse became my mandate. I was hungry to know God more, and I also desperately wanted to heal my mind. From 1974 to 1975, I faithfully memorized one chapter of the Bible each week. One of the gifts that God has given me is that I am very routine. People will say that it is discipline, but once I have decided to set a goal for myself, I will do what it takes to accomplish it. By the grace of God, I memorized 55 chapters in 55 weeks.

Whenever I teach in front of a group of people today, I quote Scriptures constantly. Often, people will ask me, "How did you learn that many Bible verses?" Well, many of those verses are the ones I memorized in my second full year of walking with the Lord. And sure enough, God healed my mind, just as He promised. By absorbing God's Word and meditating on it over and over, I opened myself up to the transformative and restorative power of a renewed mind (Rom. 12:2).

The truth is that I had a voracious desire to know God when I came to Christ. So, I was able to get my mind healed and also get to know His Word. The transformation was not the primary motivation, but it *was* the main thing that happened to me during that season. I also started to think according to the way God thinks. God's wisdom would come to me. If I had a problem, I asked myself, "What Bible verse applies to this situation?" If I didn't have a verse that came to mind, I looked up a key word in my Bible concordance and found a passage that spoke to my situation.

After finishing high school, I chose to become a history major at the University of Maryland. Now that my mind was restored, I could remember important dates, quotes, and historical chronologies. I started to get As in college, although not in every subject; I was still far behind in other areas, like English, where I needed special tutoring just to get my grammar and spelling up to par. By the time I went to Fuller Seminar at a graduate level, I completed my Master of Divinity and Doctor of Ministry, ending up with a GPA of around 3.9. Thus, God took me from a 2.0 to practically a 4.0—and I give all the glory to Him.

The principle is clear: Meditating on the Word of God will make you successful and prosperous. God showed me that reality on a micro level, as He was blessing my grades and prospering me with my studies. I believe this is part of what it means to love God *with all your mind* (Matt. 22:37). All our mental faculties are God-given, and naturally, He wants us to use our minds to love Him. Meditating on God's Word and acting on it are crucial ways we can live this out. The truth in Joshua 1:8 that brought personal transformation to me can do the same for you—and much more.

KNOWING GOD, HIS WAYS, AND HIS WISDOM

Many of us are passionate about enacting change in society, but we must start in our own lives first. Just as I learned how to meditate on God's Word as a new believer, all believers—young and old alike—must appropriate this truth into our daily living. Personally, the highlight of my day is spending time in God's Word and prayer each morning. Maintaining this habit has kept my love for Jesus burning brightly throughout all seasons of life and ministry.

When you love God, who is limitless and eternal, you will want to know Him and discover new facets of who He is. When you know God's Word, you will know Him. You will become better acquainted with His ways. How should you deal with a coworker who offends you? How should you treat your family members who irritate you? How should you respond to someone asking for money on the sidewalk? Familiarize yourself with God's Word, and you will find the answers you seek. Getting to know Jesus' nature and character empowers us to imitate Him. That is part of our journey of becoming more Christlike and living out our faith in community with others.

As we saw in an earlier chapter, the Word of God also allows us to tap into the endless fountain of His wisdom, which is a key to seeing transformation. Colossians 3:16 (NKJV) tells us, "Let the word of Christ dwell in you richly in all wisdom, teaching and admonishing one another in psalms and hymns and spiritual songs, singing with grace in your hearts to the Lord." I like how this verse specifically refers to "the word of Christ." Jesus Himself *is* the Word (John 1:1), and He *is* our wisdom (1 Cor. 1:30). Again, in the context of community, we are called to immerse ourselves in God's Word and let it permeate our lives.

According to the above verse in Colossians, the purpose of singing God's Word is to help us memorize the Word. During the Jesus People days, the musical group *Scripture in Song*, founded by David and Dale Garratt of New Zealand, led the way in creating a new genre of Christian worship music. Their prolific albums helped us memorize and know God's Word by setting Scripture to the contemporary sounds of that era. Each generation has a unique sound released by a new wave of worship leaders, and I believe those who embed the Word into their music will be the ones who make an eternal impact on their generation.

TAKING OUR PROMISED LAND

One of the things I love about the Word of God is how dynamic and multilayered it is. Just as the promise in Joshua chapter 1 can apply on a personal level, it also has larger implications for the world in which we live. The context for the opening verses in the book of Joshua gives us a clue as to the bigger picture that God had in mind.

Following the death of Moses, God appointed a young leader named Joshua to lead the nation of Israel (v. 1–2). The Lord emphatically tells Joshua to "be strong and very courageous" as he receives his divine assignment for the days ahead (v. 6–7, 9). As a successor to the man who spoke "face to face with God" and wrote the entire Torah, Joshua had big shoes to fill, to say the least.

Remember at this point that God's people had just emerged from 40 years in the wilderness and had not yet entered the land of Canaan, the territory that God had promised them. In fact, they would yet have to fight tooth and nail to defeat 31 kings just to take initial possession of the Promised Land (Josh. 12:24). Joshua was the new leader of Israel's army, and God knew exactly what marching orders to give him. Let's read the following three verses with that in mind:

> Only be strong and very courageous, that you may observe to do according to all the law which Moses My servant commanded you; do not turn from it to the right hand or to the left, that you may prosper wherever you go.

> This Book of the Law shall not depart from your mouth, but you shall meditate in it day and night, that you may observe to do according to all that is written in it. For then you will make your way prosperous, and then you will have good success.

> Have I not commanded you? Be strong and of good courage; do not be afraid, nor be dismayed, for the Lord your God is with you wherever you go. (Josh. 1:7–9 NKJV)

Notice the commands that God repeats in verses 7 and 8. Joshua, and all of Israel with him, are to *meditate* on the Word of God and to *observe* and *do* the Word. Obedience to these commands would ensure that they will be successful in everything they undertake. It also includes the promise of the Lord's abiding presence: "for the Lord your God is with you wherever you go" (Josh. 1:9). Thus, Joshua's strength and courage would stem from his intimacy with God, not his own power.

Most notably, obeying this command would enable Joshua and the nation of Israel to conquer the land destined for their taking. I believe this is a metaphor for us today. Joshua 1:8 gives us a picture of what it takes to see national transformation. Does that mean there will be many battles ahead of us? You better believe it. Of course, we aren't engaging in physical warfare, "for our struggle is not against flesh and blood" (Eph. 6:12), yet the principle still applies. On the macro scale, God has already won the war, but in the here-and-now, there are battles that still rage on. The key strategy is to know and meditate on God's Word in order to take action and realize the victory.

KNOWING GOD AND KEEPING HIS COMMANDMENTS

The Word of God is essential to knowing and loving God. When you have a genuine love for God, the Bible says that you will keep His commands. This is central to the idea of not only *hearing* God's Word but *doing* His Word. To love God is to obey God and, therefore, to obey His Word. During the Last Supper, Jesus repeated this truth several times as He spoke with His closest friends:

> If you love Me, keep My commandments. (John 14:15 NKJV)
>
> He who has My commandments and keeps them, it is he who loves Me. And he who loves Me will be

loved by My Father, and I will love him and manifest Myself to him. (John 14:21 NKJV)

Jesus answered and said to him, 'If anyone loves Me, he will keep My word; and My Father will love him, and We will come to him and make Our home with him.' (John 14:23 NKJV)

He who does not love Me does not keep My words; and the word which you hear is not Mine but the Father's who sent Me. (John 14:24 NKJV)

The point could not be any clearer. We cannot say that we truly love God if we disrespect and ignore His commands. It takes a humble heart to submit ourselves to and live in obedience to His Word at all times. Thankfully, the power of the Holy Spirit and the grace of God upon our lives are the catalysts to see this personal transformation take place. When we continually tap into the love that God has for us, we will have everything we need to reciprocate that same love for Him. Loving God by meditating on His Word is a joy and a privilege, and we will see the fruit of acting on the Word as we follow the Holy Spirit's lead throughout our lives.

A FRUITFUL LIFE FROM A BIBLICAL WORLDVIEW

As we've touched on already, according to Joshua 1:7–8, our mandate is to meditate on the Word and to act on it. Here is my paraphrase of these two verses: "Keep My Word constantly before you. Talk about it and think about it around the clock. Remind yourself of it every moment of every day. Ponder what I've said. Then put My Word into practice—all of it—in every area of your life. Lead a life of obedience to My Word."

What is the result? God says three times that you will *prosper* and have *success*. We see very similar wording in the first Psalm:

> How blessed is the man who does not walk in the counsel of the wicked, nor stand in the path of sinners, nor sit in the seat of scoffers! But his delight is in the law of the Lord, and *in His law he meditates day and night*. He will be like a tree firmly planted by streams of water, which yields its fruit in its season and its leaf does not wither; and *in whatever he does, he prospers*. (Ps. 1:1–3 NASB1995)

Meditating on the words of God day and night will lead to a fruitful life. An integral part of this process is to see how the Word will shape and mold your worldview. As my good friend James Garlow writes in his book *Reversed*, everyone has a worldview—from the homeless person down the block to the corporate executive on Wall Street. A worldview is formed through your education, upbringing, environment, consumption of media, and other factors throughout life.[43] But how can you differentiate your worldview from the per-

---

[43] James L. Garlow. *Reversed: From Culturally Woke to Biblically Awake*. Well Versed Publishing, 2024, p.21-22.

vasive humanistic worldview? In order to have a biblical worldview, you need to be a person of the Word, which will set you up to benefit in many practical ways.

By meditating on God's Word, you will...

1. Deepen your relationship with Jesus, because He *is* the Word (John 1:1–14).

2. Become more Christlike in character (2 Cor. 3:18).

3. Be transformed by the renewing of your mind (Rom. 12:2b).

4. Not be conformed to the world's ideologies (Rom. 12:2a).

5. Experience supernatural prosperity and success (Josh. 1:8).

6. Gain wisdom because wisdom comes from the knowledge of His Word (Prov. 2:1–6).

7. Discern truth in a culture full of "fake news" (John 16:13–15).

8. Have a biblical understanding of current events and social issues. This, in turn, will help you to know who to vote for. I encourage you to do your homework and support candidates whose policies and lives reflect Judeo-Christian values more than their competition.

THE BIBLE HAS TRANSFORMED THE WORLD

Have you ever stopped to consider how much impact the Bible has had on our society? If you begin just on a national level and branch outward, you will soon discover that the scope of Scripture's impact on the world, especially Western culture, is nearly limitless. A brilliant scholar named Dr. Vishal Mangalwadi undertook the challenge to investigate this global phenomenon, and the results of his studies are stunning.

Mangalwadi's *The Book That Made Your World* unpacks how the Bible has literally shaped and transformed nations over the course of human history. His book demonstrates that a biblical worldview forged the soul of modern civilization.[44] From morality to law and order to human rights, dignity, and liberty, the truth found in God's Word has left a profound imprint on countless areas of society that we simply take for granted. "No art historian can understand Western art; no musician can understand classic music; no professor can understand languages such as English, Dutch, or German, without understanding the Bible."[45]

Why are universities, hospitals, and modern medicine nearly ubiquitous today? Why have the realms of technology, science, and education seen so many breakthroughs over the centuries? It is due to a pervasive biblical worldview and the resulting efforts of Christians who acted on that worldview. Even the modern awakening of human reason—and its far-reaching ripple effects—had roots in the foundational tenets of Scripture:

---

[44] Vishal Mangalwadi. *The Book that Made Your World*. Thomas Nelson. Kindle Edition, p.17.
[45] Mangalwadi. *This Book Changed Everything*. Pasadena, CA: SoughtAfterMedia, 2019, p.284.

If God is Truth, if he can speak to us in rationally understandable words, then human rationality is really significant. The way to know the truth is to cultivate our minds and meditate on God's Word. These theological assumptions constituted the DNA of what we call Western civilization.[46]

By producing an unprecedented hunger for the knowledge of truth, biblical revivals [the Great Awakenings] lifted Protestant countries out of the poverty that was chronic worldwide.[47]

If the positive effects of a biblical worldview are that significant, what might happen if that worldview were reversed? Unfortunately, we don't have to look too far today to see the repercussions of that happening on our very own soil. The virtues of American culture have been gradually decaying as the Word of God has been increasingly devalued and dislodged from Western culture. That has directly impacted the family unit, our education system, and government policies. In California alone, so many unbiblical laws and bills have been passed by our government officials that it is truly mind-boggling. A return to our roots—in the truth and practice of God's Word—is needed to bring about lasting reformation in our nation.

FROM FAKE NEWS TO GOD'S TRUTH

Restoring a biblical worldview to our culture is paramount to upholding truth in a society plagued by fake news. Americans

---

[46] Mangalwadi. *The Book that Made Your World*, p.82.
[47] Ibid., p. 89.

have been led to believe that truth is relative and subjected to your feelings. If you want to believe in all 56 genders available on Facebook,[48] that is "your truth." However, for those who have eyes to see, God's truth is absolutely indispensable to keep society from chaos and anarchy. One practical example is that truth develops trust and credibility. You cannot do a business deal or transaction without truth as the foundation. James Garlow writes, "In order to have a biblical worldview, we must have a new, spiritually alive mind rooted in the fear of God (Prov. 9:10). This is the beginning of wisdom and insight into all of life; in other words, that is what produces a proper worldview."[49]

Truth is a huge deal to God. In John 8:31–32 (NASB1995), Jesus said, "If you continue in My word, then you are truly disciples of Mine; and you will know the truth, and the truth will make you free." Several chapters later, Jesus revealed that He *is* the truth: "I am the way, and the truth, and the life; no one comes to the Father except through Me" (John 14:6). This harmonizes with the Old Testament, for two of the Ten Commandments have to do with truth. Exodus 20:15–16 (NASB1995) says, "You shall not steal. You shall not bear false witness against your neighbor." Then in Proverbs 6:16–19, seven sins are listed that are an abomination and hated by the Lord; two of the seven are "a lying tongue" (v.17) and "a false witness who declares lies" (v.19).

---

[48] Peter Weber. "Facebook offers users 56 new gender options: Here's what they mean." *The Week*. January 8, 2015. https://theweek.com/articles/450873/facebook-offers-users-56-new-gender-options-heres-what-mean
[49] Garlow, *Reversed*, p.24.

With each passing year, society feeds us more lies. Let's take a look at a few examples that form the tip of the iceberg.

On March 22, 2022, Judge Ketanji Brown Jackson, a Harvard graduate, was unable to define the word "woman" when prompted during her confirmation hearing as she was being vetted to become a Supreme Court justice. "Can I provide a definition? No, I can't," she said. "Not in this context; I'm not a biologist."[50] This statement was deeply troubling, as it reflected Jackson's "woke" ideology. In today's cancel culture, she felt the need to err on the side of being politically correct and avoid any definitive truth statements on basic biology. Regardless of your political affiliation, I believe that everyone—including Judge Jackson—knows deep down inside that a woman is defined as a female adult with two X chromosomes. To say otherwise is completely irrational and out of touch with reality.

Another headline that follows suit is the lie that men can menstruate.[51] Transgenderism would have you believe that you cannot define what a woman is and that a man can, in fact, be a woman if he wants to be one. This type of extreme ideology, which blurs the lines between manhood and womanhood, concerns me not only as a pastor but as a parent of four adult children and a grandparent of nine

---

[50] Alexa Moutevelis. "Outrage after Ketanji Brown Jackson says she 'can't' define the word woman..." *Fox News*. March 23, 2022. https://www.foxnews.com/media/outrage-ketanji-brown-jackson-tells-senators-woman-bizarre

[51] Chloe Atkins. "For transgender men, pain of menstruation..." *NBC News*. January 11, 2020. https://www.nbcnews.com/feature/nbc-out/transgender-men-pain-menstruation-more-just-physical-n1113961

grandchildren. (Let me pause for a moment to say to those who may have gender dysphoria that I feel for you, and my heart goes out to you. The confusion many feel about their identity is a reality we need to recognize and address. Ultimately, I believe this confusion stems from the presence of sin on our broken planet, and the Bible offers us the answer to our sin and brokenness through the saving work of Jesus Christ.)

The nonstop lies extend from individual gender roles to the mass-scale crisis affecting the southern border of the United States. In April 2024, U.S. Secretary of Homeland Security Alejandro Mayorkas blatantly lied in front of Congress when he said the southern border was "as secure as it can be."[52] Just three months earlier, he made the startling admission that over 85 percent of illegal migrants apprehended at the U.S.-Mexico border are routinely released onto American soil.[53] As a result of the Biden-Harris administration's open-borders policy, our borders remained wide open for fentanyl, organized crime, domestic terrorists, and human trafficking to come in. This is unmistakably evil. We saw an influx of upwards of 10 million illegal immigrants

---

[52] Josh Christenson. "Mayorkas tells Congress border 'as secure as it can be'..." *New York Post*. April 16, 2024. https://nypost.com/2024/04/16/us-news/mayorkas-tells-congress-border-is-as-secure-as-it-can-be-cannot-recall-saying-over-85-of-migrants-are-released-into-us/

[53] Adam Shaw, Bill Melugin, and Griff Jenkins. "Mayorkas tells Border Patrol agents..." *Fox News*. January 8, 2024. https://www.foxnews.com/politics/mayorkas-tells-border-patrol-agents-illegal-immigrants-released-into-us-sources

under President Biden's watch, but those statistics are only estimates.[54]

When inaugurated, the president swore on the Bible to uphold the Constitution and defend our country against both domestic and foreign enemies. With President Biden's nonsensical policies that left our southern borders flung wide open, he did just the opposite. I believe this was intended to be a direct attack in retaliation against President Trump, to do the polar opposite of what he wanted to accomplish with the construction of the border wall. The other motivating factor behind the Democrats' open-borders policy is to buy voters from the outside. It is a power play, promising benefits and asylum to undocumented border crossers, which is a slap in the face to all the law-abiding immigrants who go through the process of obtaining legitimate citizenship.

Some of the worst fake news of all has revolved around President Trump's entire political career. The four-year Russian collusion investigation was all a lie, but Nancy Pelosi and the Congress swore that it was true. They said January 6, 2021, was an insurrection. As someone who was present in Washington, D.C., that day (not inside the capitol building), I can say that claim was also a lie.

We could also talk about the further weaponization of the Department of Justice (DOJ) against President Trump. In his May 2024 trial in New York, Trump was indicted on 34 counts by a jury made up of 95 percent Democrats, a

---

[54] Merrill Matthews. "Illegal immigrants double under Biden—and that's just the start." *The Hill.* January 23, 2024. https://thehill.com/opinion/4423296-matthews-illegal-immigrants-double-under-biden-and-thats-just-the-start/

Democrat judge whose daughter leads a fundraising firm supporting President Biden, and a district attorney who campaigned on the promise that he was going to put Trump in jail.[55] The unjust verdict of that trial was a travesty of justice. It was also a clear sign of the repercussions that arise when truth is absent from the judicial system.

TRUTH UNLOCKS REFORMATION

The good news is that the truth can reverse the damage done by lies. Reformation is unlocked when we become people of God's Word and influence society with the truth of Jesus Christ. The *proclamation* of truth is an important key that cannot be overlooked.

The Bible says we are to "speak the truth in love" (Eph. 4:15). Just as in Psalm 89:14, we again see love and truth paired in Scripture. First and foremost, we are called to love people, but we have to be vocal and declare the truth. This responsibility begins with the church. As I shared before, many pastors are not preaching the whole counsel of God. We have so much cowardice in the pulpits as sermons shy away from the truth in God's Word regarding controversial

---

[55] James Gordon. "Donald Trump rips '95 percent Democrats' hush money trial jury…" *Daily Mail*. April 22, 2024. https://www.dailymail.co.uk/news/article-13338619/Trump-rips-hush-money-jury-contempt-hearing.html; Theo Burman. "Did Alvin Bragg Campaign on a Promise…" *Newsweek*. May 31, 2024. https://www.newsweek.com/did-alvin-bragg-promise-trump-prosecution-hush-money-guilty-conviction-1906705; Robin Levinson-King and Kayla Epstein. "Who is Juan Merchan…" BBC. May 31, 2024. https://www.bbc.com/news/world-us-canada-65182727

issues. That is why we need revival—for the church to be revived by the Spirit of Truth.

As truth is proclaimed, that truth will develop biblical values in individual lives, and biblical values *that are lived out* will lead to cultural change. The essence of our culture becomes a kingdom culture, not a worldly culture. The changes in our culture will then lead the laws of the land to change. Godly, just laws will be passed because people are all on the same page, united by a cultural narrative established on truth. Thus, the power of proclaiming and acting on God's Word can bring about lasting reformation in society.

BE A DOER OF THE WORD

At the finale of the Sermon on the Mount, Jesus concludes with these words: "Therefore whoever hears these sayings of Mine, *and does them*, I will liken him to a wise man who built his house on the rock: and the rain descended, the floods came, and the winds blew and beat on that house; and it did not fall, for it was founded on the rock" (Matt. 7:24–25 NKJV). Hearing the truth is an essential part of following Jesus, but it is only the starting point. In other words, going to church once a week and mentally assenting to a biblically based message isn't going to cut it. When the rubber meets the road, you will have to act on what you've heard to prove that you are a true disciple of Christ.

Both hearing and doing the word of Christ are critical to ensuring that your life has a firm foundation. In his epistle, James, the Lord's brother, echoes the sentiment from the Sermon on the Mount: "But *be doers of the word*, and not hearers only, deceiving yourselves" (James 1:22 NKJV). Our faith is meant to be lived out, not just thought about. Let the Word of God color your worldview and influence every decision you make. By partnering with the Holy Spirit and obeying His Word, we will find immeasurable joy, satisfaction, and success as we reap the benefits of walking with God (Ps. 103:1–5). By being doers of the Word, we will bring transformative change to our lives and the lives of others.

Pray this with me:

> *"Heavenly Father, thank You for Your Word. Give me a greater hunger for Your Word like never before. Jesus, I want to know You more. Help me to meditate on Your ways and Your wisdom in every circumstance. Holy Spirit, help me to be a doer of the Word. By Your grace, I will follow and obey You—today and all the days of my life. In Jesus' name, amen!"*

Chapter 8:

FROM WINNING SOULS TO DISCIPLING NATIONS

And Jesus came up and spoke to them, saying, 'All
authority has been given to Me in heaven and on earth.
Go therefore and make disciples of all the nations,
baptizing them in the name of the Father and the Son and
the Holy Spirit, teaching them to follow all that
I commanded you; and behold, I am with you always, even
to the end of the age.' (Matt. 28:18–20)

Winning souls has been part of my MO since day one of being a follower of Jesus. From the get-go in 1973, following my conversion experience, I have passionately shared the good news with the lost in every setting imaginable. I share my testimony whenever I am traveling (which is often), at the gym, in restaurants, and even over the phone. I also carry my personal tract with me, sharing the concise story of how I got saved. This has led to many people giving their lives to Jesus, including my siblings and relatives. Now, I have to acknowledge that as a major part of my ministry calling, I believe I am called to be an evangelist (Eph. 4:11). Whether one is called to be an evangelist or not, we are all called to be a witness for Jesus (Acts 1:8). I cannot underscore enough the vital importance of sharing the gospel with unbelievers.

That said, there is much more to the story. For years, I looked at the Great Commission as simply winning souls and making individual disciples. Much of the church has that paradigm, and the Great Commission undoubtedly begins there. But that is not the full counsel of what the Bible actually teaches.

My eyes were opened to the broader meaning of Matthew 28:19— "Go therefore and make disciples of all the nations"—through my relationship with Peter Wagner, who was a professor of church growth. Peter and I were good evangelicals (my dad was the first Korean Southern Baptist pastor in America in 1958), and we felt like that simply meant we had to see souls saved. However, Peter ended up studying under Donald McGavran, a missionary-turned-scholar who served in India for 60 years. Donald McGavran talked about discipling whole nations, not just individuals in nations. As a result of Peter Wagner's personal paradigm shift in the 1990s, the theology of transforming society also crystallized in my own life.

The Koine Greek text of the Great Commission is illuminating. The key words in verse 19 are *panta ta ethne*. They are translated in my Bible as "all the nations." The final word, *ethne*, has a much richer meaning than just geopolitical nations.[56] *Ethne*, or *ethnos* in the singular, is where we get the

---

[56] "Lexicon: Strong's G1484 – *ethnos*." Blue Letter Bible. Accessed August 1, 2024. https://www.blueletterbible.org/lexicon/g1484/kjv/tr/0-1/

term "ethnic group" from. This word can be best defined as "people groups." According to Peter Wagner, *ethne* refers to "groups of people who live with each other because of a certain set of commonalities that bind them together," which would include tribes, races, tradesmen, guilds, and people of the same profession.[57] I have concluded that this logically includes groupings within the seven mountains of society: church, family, business, education, government, media, and arts and entertainment. (By the way, I recommend my book *The Reformer's Pledge*, in which my good friend Lance Wallnau gives the best synopsis on the seven mountains in his chapter "The Seven Mountain Mandate.")

To be clear, the Great Commission does involve winning souls and discipling them, but it also includes discipling nations and entire people groups with biblical values.[58] That is a huge difference when you consider the ramifications of what Jesus is calling us to do. Jesus is talking about transforming culture. He is talking about transforming nations.

In Matthew 24, Jesus speaks of the separation of the sheep nations from the goat nations at His second coming. In this light, we must understand that we all have a part to play to see God's kingdom culture transform the society in which we live. This isn't just a cute idea. It is a call to be reformers in our culture. It is a mandate to transform entire nations and people groups. It is inculcating the nations with the culture of heaven.

---

[57] C. Peter Wagner. *This Changes Everything*. Baker Publishing Group. Kindle Edition, p.175. (See also Acts 19:24-28 and Revelation 5:9.)
[58] Wagner, *This Changes Everything*, p.175.

LAW OF FIRST MENTION IN THE BIBLE

We see God's ultimate purpose for His creation and the crowning achievement when He created man in His image and gave man "the Great Commission" mentioned in Genesis 1:28. Keep in mind that this is before Adam and Eve's fall, which takes place in Genesis chapter 3.

> Then God blessed them, and God said to them, 'Be fruitful and multiply; fill the earth and subdue it; have dominion over the fish of the sea, over the birds of the air, and over every living thing that moves on the earth.' (Gen. 1:28 NKJV)

First, God blesses Adam and Eve. Later, we see God blessing Abraham in Genesis 12, but this is the first time God blesses anyone. This is a good example of the Law of First Mention. To bless in the Hebrew is the word *barak*. This is a rich, multifaceted word and can mean different things like "give, grant, bring, invoke, share, worship, praise, greet, or congratulate," depending on the context of the word.[59] But for our context, the word *bless* means "to bestow favor and goodness out of a heart of love."

From this one word, we see why God created humanity. He created Adam and Eve because God is love (1 John 4:8, 16), and He wanted to express His love to humanity and be loved by them in return. Please note that God is perfect and complete in Himself. He doesn't *need* love like we do, but He

---

[59] *International Standard Bible Encyclopedia, Volume I*. Edited by Geoffrey W. Bromiley. Eerdmans Publishing Company, 1979, p.523.

is love, and as the poem goes, "Love in your heart wasn't put there to stay—love isn't love till you give it away!"[60]

So, God created Adam and Eve, but it didn't end with them. He wanted a family, and that is why His first commandment to Adam and Eve was that they were to "be fruitful and multiply" and "fill the earth" (Gen. 1:28a). This is the Great Commission in the Old Testament. His purpose was to create a big family made in the image and likeness of God. Today, He still wants a big family. Although man sinned and death entered into the world (Rom. 5:12), Jesus Christ, God's Son, came to earth to be the substitute for our sins so that those who believe in Him (surrender their lives to Him) would be forgiven of our sins, receive His Holy Spirit within us, and be adopted as His eternal family. Jesus gives us the Great Commission in Matthew 28:18–20 for this same reason: He wants the nations to be part of His family.

This is the beginning of the Great Commission in Genesis. But notice that God does stop with Adam and Eve being fruitful and multiplying. The next phrase of the Great Commission is to "fill the earth" (Gen. 1:28b). Why? Adam and Eve were in paradise, which represents heaven on earth. We see that God put them in a specific location that Genesis 2:8–15 outlines. God never intended that heaven on earth should confined to a small location. His desire with the commandment to "fill the earth" was for all the world to become heaven on earth. That is why Jesus gave us the most

---

[60] https://rodgersandhammerstein.com/song/the-sound-of-music/sixteen-going-on-seventeen-reprise/

significant prayer to pray in the Bible: "Your kingdom come. Your will be done, on *earth* as it is in *heaven!*"

Genesis 1:28 confirms God's heart not just to see souls saved but to see nations being transformed so that heaven's culture permeates society. It won't ever be perfect this side of the Second Coming of Jesus, but I do believe that He wants as much of His righteousness and justice on earth as it is in heaven.

The next word in Genesis 1:28c that is critical in fulfilling the Great Commission is the word *subdue*. The Hebrew word here is *kabash*, which means "to subdue the enemy." Now, who is the enemy in the garden? When preaching, I often make the rhetorical joke by asking, "How many of you know that your spouse is not the enemy?" This should go without saying, but keep in mind that God spoke this commandment to only two people, Adam and Eve.

The truth is that satan is the enemy, and we see that he had already been cast out of heaven and was in the garden in Genesis 3. Why did God—who is all-powerful and uncreated, who could have destroyed satan with one look—allow satan and his cohorts to be cast down on earth? I believe it was so His children could finish the job that God began by vanquishing satan and his demons. The next word in Genesis 1:28d reveals much of God's heart for His children and His purpose for us today. The word is *radah*, which means "to rule." God the Father wanted His family to rule and reign with Him as co-regents with the Godhead! But you know the rest of the story in Genesis. Instead of us vanquishing the enemy, satan subdued us, and he became the ruler of this world (John 14:30). *But God!*

ALL AUTHORITY BELONGS TO JESUS

"...All authority has been given to Me in heaven and on earth." (Matt. 28:18 NASB1995)

Why did Jesus begin the Great Commission by making a statement that seemed obvious? Did Jesus have all authority on earth before the resurrection? And if not, what happened at the cross and His resurrection that would lead Jesus to begin His final instruction to the church before His ascension by saying, "all authority has been given to me ... on earth"?

I believe that Jesus had all authority in heaven, and God never lost it in heaven. However, God had delegated His authority to man in Genesis 1:28, and when man fell, he lost his authority to satan. We know that satan had authority on earth by the conversation he exchanged with Jesus in the wilderness. The third temptation of Jesus went this way:

> Again, the devil took Him up on an exceedingly high mountain and showed Him all the kingdoms of the world and their glory. And he said to Him, 'All these things I will give You if You will fall down and worship me.' (Matt. 4:8–9 NKJV)

I want to pause here because if satan was lying—if he had no authority to give to Jesus over "all the kingdoms of the world and their glory"—then this would not have been a real temptation. But the truth of the matter is that satan became "the ruler of this world" (John 14:30), "the god of this age" (2 Cor. 4:4), and "the prince of the power of the air" (Eph. 2:2b).

Then Jesus said to him, 'Away with you, Satan! For it is written, "You shall worship the LORD your God, and Him only you shall serve."' (Matt. 4:10 NKJV)

So, what happened on the cross that Jesus would say before His ascension, "All authority has been given to Me in heaven and on earth"? We don't know exhaustively all that happened on the cross, but a number of key passages in the Bible give us an idea of how Jesus took back the authority that was abdicated and lost by Adam and what that regained authority means for the Ekklesia, the church.

The Bible says that before Jesus ascended into heaven, He first descended to the lower regions of hell. "Now this, 'He ascended'—what does it mean but that He also first descended into the lower parts of the earth? He who descended is also the One who ascended far above all the heavens, that He might fill all things" (Eph. 4:9–10 NKJV). What did Jesus do in hell? He definitely didn't go there because He had sinned. Jesus never sinned. But I believe that Jesus descended there to take back the authority that was lost in the garden. Colossians 2:15 (NKJV) says, "Having disarmed principalities and powers, He made a public spectacle of them, triumphing over them in it."

Finally, Revelation 1:18 (NKJV) affirms that He has now all authority over death and hell. "I am He who lives, and was dead, and behold, I am alive forevermore. Amen. And I have the keys of Hades and of Death."

We know in Scripture that keys represent authority (Matt.16:18–19). When Harvest Rock Church bought the performing arts center Ambassador Auditorium in 2004, the money was wired from the escrow account. After signing the necessary papers, the previous owner gave me all the keys to the auditorium. I now had the authority to use the building for God's will and purposes.

That is what Jesus did. Again, we don't fully understand all that took place on the cross, but the bottom line is that Jesus has "all authority in heaven and on earth," and He has now given it back to His children, the church (Rom. 8:14–17, Gal. 4:6–7). As sons and daughters of God, we have received the kingdom as our inheritance and the "keys to the kingdom" to exercise authority over satan and his cohorts. This doesn't mean that satan is completely vanquished; on the contrary, he still has power, and his wrath is great, especially in these last days, because he knows his time is short (Rev. 12:12).

FROM D-DAY TO V-DAY

One of the best analogies for how we're to wield authority and advance the kingdom I have heard over the years is the difference between D-Day and V-Day. These are two of the most important dates in the timeline of World War II. D-Day was when the Allied Forces, including the long-awaited U.S. troops under Supreme Commander Gen. Dwight Eisenhower, invaded Normandy on June 6, 1944. Historians and military strategists unanimously agree that the successful landing of the Allied Forces on the shores of Normandy, France, effectively won World War II for the Allies. Nevertheless, some of the fiercest fighting took place in the 11 months between D-Day and V-Day—May 8, 1945—when Germany unconditionally surrendered to the Allied Forces.

So, too, Jesus already won the battle on the cross. For us as believers, that was our D-Day. It is essentially a done deal. Revelation 11:15 tells us, "Then the seventh angel sounded; and there were loud voices in heaven, saying, 'The kingdom of the world has become *the kingdom* of our Lord and of His Christ; and He will reign forever and ever.'"

We know that our ultimate V-Day—when God destroys satan and judges the earth—will be at the second coming of Jesus (see Rev. 21 and 22). Until then, Jesus has commanded us to disciple nations. Just like the Allied Forces used every weapon of warfare to accomplish the victory over the Axis Forces (Germany, Japan, and Italy), we also must use every means to advance God's kingdom. The primary weapon we have is our God-given authority to engage in spiritual warfare, which is the next thing that we have to shift to see revival and reformation.

Let's seal this together in prayer:

> *"Father, I believe You have given all authority in heaven and earth to Jesus. Thank You for giving me Your authority and Your Holy Spirit to empower me to do Your will on the earth today. I pray that my nation will be baptized in Your love, character, and power so that it will look more like the kingdom of heaven. In Jesus' name, amen!"*

Chapter 9:

FROM PETITION TO SPIRITUAL WARFARE

*For our struggle is not against flesh and blood, but against
the rulers, against the powers, against the world forces of
this darkness, against the spiritual forces of wickedness in
the heavenly places. (Eph. 6:12)*

*Praying always with all prayer and supplication in the
Spirit, being watchful to this end with all perseverance and
supplication for all the saints— (Eph. 6:18 NKJV)*

I'll never forget the day I met Lou Engle. It was back
in the late 1970s when I was part of a pastoral team
overseeing a church of around 2,000 people in Maryland.
I had already met Lou's wife, Therese, who was part of our
ACTS (Active Christians That Serve) Bible study I launched
at the University of Maryland, and she was a member of
our church. But some time went by before I formally became
acquainted with Lou.

As one of the initial icebreakers, I asked Lou what he did
for a living. He said, "I cut lawns for Leisure World."

"I beg your pardon?"

"I mow lawns," Lou reiterated.

In my mind's eye, I could visualize Leisure World, which was a large retirement center in our area. They had acres upon acres of land. "So, do you ride a tractor lawnmower and cut the grass?" I asked.

"No, they want the lines to be perfect," Lou told me. "So, it takes me eight hours a day, every day, to use a push mower to have lines that are perfectly aligned."

"You do this eight hours a day, five days a week?" I asked incredulously.

"Yes, I do."

"Dude, that must be the most boring job ever," I said.

"No, it's the best job," Lou countered, "because I just pray in tongues every day. I just pray and commune with God."

At that point in our conversation, something clicked within my spirit. In the season leading up to this, I knew that God was calling me to plant a church, and I could pick 12 people to be on my team. I immediately said to myself, "I want Lou on my team." I had heard enough in our brief exchange to know that he was the man for the hour. Now, I didn't know much as a young pastor, but I did know that prayer was the key to having any success in ministry.

Over 45 years later, I can say that Lou was the best hire I have ever made as a pastor. Looking back, I know that God divinely brought Lou and Therese into my life, and I will be forever grateful for our covenant friendship. Lou has had tremendous influence in my life, but perhaps the most important thing is that he taught me how to pray.

By the time God called me and Sue to move to California, I extended the invitation for Lou and Therese to make the journey with us. They heartily agreed to do so. Once we arrived in SoCal in 1984, revival was not breaking out as we had expected, and we had to persevere when there was seemingly nothing going on. Nevertheless, I believe our prayers in that season positioned us for what happened 10 years later.

Our church held an early morning prayer meeting every weekday. We saw some measure of growth in our church, and God's presence showed up. Meanwhile, I was stuck in the rut of personal prayer and needed to be pushed outside my comfort zone. Well, God knew Lou was the one to make that happen.

I told Lou one day, "I am paying you to be on staff, and I want you to lead the prayer meeting. I'm the senior pastor, so I don't need to be there."

Lou responded, "With all due respect, you are the main person who has to be there. Because you, as a senior pastor, have to lead by example for the rest of the people in the church, as 'My house is a house of prayer for all nations.'"

In that moment, the conviction of the Lord came upon me, and I realized he was speaking the truth. *I can't just delegate prayer away to others. I need to be a person involved in corporate prayer.* Thus, my covenant brother Lou Engle set the tone for me to lean into fervent prayer that went beyond my prior understanding of prayer and petition.

CALLED TO BE A HOUSE OF PRAYER

"Then He taught, saying to them, 'Is it not written,
"My house shall be called a house of prayer for all
nations"?'" (Mark 11:17 NKJV)

The moment you are born again, you are called to pray. You are now a priest in God's house (see Rev. 1:6). You will notice that God didn't say, "My house will be a house of preaching or fellowship," both of which are fine and scriptural. But Jesus wants to make a point that the primary purpose for God's house is to pray. "Do you not know that you are a temple [or the house] of God and that the Spirit of God dwells in you?" (1 Cor. 3:16).

From the very beginning, God created man to have fellowship with Him. He would walk with man in the cool of the day (Gen. 3:8). Through prayer, God communicates with us, and we with God. Just like my relationship with Sue, it is not one-way communication. The deepest communication, after all, is sharing our hearts with one another. Abraham is called the father of our faith because he had an intimate relationship with God, where God calls him His friend (James 2:23).

Prayer is hearing from God and speaking out what He wants us to pray. Jesus said in John 15:7 (NASB1995), "If you abide in Me and My words abide in you, ask whatever you wish [that is in accordance with My word], and it will be done for you."

FROM DUTY TO DELIGHT

The impartation I received from Lou Engle has transformed my prayer life. I first went from prayer as a *duty* to sheer *discipline*, but now I can honestly say before the Lord that it is a *delight*. What I mean is that my daily time with Jesus is the highlight of my day. I look forward to going to bed early so I can get up, get into His Word, and pray. Before I talk about prayer any further, I want to give you a glimpse into my prayer life.

I journal my prayers every morning. By journaling, I get several things accomplished during my time of prayer. First, I am consistent. Because I'm recording or journaling my prayer, it holds me accountable because I don't want to miss a day's entry. As a result, I can't remember the last time I missed journaling and thus missing my time of intercession. Secondly, I use this time to keep a brief diary of what transpired the day before. In fact, that is my way of entering His gates with thanksgiving and into His courts with praise (Ps. 100:4). I begin by worshiping and giving thanks for specific things that took place the day before.

For example, I was in Hawaii working on the final chapters of this book. We just had our family vacation, and I used the few extra days in Hawaii to finish the manuscript. Let me give you an actual entry of what took place yesterday. (By the way, before you read on, I am not prescribing that you need to journal, but this is what I do, and if it helps you to be consistent, great!)

Friday, August 16, 2024, Honolulu.

Father, I love You and worship You. Thank You for Your grace yesterday. I was able to find a new great restaurant, Rob's Good Time Restaurant with one of the best hamburgers, and I was able to turn in the car, check out of the hotel and catch the next flight, even though my flight was canceled. Although there is no lounge in Lihue airport, I was able to work three hours at the Starbucks on my book. God, You are so good to me! I love and worship You! Thank You for dinner with the Yamada's last night.

Thank You for the revelation that heaven is inviting me into the intimate relationship with the Tri-une Being. Father, I pray that I may be one as You are in me and I in You, that You may be in me that the world might believe that You sent Jesus. **John 17:21 — 'that they may all be one, just as you, Father, are in me, and I in you, that they also may be in us, so that the world may *believe* that you have sent me. 22 The glory that you have given me I have given to them, that they may be one even as we are one, 23 I in them and you in me, that they may become perfectly one, so that the world may know that you sent me and loved them even as you loved me.'** Father, help me to walk in union with You, Jesus, and the Holy Spirit. You in me, I in You—Jesus and the

Holy Spirit and the Father within me. Thank You that You have loved me as You have loved Jesus. I worship You and magnify Your name.

The next day, I had a rough day after not getting enough sleep because the hotel room they gave me was on the street side of the busy Kalakaua Ave. Then I had to speak at a conference in Nashville using an online platform that I wasn't familiar with. Here is my entry:

Saturday, August 17, 2024, Honolulu.

Father, I love and worship You! You do exceedingly abundantly beyond all that I could think or ask. Thank You for the upgraded room. Thank You for 5,000 points added to my Bonvoy account due to the fact that they put me on the street side of the hotel and bikers were keeping me up at night. Thank You that the Zoom went well even though I had no idea if I was on or not. Truly I spoke in faith. Thank You that You allowed me to have a great meal at the Beach House here at the Westin. Thank You that I was able to get much writing done and I was able to work out. I give You all the thanks and praise. Your goodness and favor are beyond anything that I can ask or think.

(By the way, you'll notice how I journal the restaurants I eat in. I am such a foodie; I could be a journalist on the Food Channel!)

Finally, I love to journal because when I do, it holds me accountable to pray for people by name. I am not going to reveal my prayer list because that is between me and the Lord, but when I tell people that I pray for them daily, it is not hyperbole. I write down their names and pray for them as I journal. And because my list is long, I end up praying for over an hour each day, not including my time in prayer with Sue or my time in the Word, which is what I give myself the most margin for.

So, when I entitled this chapter "From Petition to Spiritual Warfare," I did so with the recognition that I am absolutely a petitioner and an intercessor. I am not a world-class intercessor like some of my friends, but I love to pray. However, I know that in order to see revival and reformation, we have to learn how to do effective spiritual warfare—specifically strategic-level warfare—and we need to value corporate prayer meetings.

THE CASE FOR STRATEGIC SPIRITUAL WARFARE

I want to focus on spiritual warfare because the real battle for "the soul of any nation" is first a spiritual one. I believe that we have to bind the forces of darkness and loose God's kingdom in order to change the culture of a nation. This is the battle that is holding people back from salvation because "the god of this age has blinded the eyes of unbelievers" (2 Cor. 4:4 NIV). Therefore, we need to win the battle in the heavenlies to see the changes in salvation as well as the government. The second way we change our culture is through truth and biblical values. In my opinion, it is not either-or. We have to engage in both arenas.

The apostle Paul writes in Ephesians 6:12 (NKJV), "For we do not wrestle against flesh and blood, but against principalities, against powers, against the rulers of the darkness of this age, against spiritual hosts of wickedness in the heavenly places."

In Ephesians 6, the context for spiritual warfare is the corporate church. Paul was not presenting an individualistic perspective on prayer. He was encouraging the believers at Ephesus to stand strong in the faith together as the unified corporate Body of Christ (Eph. 6:10–18; Eph. 2:14–16). Peter Wagner, in his book *This Changes Everything*, comments on Ephesians 6:12:

> Our assignment is to attack aggressively. Now is not the time for passivity! Sitting back and hoping against hope that God will save the world without us is misguided thinking ... God is sending us into the invisible world to do hand-to-hand combat. Paul used the word 'wrestle' to describe this combat. Wrestling was the closest and most intense contact sport in the Roman Empire ... We must not back off from our assignment. [61]

Please note that Peter Wagner is advocating aggressive, offensive prayer. Jesus declared war against satan. He said, "I

---

[61] C. Peter Wagner. *This Changes Everything*. Baker Publishing Group. Kindle Edition, p.98-99.

will build My church, and the gates of hell will not prevail against it" (Matt. 16:19). Gates don't attack you; you attack the gates of hell. For too long, the church has been on the defensive, just holding onto life until Jesus comes back and raptures us out of here. My Bible teaches that Jesus came to destroy the works of the devil (1 John 3:8), and I am here to reinforce the victory that Jesus won on the cross with the declaration, "It is finished!"

Jesus reflected this call for corporate spiritual warfare in Matthew 18:18–20, where He talks about using our authority to bind and loose in corporate prayer. (Note: Each occurrence of the word "you" in these verses is plural in the Greek.)

> Truly I say to you, whatever you bind on earth shall have been bound in heaven; and whatever you loose on earth shall have been loosed in heaven. Again I say to you, that if two of you agree on earth about anything that they may ask, it shall be done for them by My Father who is in heaven. For where two or three have gathered together in My name, I am there in their midst.

Training for Reigning

In light of what Scripture so clearly articulates, the war has already been won. We have read the end of the story—every knee will bow before King Jesus (Phil. 2:9–11). At the same time, there are still battles to be fought in order to arrive at that final victory. Jesus has given us the authority—*His* authority—to destroy the works of the enemy and to advance His kingdom on the earth (1 John 3:8, 4:17). He gave us the

Great Commission to disciple nations and inculcate them with heaven's kingdom culture (Matt. 28:18–20).

The ongoing reality of spiritual warfare is meant to train us for ruling and reigning with God. From the very beginning, God made us in His image and likeness, and He gave us a commandment to subdue the enemy and co-rule with Him over the earth (Gen. 1:27–28). This dominion mandate has never changed!

The late author Paul Billheimer, in his book *Destined for the Throne*, affirms that we are currently training for reigning. Billheimer presents a compelling case that engaging in spiritual warfare and being proactive in prayer are preparing us for our eternal destinies. As we put our faith into action in the here and now, all of it constitutes on-the-job training for our divine assignments in the new heaven and the new earth to come.

THE 3 LEVELS OF SPIRITUAL WARFARE

The first level of spiritual warfare is the *ground level*. This is where we are to cast out demons from individuals and bring freedom from demonic oppression on a person-by-person basis.

Second is the *occult level*. This includes everything from witchcraft to black magic, seances, New Age practices, cards, horoscopes, and the like. We need to be aware of—not scared of—this level of warfare, and we must be equipped to strategically overcome it.

Third is the *strategic level*. This is where we must confront the principalities and powers that influence nations. One of the most significant strongholds, as noted in *The Last of the*

Giants by George Otis Jr., is Islam. Otis identified it as a powerful spiritual stronghold, and I believe there are even more forces at work than he discussed.

Islam, as Otis notes, is a major stronghold, with over 1.25 billion Muslims living under spiritual deception. The ideology that Muhammad received, claiming that Allah is the God of Abraham, Isaac, and Jacob, is different from the God of the Bible. The oppressive practices within Islam— such as the mandate to kill apostates, the concept of Jihad, and the use of human shields—are manifestations of an underlying spiritual principality. For example, the book of Daniel mentions the Prince of Persia, a principality that was locked in spiritual warfare contesting Daniel's prayers. The events of October 7, 2023, highlight the darkness behind this ideology, as acts of violence were justified in the name of religion. Moreover, the enforcement of Sharia law, which oppresses women and promotes injustice, is a clear example of unrighteousness. As the Bible says in Ephesians 6:12, we do not wrestle against flesh and blood but against spiritual forces of evil.

Another significant principality I see is Communism. The economic policies being advocated by leaders like Kamala Harris are pure socialism, which I believe would devastate our nation, much like what happened in Venezuela. This shift toward Communism, socialism, and Marxism is another manifestation of a spiritual stronghold, aiming to undermine our values and freedoms.

Therefore, we need to engage effectively. This involves not only prayer but also being led by the Holy Spirit to do prophetic acts that bring the kingdom of heaven to earth.

PROPHETIC INTERCESSION AT DEVIL'S GATE

To illustrate what I mean by prophetic acts, I want to share a story with you from Lou Engle's book, *Digging the Wells of Revival.* The story starts when God gave him a dream and led him to do an act of prophetic intercession over our region in Southern California:

> Devil's Gate was the name of a dam that protected the original water source for Pasadena and Los Angeles ... Several people were killed during the construction of the freeway near the dam, and numerous murders and suicides have occurred along the river, the Arroyo Seco, that flows from the dam. Intercessors in Los Angeles have sensed that the name literally brought a curse on the city.
>
> As I recalled the words in my dream, I understood that the Lord wanted me to pour salt into the stream as a sign of cleansing, to ask for forgiveness on behalf of our forefathers for cursing the water, and to entreat God to pour out the rivers of revival on Pasadena and Los Angeles ... God was asking me to do the same for Los Angeles [as Elisha had done in 2 Kings 2:19-22] to bring healing and fruitfulness to the waters that were producing spiritual death.
>
> Shortly after my dream, an intercession team joined me at Devil's Gate, where we poured salt into the stream and called for a renewal of God's covenant mercies ... We prophesied a changing of the demonic name and the removal of the curse

cast by the giving of the name. We also asked God to forgive the people of Los Angeles for breaking covenant with Him.

At the time of our visit to Devil's Gate, southern California was in the midst of a five-year drought. Many thousands of Christians were praying for rain. Eight days after our intercessory act on behalf of the city, the rains began to pour, so much so that the newspapers hailed that month 'Miracle March.'

…For two years we saw no visible evidence that our acts of prophetic intercession had accomplished anything more. One day Angela Blair, an intercessor on the team that had gone to the dam, asked the Lord why the name of Devil's Gate had not yet been changed. The Lord answered her that the name was indeed changing, and that in the days ahead the dam and the surrounding area would be called by an Indian name. Imagine our joy when one month later we read this announcement in the 'Pasadena Focus,' the official city newsletter: '*Haha-mongna*. That's the name the Gabrielinos (early Pasadena Indians) gave to what now is known as "Devil's Gate…." The English-language translation is "Flowing Waters: Fruitful Valley." Nearly everyone agrees that *Hahamongna* will be a more appropriate name for this long-neglected community asset after it is restored to its natural state.'

The very words we had proclaimed prophetically were now proclaimed publicly! We had specifically prayed that the curse of barrenness would be broken, as it was when Elisha cleansed the water of Jericho. Now the official Pasadena newsletter reported the reinstatement of the original Indian name, Flowing Streams and Fruitful Valley. It was a sign for us that revival would come to Pasadena and flow to Los Angeles.[62]

BINDING THE PRINCE OF PERSIA

A more recent example of strategic-level warfare took place on May 8, 2024. I had the opportunity to facilitate the United for Israel March at USC, where we experienced a powerful time of prayer, identification repentance, and reconciliation.

During this gathering, we heard from a young man who was originally a Muslim from Iran. Ten years ago, he was suicidal, but he had a radical encounter with Jesus and is now passionately following Him. This young man publicly repented on behalf of Iran for the genocide committed on October 7, 2023. We also had a Jewish mother, fluent in Hebrew, who was deeply moved by the atrocities of October 7. The day after, on October 8, she felt compelled to attend a church service, where she gave her life to Yeshua. She publicly forgave Iran and Hamas, and we sealed this moment with a communion service.

We then prayed for revival and spiritual awakening among both Muslims and Jewish people worldwide, with the hope

---

[62] Lou Engle. *Digging the Wells of Revival*. Destiny Image. Kindle Edition, p.181-185.

of seeing them come to Jesus. We also corporately bound the spirit behind the Prince of Persia and antisemitism, which has surged in recent months, especially in America. It was truly a powerful and transformative gathering.

Less than two weeks later, on May 19, 2024, the breaking news hit that Iranian President Ebrahim Raisi died in a helicopter crash. We also witnessed similar outcomes with leaders of Hamas and Hezbollah, who were either taken out by targeted attacks or by what appeared to be accidents. These events came in the wake of our prayers, as the demonic principalities protecting these leaders were confronted and weakened. I am not claiming that we were the only ones doing strategic spiritual warfare during this time frame, but I want to recognize what *God* did as a result of our obedience to pray the way He was leading us to pray.

RULES OF ENGAGEMENT

When doing spiritual warfare, and especially the higher levels of warfare, it is essential that we follow certain rules of engagement. I will summarize them below:

First, make sure there are no holes in your armor. As we see in Ephesians 6, we must proactively walk in obedience to God to ensure that we have the armor of God equipped in the following areas:

- Belt of Truth: Live in truth and integrity (Eph. 6:14a).
- Breastplate of Righteousness: We must walk in holiness and righteousness (v.14b).

- Gospel of Peace: Prepare yourself to spread the message of the kingdom, which brings peace, joy, and righteousness in the Holy Spirit (v.15).

- Shield of Faith: Strengthen your faith to stand against principalities and powers (v.16).

- Helmet of Salvation: Be secure in your identity in Christ (v.17a).

- Sword of the Spirit: Use the Word of God in your declarations and spiritual warfare (v.17b).

Second, we must engage in corporate prayer. It is crucial to unite in prayer with others when dealing with higher-level spiritual battles.

Third, have a prayer shield around you. Recruit other intercessors to actively cover you in prayer, thus providing a spiritual shield. I believe all fivefold leaders should have a prayer shield covering them, whether that is a group of volunteers or paid intercessors.

APOSTOLIC AND PROPHETIC DECREES

Apostles and prophets work together in spiritual warfare by making apostolic and prophetic decrees. This is grounded in Matthew 16:18–19 and Matthew 18:19–20, where Jesus gives the church the authority to bind and loose on earth as it is in heaven. This authority enables the church to spiritually attack the gates of hell, following God's direction through prophetic insight.

While all believers have authority over the enemy, apostles are entrusted with extraordinary authority to wage spiritual warfare (see 1 Cor. 12:28). This collaboration between apostles and prophets in strategic-level prayer can bring significant breakthroughs in society, as illustrated by the following story.

The California Recall

In late 2002, during a season of intensive prayer, Lou Engle received a dream about Gray Davis, the governor of California at the time. In the dream, Lou saw Gov. Davis attending TheCall in San Francisco, which was coming up the following year. Although he knew Davis was not going to come to that event, Lou felt led to intensify our prayers for the governor. Davis's leadership had led California into a significant economic crisis, with billions of dollars in deficit, and his policies were as problematic as those of Gov. Newsom today. Although the radical transgender and LGBTQ movements had not fully developed by then, Davis's policies were already heading in that direction. We corporately bound the spiritual forces behind his governance and prayed for his salvation.

Not long after, on February 5, 2003, the recall process against Davis officially began, marking the first time in history that a California governor was recalled. Later that year, a special election was held on October 7, and by November 17, Arnold Schwarzenegger was inaugurated as the new governor. We believe this dramatic shift in leadership was a direct result of our prayers. While some might dismiss this as coincidence, I firmly believe, as 2 Chronicles 20:20 says, that when you believe the prophets, you will succeed. This principle has proven true time and time again.

TheCall Korea

That same year, we held TheCall at Olympic Stadium in Seoul, South Korea. We had a sizable turnout with 60,000 attendees. The only problem was that it had been pouring rain for days on end, including the day of the gathering. Because of the constant downpour, there were only several hundred attendees gathered near the stage, while thousands of others were walking around the covered areas of the stadium, not really engaged in prayer.

As I stood on the stage next to Lou, he turned to me and said, "Ché, I just got a word from God. It's that you are to pray that the rain will stop."

A bit hesitant, I replied, "Lou, you're the one who got the word. You pray."

"No, you're the apostle," he countered. "You need to make the decree."

Knowing Lou was right, I conceded and walked up to the mic. I called for everyone's attention and then announced that we were going to pray together that the deluge would come to an end. My prayer was simple: "Lord, I pray that the rain will stop and the skies will clear up over this stadium in Jesus' name."

It was hardly a few minutes later when the raindrops stopped coming down, and sunlight broke out over the stadium. Awestruck, I looked around and saw that it was still raining *around* the stadium but not overhead. It was literally an open heaven over us!

We felt a fresh wind in our sails as thousands of people began to descend and engaged in prayer as a unified corporate body. If you have never been in a prayer meeting with thousands of Koreans, then you are missing out! In the end, we recognized that this miracle was the result of the important role that apostles and prophets play in tandem with one another. Lou heard the prophetic word, and I made the apostolic decree—and God did the rest.

Setting the Captives Free

This next testimony, as well as the one that follows it, took place shortly before this book's release. Britt Hancock, Founder and Director of Mountain Gateway, is an evangelist who worked with David Hogan's ministry for years before starting his own. In November 2023, Britt sent me pictures of the incredible work they have been doing in Nicaragua, where they partnered with Nathan Morris of Shake the Nations Ministries. Together, they led revival meetings in Nicaragua that reached over a million people. One of their events saw 270,000 people gather in Managua's Revolution Square, with hundreds of thousands committing their lives to Christ over various crusades. Tens of thousands of people were miraculously healed, and the movement gained significant attention.

However, this success also drew the eye of the Nicaraguan government. In December 2023, 13 pastors and attorneys affiliated with Mountain Gateway were arrested under false charges by the repressive Communist regime of Nicaraguan President Daniel Ortega. Britt's staff members were unjustly sentenced to prison terms ranging from 12 to 15 years. In total, 130 missionaries and Christians were arrested during this government crackdown.

When I recently met with Nathan Morris at the Empowered21 conference in Jakarta, he personally shared an update about the efforts to secure the release of the Mountain Gateway staff and broke the news that nothing had worked. Despite receiving recognition from many, including the U.S. State Department and prominent Christian leaders, the situation seemed desperate. I felt led by the Lord to invite Nathan to Los Angeles to help reach our Hispanic community, especially young people, with the gospel. Nathan immediately told me that he was on board. I also knew I needed to speak with Britt Hancock, as his team had been crucial to organizing the crusades in Nicaragua.

So, in early September 2024, I called Britt during a layover in Washington, D.C., and invited him to partner with us in these new initiatives in LA. "I'll be there," he said. "I am 100 percent committed." But then he added, "However, my staff is still in prison, and they are the ones who really know how to organize this citywide crusade."

At that moment, I felt that the Lord gave me a word for him from Luke 4:18. I said, "Britt, as you make this commitment to LA, the Lord is saying, 'The Spirit of the Lord is upon Me, because He has anointed Me to preach the gospel to the poor; He has sent Me to heal the brokenhearted, *to proclaim liberty to the captives* and recovery of sight to the blind, to set at liberty those who are oppressed.' I believe that the 13 captives will be set free as you make this commitment."

I released this word over him and made an apostolic decree over the phone. The date was September 4. What I didn't know at the time was that Britt and his wife, who were both listening over speakerphone, had just received word earlier that day that the pastors would be vindicated and released from jail. However, they could not legally disclose the news until it was made official. During the call, Britt's wife, astonished at the timing of my decree, wrote down the Scripture of Luke 4:18 on a piece of paper.

That very next morning, on September 5, Britt texted me with the incredible news: *The 13 captives had been released!*[63] Surely, thousands of people had been praying for this breakthrough, but I felt it was a prophetic confirmation that their release was tied to Britt's obedience and commitment to come to Los Angeles. This breakthrough was also a confirmation for us at Harvest Rock Church to move forward with a three-year outreach plan starting in 2025. Each year, we are going to hold citywide outreaches within a 30-minute radius of USC, culminating in a stadium event at the LA Memorial Coliseum in 2028. The sudden release of the captives prophetically served as a green light for us to go after the harvest in Los Angeles.

The Trump–Jehu Decree

The final story I want to share in this chapter took place while this book was in its final stages of editing prior to publication. On October 12, 2024—Yom Kippur, the Day of Atonement—we gathered at the National Mall in Washington, D.C. for an event called "A Million Women," spearheaded by Lou Engle and Jenny Donnelly. According

---

[63] "Nicaragua Update: September 5, 2024." Mountain Gateway. https://www.mountaingateway.org/update-september-5-2024.html

to a conservative estimate by the park police, we saw over 370,000 women and men in person at this prayer assembly. In addition, another 10 million participants joined in prayer via livestream from all over the globe. The turnout was awe-inspiring, as we caught a greater glimpse of the power that is released when believers come together in corporate unity to seek God's face and intercede for our nation.

That day, while standing on stage near the iconic stretch of grass facing the Washington Monument, I made an apostolic decree as the sun was setting over our nation's capital. Before I go into the specifics, I want to share the profound journey that led me to make this significant decree.

The journey began on September 2, when I was catching up with Lou Engle on a Zoom call. After inviting me to support him in leadership on October 12, Lou asked how I wanted to participate on the day of the event. The impression I had at the time was to make some sort of apostolic decree dealing with the spirit of Jezebel. As Lou can testify, we have faced the spiritual stronghold of Jezebel in California for the last 40-plus years, as the main foothold for that principality resides in San Francisco. This is significant because San Francisco was the birthplace of the sexual revolution and gay rights movement of the 1960s and 70s, and it has also given us leaders like Gavin Newsom, Nancy Pelosi, Dianne Feinstein, and Kamala Harris. (To be clear, none of these political leaders are the *personification* of Jezebel, but they are a *type* of how the spirit of Jezebel can manifest through political leadership aligned with Jezebel's value system.)

As shared previously, I often make decrees based on *rhema* words that prophets in my life have given me. However, since

I hadn't yet received a prophetic word or confirmation, I told Lou that I wanted to take more time to pray about the decree and really hear from the Lord.

Within the next three days in September, I witnessed the incredible turn of events related to the release of the 13 Mountain Gateway pastors. This powerful testimony significantly bolstered my faith to make my upcoming decree on October 12. I saw how God was clearly at work when I had made the decree on the phone call with Britt Hancock, and I knew God would move powerfully again. Still, I wasn't sure on the exact wording for the decree.

Then, one night, I was listening to a teaching by Jonathan Cahn, where he shared insights about the 2016 presidential election. He described Hillary Clinton as a type of Jezebel and Donald Trump as a type of Jehu. According to Scripture, Jehu was a military leader in Israel who was flawed but nevertheless anointed by God to accomplish His purposes in that generation (1 Kings 19:15–18). Jehu's most iconic feat was to cast out Jezebel and end her reign of wickedness (2 Kings 9:30–37). Therefore, President Trump's victory over Clinton in 2016 served as a prophetic picture of a Jehu-type leader overthrowing a Jezebel-type leader.

When I heard this, the realization clicked in my mind: I was to decree that Trump, again like Jehu, would defeat Kamala Harris, another type of Jezebel, through the 2024 election results. Lou had also shared with me that Jonathan Cahn felt prophetically led to break an altar of Ishtar, or Asherah, on October 12. This connected back to the Mount Carmel showdown between Elijah and the prophets of

Baal and Asherah, the gods that King Ahab and Jezebel worshipped (see 1 Kings 18). I now knew I would make my decree after that altar was broken, as a symbol of breaking Jezebel's power.

Thus, on October 12, after 10 hours of corporate prayer and fasting, I joined many other apostles and prophets on stage as we smashed the altar of Ishtar. (I hadn't originally realized Jonathan Cahn was planning to bring a literal stone altar to the capital!) Once most of the altar had crumbled, I picked up one of the stone pieces and threw it into a trash-can off-stage as a simple prophetic act. Then, I proceeded to make the following apostolic decree:

> *I believe what Jonathan Cahn says, that Trump is a type of Jehu, and Kamala Harris is a type of Jezebel. And as you know, Jehu cast out Jezebel … I decree in Jesus' mighty name, and I decree it by faith that Trump will win on November the 5th. He will be our 47th president, and Kamala Harris will be cast out, and she will lose, in Jesus' mighty name.*[64]

Now, as of this writing in October 2024, the election has not yet occurred, but I am fully confident in this prophetic journey leading me to decree that Trump will win. I am stepping out in faith to include this section in the book, acknowledging that by the time this book is published in December, the election will be over. I have always believed

---

[64] "A Million Women Live Stream." A Million Women. October 12, 2024. https://youtu.be/JHAMWJeVOQo?t=36501

that faith involves risk, and I feel I need to stand by what God spoke to me. This is how I understand decrees: They come about when we first hear from heaven, then we make the decree, and we stand in faith that it is a done deal based on what we have heard from God.

Ten days after making this decree in Washington, D.C., I was invited to a prayer meeting in Atlanta where President Trump would meet with 300 pastors following one of his rallies. I agreed to the last-minute plans and booked a flight to make it there in time. With 15,000 people converging on the city for the rally, the hotels were completely sold out.

After touching down in Atlanta, our HIM church pastor from the area picked me up and was planning to join me for the meeting. However, a few hours beforehand, I received a text from my contact liaison inquiring if I was still coming.

"Yes," I replied. "Is the meeting still on?"

She texted back, "Things have changed because the venue where we're going to have the prayer meeting is very small. So, we're going to only have 80 pastors come together instead of 300."

My immediate thought was to ask if I was among the 80, but I chose to surrender it to God, praying, "Lord, if You want me to be there, I believe You spoke to me to accept this invitation. I'm here to support Trump, and it will be a great rally regardless."

Just two hours before the meeting, I got word that I was included in the group of 80, which came as a wonderful surprise. I then made my way to the designated area an hour before Trump's arrival. I learned that the pastor in charge, from Charlie Kirk's ministry TPUSA, had arranged for several leaders to pray for Trump. They asked Ben Carson, Jentezen Franklin, and Jenny Donnelly to pray over him. I was surprised once again when the pastor asked if I would pray, too. It felt providential, given that my ministry isn't based in Atlanta or as widely known as some of the others.

Finally, the moment came for the four of us to meet President Trump, shake his hand, stand with him for a photo, and then lay hands on him, praying one after another. When it was my turn to pray, I declared Isaiah 11:2–3 over President Trump: "The Spirit of the Lord will rest on Him, the spirit of wisdom and understanding, the spirit of counsel and strength, the spirit of knowledge and the fear of the Lord..." I declared to him, "You will delight in the fear of the Lord" (v.3). This passage, of course, is talking about Jesus, but I believe it can also apply to all believers.

My encounter in Atlanta felt surreal, and I couldn't help but be amazed by how God had orchestrated all of this. In this remarkable season, I believe the 2024 election will prove to be a major sign of what will continue to unfold, both in the spiritual and in the natural. We are in the early stages of a Third Great Awakening, and we are going to see the greatest revival and reformation in history. It's time for the church to arise in our rightful authority and take territory for God's kingdom!

(These testimonies have provided a few examples of apostolic and prophetic decrees from my own walk with Jesus. For those interested in learning more on the apostolic, read my book *Modern-Day Apostles*.)

Join me in prayer as we close:

"Heavenly Father, I believe You have called me to be a house of prayer. Thank You for giving me Your authority and power to overcome all the works of the enemy. Give me wisdom and heavenly insight so that I may wage war effectively in the Spirit. Empower me by Your Spirit to pray prophetically and apostolically to advance Your kingdom on the earth today—in Jesus' mighty name, amen!"

Chapter 10:

FROM GOING TO CHURCH TO BEING THE CHURCH

*And He gave some as apostles, and some as prophets,
and some as evangelists, and some as pastors and teachers,
for the equipping of the saints for the work of service, to
the building up of the body of Christ; until we all attain to
the unity of the faith, and of the knowledge of the Son of
God, to a mature man, to the measure of the stature which
belongs to the fullness of Christ.
(Eph. 4:11–13 NASB1995)*

Sometime in early 2022, before my first return trip to South Korea following the lockdowns, I had a prophetic dream. In the dream, I was sitting at a desk with a blank piece of paper in front of me. My father was on my right-hand side, and my uncle was on my left. They both wanted me to write my name in Korean. The problem was that I didn't know how! I can't speak or write in Korean, although I remember being taught how to write my name when I was a little boy. Over the years, I'd completely forgotten the Korean alphabet. But in the dream, it felt crucial that I remember how to write my name—because your name is tied to your identity, and identity is intertwined with your destiny.

Still in the dream, I picked up the pen and wrote my name in Korean letters. When I woke up, I knew by revelation how to write my name again. The Lord brought it back to me, even though I had forgotten it since childhood. Even now, I can still write my name in Korean. Granted, it's a simple name, not difficult at all, but the meaning behind it in that dream was profound.

I easily understood why my father and uncle were there with me. My father was the first Korean Southern Baptist pastor in North America and so much more—an apostle, a revivalist, and a reformer. He fled from North Korea during the Korean War, escaping imprisonment by God's grace, and eventually made his way to South Korea, where he met my mother. May is a special month for me personally because my mother's birthday was May 13, my parent's wedding anniversary was May 22, and on a larger scale, Israel also became a nation on May 14, 1948.

My father came from a very humble background as a refugee from North Korea, but my mother's family was among the wealthiest in South Korea. My grandfather on her side had exclusive rights to sell rice to the Korean military during the war, making him a fortune. He even started a private bank and owned significant land in Seoul, some of which was later taken by the government to build a freeway.

My uncle, on the other hand, was a significant figure in the Korean government. He served as a cabinet member for two different presidents and was the president of Hanyang University. He represented a marketplace apostle in my family, while my father was a church apostle. In that dream, I felt like I was receiving an impartation from both—I was called to be both a marketplace and a church apostle.

This revelation changed everything for me. Before this, I had only seen myself as a church apostle. But the dream confirmed something deeper. In 2010, long before the pandemic and this dream, my wife and I started a business called Joseph's Storehouse. Our financial manager advised creating an S Corp. Since that dream, our business has flourished beyond anything we could have imagined.

One of our apostles, Leanne Goff, wrote a great book called *Missionary and Millionaire*. Leanne has been commissioned as an apostle both on the church mountain and in the marketplace; she has planted over 380 churches in Cuba and is a very successful businesswoman. Last year, we were even able to give, by God's grace, almost $2 million in one offering from Joseph's Storehouse to our church (see Acts 4:32–35). This is also why my wife and I can give our salary back to our church each year, which we have been doing for years.

Again, I want to emphasize that this is all by His grace, and Yeshua gets all the glory! As a marketplace apostle, I believe one of our roles is to lay resources at the feet of the church. And in this unique position, as both a marketplace and church apostle, I was able to do just that. For a more detailed understanding of the apostolic ministry, I recommend reading my book *Modern-Day Apostles*.

FROM GOING TO CHURCH TO BEING THE CHURCH

When we pass by a building where our church meets, how many of us have pointed to that building and said to a friend, "I go to that church"? Now, we all know that the church is not a building. Nevertheless, a building or going to a service has become synonymous with being the church. The church, *ekklesia* in the Greek, literally means "called-out ones." In ancient Greece, the *ekklesia* was a called-out assembly of citizens from the city-state of Athens as early as 621 B.C. By 507 B.C., a group of male Athenian citizens, age 18 or older, called the *ekklesia*, was responsible for making important decisions about the city, such as passing laws, selecting officials, and dictating foreign policy. The *ekklesia* was a key part of the first known democracy in the world.

Ed Silvoso, in his monumental book *Ekklesia*, states the original use of the word: "In fact, by the time He [Jesus] first uttered the word in the gospel of Matthew, it had been in use for centuries in both the Greek and Roman empire to refer to a secular institution operating in the marketplace in governmental capacity."[65] He goes on to say, "Its objective was the transformation of people and society, rather than acting as a transfer station of saved souls bound for heaven."[66]

And I also say to you that you are Peter, and on this rock, I will build My church, and the gates of

---

[65] Ed Silvoso, Ekklesia: Rediscovering God's Instrument for Global Transformation. Chosen Books, 2017, p.19.
[66] Ibid., p.20.

Hades shall not prevail against it. And I will give
you the keys of the kingdom of heaven, and whatever you bind on earth will be bound in heaven,
and whatever you loose on earth will be loosed in
heaven. (Matt. 16:18–19 NKJV)

There are several truths that I want to elaborate on from
Matthew 16:18. First, the church is *God's people*. 1 Peter 2:9–
10 (NKJV) says, "But you are a chosen generation, a royal
priesthood, a holy nation, His own special people, that you
may proclaim the praises of Him who called you out of darkness into His marvelous light; who once were not a people
but are now the people of God, who had not obtained mercy
but now have obtained mercy." Notice how Jesus did not say,
"I will build My synagogue" or "I will build My temple." He
picked the word *ekklesia* because the called-out ones are not
just to meet and gather on Sundays, but they are called out
to legislate in society through prayer (Matt. 16:19) and action
24 hours a day, seven days a week.

Second, Jesus is the foundation for the Christian life,
and thus, *Jesus is the foundation of the church*. Paul says, "For
no other foundation can anyone lay than that which is laid,
which is Jesus Christ" (1 Cor. 3:11 NKJV). Billy Graham
said, "Jesus Christ Himself founded the church. He is the
great cornerstone upon which the church is built. He is the
foundation of all Christian experience, and the church is
founded upon Him."[67]

---

[67] Billy Graham. *Peace with God: The Secret Happiness*. Thomas Nelson. Kindle Edition, p.221.

Third, the church is to be on *the offense*. We are to attack the gates of hell. I love the title of a chapter in one of Peter Wagner's books, "From Tolerating Satan to a Declaration of War."[68] God has called us to fight evil and all the works of satan. It starts with spiritual warfare ("Deliver us from the evil one" from Matt. 6:13), as discussed in the preceding chapter, but throughout the book, I have been trying to make a case for Christian activism. "The people who know their God will be strong and take action" (Dan.

I believe that real change in the church begins with apostles leading the way, and we need to recognize the apostolic ministry in the marketplace. Of the majority of Christians, only 1 percent are in vocational church ministry. So, we have developed this Platonic thinking related to the separation of church and state, of secular and sacred, of people who are going to the church on Sunday versus being the church throughout the week. We have to realize that we are all kings and priests, and we are His church.

The real change that will take place in society will be in the marketplace—where 99 percent of Christians are. It is ridiculous to think that only 1 percent of the church received the ascension gifts of being apostles, prophets, evangelists, pastors, and teachers (Eph. 4:11). God gave these gifts to the whole Body of Christ. However, since the majority of the people are not vocationally involved, their ministry has to be wherever they go—in any home, work-place, or meeting place.

---

[68] Peter Wagner, *This Changes Everything*, p.89.

THE CASE FOR MARKETPLACE APOSTLES

Strategically speaking, how we transform society is by recognizing and raising up marketplace apostles. I want to share some examples of people I feel God called to be marketplace apostles, whether they would call themselves that or not.

R.G. LeTourneau (1888–1969) was a shining example of a marketplace apostle. He was a pioneering inventor and businessman known for his significant contributions to the development of heavy machinery. LeTourneau was so successful that he chose to give 90 percent of his income to ministry while living off only 10 percent (which was still substantial). He generously funded missionary work, evangelistic campaigns, and Bible translations through the Christian Missionary Alliance. LeTourneau acquired land and planted more churches than potentially any other church apostle of his generation. He also founded LeTourneau University in 1946, a school focused on technical education and discipleship.

One of the marketplace apostles of our current day I want to honor is Phil Liberatore. Phil is a dear friend, a CPA and tax-resolution specialist based in Southern California. Through his generosity and giving, he has done more to advance God's kingdom than anyone I personally know. This has been done across the board, from international and national ministries to regional and local initiatives.

Jenny Donnelly is another marketplace apostle on a mission to transform the world. She has been ordained as both a marketplace and church apostle. She had an extremely successful company, making $100,000 a month before she became a pastor. Now, Jenny is applying her marketplace anointing to a ministry called Her Voice Movement. (See more in Appendix B.)

There are many different organizations bringing reformation today, and I encourage you to make note of each one and pray about getting involved:

- *Revive California* is a 501c4 that was birthed in February 2021 with the vision to see historic revival and reformation come to California. We have brought together over a dozen apostolic leaders from California, many of whom are marketplace apostles, like Dr. Marc Little, attorney; Senator Shannon Grove, State Senator; Dr. John Jackson, President of Jessup University; Dave Dias, businessman and former dot-com owner in Silicon Valley; and Phil Liberatore, founder and owner of one of the largest accountancy firms in LA. Go to revivecal.org for a complete list of the advisory board, including leaders from the government, education, business, and church mountains of culture.[69]

- *America Upheld* is an FEC-approved PAC committed to supporting conservative candidates running for office with a biblical worldview.[70] (See the chapter on "Poverty to Prosperity" to read more of the story about America Upheld.)

---

[69] https://revivecal.org
[70] https://www.americaupheld.org

- *The Salt & Light Council* with Dran Reese is on a mission to "see America's biblical and moral foundations restored by training and equipping churches" to "defend and promote life, natural marriage, our constitutional and religious liberties."[71]

- *Turning Point USA*, founded by Charlie Kirk, was created "to empower informed civic and cultural engagement grounded in American exceptionalism and a positive spirit of action."[72]

- *Family Research Council* with Tony Perkins has a mission "to serve in the kingdom of God by championing faith, family, and freedom in public policy and the culture from a biblical worldview."[73]

- *Give Him 15* with Dutch Sheets is a daily devotional series leading Christians in prophetic intercession and decrees to make an impact in our nation and around the globe. (See Appendix C for an important essay by Dutch Sheets on the topic of reformation.)

- *FlashPoint*, hosted by my good friend Gene Bailey, is a weekly televised program bringing truth on the media mountain through insightful news and commentary.[74]

---

[71] https://www.saltandlightcouncil.org/home/
[72] https://www.tpusa.com/about
[73] https://frc.org
[74] https://flashpoint.govictory.com

THE CASE FOR MENTORING THE NEXT GENERATION OF REFORMERS PERSEVERING FOR REFORM

Reformation takes time. The First Great Awakening began in 1738 in England. At the time, England had a monopoly on the slave trade. John Wesley, one of the key apostolic revivalists of that Awakening, wanted to abolish slavery and the slave trade in his lifetime. He wrote a treatise on slavery called "Thoughts on Slavery" in 1774, two years before our Independence was declared. He highlights the total injustice of slavery:

> Where is the justice of inflicting the severest evils on those that have done us no wrong? Of depriving those that never injured us in word or deed, of every comfort of life? Of tearing them from their native country, and depriving them of liberty itself, to which an Angolan has the same natural right as an Englishman, and on which he sets as high a value? Yea, where is the justice of taking away the lives of innocent, inoffensive men; murdering thousands of them in their own land, by the hands of their own countrymen; many thousands, year after year, on shipboard, and then casting them like dung into the sea; and tens of thousands in that cruel slavery to which they are so unjustly reduced? ... I absolutely deny

all slave-holding to be consistent with any degree
of natural justice.[75]

John Wesley had a tremendous influence with what
would become the Methodist movement, which was a movement of abolitionists—people who were against slavery.

Slavery was the number-one injustice issue of England,
the British Commonwealth nations, and the United States.
But in England, God raised up William Wilberforce and
the Clapham Group, who were tremendously influenced by
John Wesley and the Methodist movement.

Eric Metaxas tells the story of how Wilberforce, as a
boy of 10 years old, went to live with his uncle and aunt,
who were ardent Methodists and abolitionists. "When Wilberforce's mother and grandfather sent him to live with his
aunt and uncle, they hadn't the slightest idea that they were
sending the boy into a glowing hotbed of Methodism. And
the idea that he would be parleying with a rough former sea
captain on the horrors of slavery [John Netwon]!"[76]

Wilberforce went on to bring an end to the slave trade
with Parliament's passing of the Slave Trade Act of 1807
and the emancipation of all slaves in the British Empire by
1833. The point is that from the time when revival broke out
in 1738 until the emancipation of all slaves, it took almost
100 years to reform England on just one injustice issue.

---

[75] John Wesley. "Thoughts Upon Slavery." *The Works of John Wesley.*
https://msa.maryland.gov/megafile/msa/speccol/sc5300/sc5339/000091/
000000/000001/restricted/2002_09_10/wesley/thoughtsuponslavery.html
[76] Eric Metaxas. *Amazing Grace.* HarperOne. Kindle Edition, p.10-11.

The other point I want to note is that what Wilberforce did, trying to pass this bill for over 27 years, had a profound impact on the United States. One year later, the United States officially banned the importation of slaves on January 1, 1808, when the "Act Prohibiting the Importation of Slaves" took effect. This law was signed by President Thomas Jefferson on March 2, 1807, after passing the Senate on December 17, 1805, and the House on February 13, 1807. The law made it illegal for Americans to import slaves from Africa, but unfortunately, the domestic slave trade between ports in the United States continued. It continued until the 13th Amendment was passed on January 31, 1865, and ratified by December 1865, almost a year later.

The Bible says love is patient (1 Cor. 13:4). But the Greek word *makrothumaei* means "to suffer long." When you love God and love others, including America, you are willing to suffer for a long time until the change takes place.

It took 49 years to overturn *Roe v. Wade* with the *Dobbs v. Jackson* case, but still, abortion is not abolished. Now, thank God for the thousands of babies that are alive today because of this Supreme Court decision. James and Rosemary Garlow, founders of the reformation ministry Well Versed, wrote on a recent blog, "Since the Dobbs case (a great victory) two years ago, the lives of 8,000 babies a year have been saved in just one state (Missouri) alone, but that will change this November if we do not defeat the abortion amendment in that state and 10 others" (Aug. 28, 2024). Each state will decide the law of legalization of abortion. Garlow goes on to write:

Every state that has voted on abortion since the overturning of *Roe* has enshrined the killing of babies into their state constitution. All of them! There are 10 or 11 states that will vote on pro-abortion amendments in November, just a few weeks from now, likely one in which many of you reading this live: FL, MD, NY, AR, MO, NE, SD, MT, NV, ID, CO. Once it is in the constitution, it is extremely difficult to get it removed. It only requires a 50% plus one vote to pass these murderous amendments in every state, except in Florida, where it requires a 60% vote. We must vote 'no' on every amendment in every state, but the language for the titles of the amendments are very deceiving (just like they were in the Kansas case, where some pro-life people were confused how they should vote).

I agree that we must battle each bill until an Amendment is passed recognizing that a baby is a human being, with all the civil rights that are true in America, making it illegal to kill a baby. We, as reformers, can never give this issue a rest. We must also pass on the mantle of being a reformer for justice like William Wilberforce's Uncle William and Aunt Hannah in Wimbledon inculcated their values of being an abolitionist to little William.

Behold, I will send you Elijah the prophet before the coming of the great and dreadful day of the

LORD. And he will turn the hearts of the fathers to the children, and the hearts of the children to their fathers, lest I come and strike the earth with a curse. (Mal. 4:5–6 NKJV)

I want to share an encouraging true story recounted by my good friends Gene and Teri Bailey, who gave me permission to share this story in this book. It carries the heart of Malachi 4:5–6 and shows the crucial role that spiritual parents are meant to play in raising up the next generation of reformers.

"DUTY IS OURS; RESULTS ARE GOD'S"

Even though the founding fathers intended the United States of America to be a nation without slavery, this didn't happen right away. In the beginning years of our nation's history, the majority of Congress was opposed to the emancipation of slaves. Despite this fact, one man fought tirelessly for the freedom of America's slaves. This man was John Quincy Adams. For 28 consecutive years, he consistently fought for this cause—even when it seemed that he was making no progress at all. One day, while he was leaving the Capitol building, a reporter stopped him and asked why he kept pushing for the emancipation of slaves when it seemed hopeless. Adams turned, looked at the reporter, and said simply, "Duty is ours; results are God's." He then walked on.

In 1847, a man who looked up to Adams came to serve in Congress as a freshman legislator. Soon, Adams took this man under his wing and became his mentor—they grew so close that this man was a pallbearer at Adams's funeral. After one term in the legislature this man went home, and Adams later died after serving 28 years in the legislature—seeing none of the fruits of his labor. Now some time after Adams's protégé returned home, he ran again for office, and again, and again. In fact, he lost multiple elections, but one of the elections he did win was the most important one—the race for the seat of the President of the United States. This man's name was Abraham Lincoln. He went on to be one the most important presidents in our nation's history.[77]

A FRESH CONSECRATION AND COVENANT

When Lou Engle and I led TheCall prayer movement, the purpose was more than to pray and fast for revival and reformation in America. (Lou was the visionary founder of The-Call, and I was the co-founder and president from 2000 to 2003.) Yes, the focus was prayer and specifically that *Roe v. Wade* would be overturned by the Supreme Court, just like the Dred Scott Decision of 1857—which determined that black slaves could never be citizens of the U.S. and therefore never have the privilege to vote—was overturned by the 14th Amendment and the 15th Amendment.

---

[77] Gene Bailey and Teri Bailey. *Killing America*. Harrison House Publishers. Kindle Edition, p.109.

I pulled my only copy of *TheCall Revolution*, which was published in 2001 and has been out of print after thinking that TheCall was over in 2003. (TheCall would be resurrected in 2007 with TheCall Nashville and officially ended with TheCall Azusa in 2016, but you never know what might result from the momentum following the Million Women gathering in October 2024, also founded by Lou Engle and Jenny Donnelly.)

Here are some quotes of the covenant declarations we made with the 400,000-plus young people at TheCall on the Mall in Washington, D.C., in 2000. This is an edited version of the last chapter entitled "TheCall Covenant":

> *WE COVENANT to love You, Father God, with all our hearts, souls, minds, and strength. In humility and led by the Holy Spirit, we will keep communion with You and love others.*
>
> *WE COVENANT to fight for the life of every unborn child.*
>
> *WE COVENANT to show practical love to the widow, the fatherless, the poor, and the rejected as we seek deliverance from religious pride and hypocrisy.*
>
> *WE COVENANT to invade every arena of our culture with kingdom love and kingdom authority instead of abdicating our responsibility to it.*
>
> *WE COVENANT to reclaim the historic call upon America to send its sons and daughters to the people groups of the earth, fulfilling the Great Commission.*

WE COVENANT to fast and pray for a great spiritual awakening in America and the other nations of the earth.

(I added this last one specifically for this book as a call for reformers and revivalists.)

WE COVENANT, by Your grace, to be revivalists and reformers until the kingdoms of this world become the king-doms of our Lord and of His Christ, in Jesus' mighty name, amen.

As I read this, I thought this would be an excellent way to end this chapter by calling the church to make a fresh consecration with these seven covenants. Go ahead and say these covenants out loud. And if you really meant it, sign your name below:

I, _____, make this covenant before God today, in the name of Jesus and by the grace of the Holy Spirit.

Chapter 11:

FROM PROCLAMATION TO POWER EVANGELISM

And He said to them, "Go into all the world and preach
the gospel to every creature. He who believes and is bap-
tized will be saved; but he who does not believe will be
condemned. And these signs will follow those who believe:
In My name they will cast out demons; they will speak
with new tongues; they will take up serpents; and if they
drink anything deadly, it will by no means hurt them; they
will lay hands on the sick, and they will recover."
(Mark 16:15–18 NKJV)

But you shall receive power when the Holy Spirit has come
upon you; and you shall be witnesses to Me in Jerusalem,
and in all Judea and Samaria, and to the end of the earth.
(Acts 1:8 NKJV)

The invitation to join my friend Billy's youth group on
a trip to Buffalo, New York, came at a good time. Billy
was my only Christian friend at Magruder High School after

my dramatic conversion in 1973. Now, it was nearing Easter of 1974, and I was lonely and longing for fellowship.

The trip was sponsored by a conservative evangelical Presbyterian church called the Church of the Atonement in nearby Silver Spring, Maryland. The high school and college students would leave on the Friday before Palm Sunday, do some sightseeing, and then visit two Presbyterian churches in the Buffalo area on Sunday before returning home on Monday. I did not know any of the students in the youth group except for Billy. This seemed like a great opportunity to meet other Christians and find out if I wanted to be involved with their church. Of course, a sightseeing trip to Niagara Falls was also enticing, so I accepted. I had a simple, logical agenda.

But God had other plans.

The trip up went well, and experiencing Niagara Falls was truly amazing. Yet I found myself hungry for God and looking forward to the Palm Sunday services. The first one was held in a large, dynamic church. The senior pastor preached the gospel and invited people to come forward and give their lives to Jesus. I loved the service because the minister sounded and preached like Billy Graham, who was my ultimate role model as a young believer.

The evening meeting, by contrast, was at a small Presbyterian church, and the youth group was invited to do the whole service. We were asked to lead worship, and the youth pastor preached that night. We had around 30 people in our group, and we were all asked to be part of the choir, whether we could sing or not. We were singing a popular song called "Day by Day" from the recent Broadway hit *Godspell*. The words are powerful: "To see Thee more clearly ... love Thee more dearly ... follow Thee more nearly ... day by day..."

As I sang these words, I began to worship Jesus and make the words my prayer. I sang and prayed in my heart, "Jesus, I really want to see You, love You, and follow You with all my heart!"

All of a sudden, my feet started to vibrate with growing intensity. It felt as if my feet had fallen asleep, but I was still standing. Then the tingling shot up my legs, to my head, and down through my arms. I was vibrating all over. My hands were so overcome that I could not close my fingers to make a fist. At the same time, I was being baptized with God's presence and love so deeply that I began to weep profusely. I was making a scene.

The youth pastor came up, put his arm around me, and whispered into my ear, "Whatever is going on with you, you have to take it to the men's room." I quickly left the sanctuary and went to the men's room alone. The intensity remained, and I didn't know what was going on. I had been a believer for less than one year and had never experienced this before.

Without knowing much of the Bible or any specific theology, I knew that God was calling me for service. It was two weeks later that I talked to an older couple, the Blakeslees, who explained to me that I had been baptized in the Holy Spirit. That night, they prayed for me to pray in tongues, and the tongues flowed out immediately upon asking.

MOVING INTO A HEALING MINISTRY

Shortly after, Rob and I started a Bible Study with the teenagers and children of the Blakeslees' adult friends. The Bible study was struggling to gain traction, so one of the adults suggested that we invite a high school teacher named Jim Woodward, who had a healing ministry. Perhaps he could minister and get things going for our little study. So, Jim came on a Friday night, the night of our get-together. He taught from the Word how Jesus heals today. Then, he began to demonstrate the healing power of God.

Jim explained that for most people, one leg is longer than the other, and as a result, people have backaches and other problems with their legs or their backs. He asked for a volunteer, and sure enough, the first person's leg was longer than the other. Holding the feet lightly in his hands, Jim commanded the leg to grow and be even, and I watched wide-eyed as the shorter leg grew out. Within seconds, the legs were even.

Jim did this a few more times and then asked if I wanted to try. At first, I was surprised because I had never prayed for anyone to get healed at that point in my life. I did what Jim told me to do, and as I prayed in Jesus' name, the legs of the person I prayed for grew even. I knew without a doubt that God had healed the leg!

That learning experience changed my life. The encounter gave me faith to pray for people who were sick. I began to pray for others as an usher at a large Bible study called "Take and Give" (TAG), meaning to *take* what God has done for you *and give* it to others. As people walked in, I greeted them and asked how they were doing. Inevitably, someone always came through the door who was sick or had something wrong with them physically (e.g., a sprained ankle, a hurt back, a cold, etc.) I would pray for them in Jesus' name, and as far as my recollection goes, most got healed.

The word spread to the leaders of this Bible study of 2,000 people, and one of the leaders came to me and said, "We have had too many reports of people getting healed after you prayed for them, and we believe you have the gift of healing. How would you like to pray for people needing healing each Tuesday night? We will give an invitation for salvation, the baptism of the Holy Spirit, and healing. We want you to pray for the sick, and we will evaluate as we go."

So, I ended up praying for the sick for the next three years, and that is how I got involved in the healing ministry. Now I believe that these signs will follow everyone who is a believer, as Jesus says in Mark 16:17–18 (NKJV): "And these signs will follow those who believe: In My name they will cast out demons; they will speak with new tongues; they will take up serpents; and if they drink anything deadly, it will by no means hurt them; they will lay hands on the sick, and they will recover." However, I believe as Peter Wagner taught in his book, *Your Spiritual Gifts Can Help Your Church Grow*, God specifically gives some "the gifts of healing" (1 Cor. 12:9).

It was during this time that I began to pray for non-Christians to get healed, and they not only got healed, but their healing led to their salvation. This is what is known as power evangelism.

The late John Wimber, founder of the Association of Vineyard Churches, wrote the seminal book on this topic, *Power Evangelism*. John was a pioneer in helping my generation understand how the giftings we have in the Holy Spirit are the most powerful tools we can employ in sharing the gospel. In his book, he gives the biblical basis for power evangelism and uses personal testimonies to back up his theology. Here I will give a summation of the key passages and then close with the story that launched me into being a "power evangelist."

JESUS NEEDED POWER

In His three years of ministry, Jesus did everything in complete reliance on the Holy Spirit. He healed the sick, cast out demons, raised the dead, multiplied food, and walked on water in response to what He saw and heard the Father doing (John 5:19). He did all of this in His humanity, as a man filled with the power of the Holy Spirit.

We know this is true because Jesus Himself received the Holy Spirit coming upon Him as a dove at His baptism in the Jordan River (Luke 3:21–22). The Spirit led Jesus into the wilderness to be tempted, and He overcame all temptation (Mark 1:12–13). Jesus then returned from the wilderness in the great power of the Spirit (Luke 4:14) and began His ministry operating in the miraculous.

> When all the people were baptized, it came to pass that Jesus also was baptized; and while He prayed, the heaven was opened. And the Holy Spirit descended in bodily form like a dove upon Him, and a voice came from heaven which said, 'You are My beloved Son; in You I am well pleased.' (Luke 3:21–22 NKJV)

The anointing and power of the Holy Spirit was a necessity for Christ's mission to be accomplished. In Luke 4:18–19, Jesus fulfilled the prophecy in Isaiah saying, "The Spirit of the LORD is upon Me, because He has anointed Me to bring good news to the poor. He has sent Me to proclaim release to the captives, and recovery of sight for the blind, to set free those who are oppressed, to proclaim the favorable year of the LORD."

THE EARLY CHURCH NEEDED POWER

Even though Jesus' disciples were with Him throughout His entire earthly ministry, they, too, needed something more. In John 14, Jesus told His inner circle of friends that they were being empowered to do the same supernatural works that Jesus Himself did—and even beyond that. The key was the promise of the Holy Spirit:

> Most assuredly, I say to you, he who believes in Me, the works that I do he will do also; and *greater works than these he will do*, because I go to My Father. And whatever you ask in My name, that I will do, that the Father may be glorified in the Son. If you ask anything in My name, I will do it. If you love Me, keep My commandments. And I will pray the Father, and *He will give you another Helper*, that He may abide with you forever—*the Spirit of truth*, whom the world cannot receive, because it neither sees Him nor knows Him; but you know Him, for He dwells with you and will be in you. I will

not leave you orphans; I will come to you. (John 14:12–18 NKJV)

By this point in their discipleship journey, the 12 apostles had already done the works of Jesus to a certain degree. They had seen sick people healed and demons cast out as a direct result of their ministry, which was based on the authority that Jesus gave them (see Luke 9:1–6; 10:9, 17). They had experienced the external power of the Holy Spirit but did not yet have the Spirit living inside them. The "greater works" that Jesus mentioned would come from a more radical relationship with God. The Father was planning to give His sons and daughters the *indwelling presence of the Holy Spirit*, who would abide with them forever.

Before He ascended into heaven, Jesus commanded them to receive the power of the Holy Spirit by waiting in the upper room (Acts 1:4, 8). The Holy Spirit was then poured out on the day of Pentecost (Acts 2:1–4), not just for a one-time showcase of God's power but for a lifetime of walking in the supernatural power of Christ's kingdom.

With this gift, the "apostles performed many miraculous signs and wonders among the people ... [And] more and more men and women believed in the Lord and were added to their number" (Acts 5:12, 14 NIV). Great miracles were done through the apostle Peter, whose shadow healed people in the streets of Jerusalem (Acts 5:15–16), and through Philip, who preached Christ in Samaria.

And the multitudes with one accord heeded the things spoken by Philip, hearing and seeing the miracles which he did. For unclean spirits, crying with a loud voice, came out of many who were possessed; and many who were paralyzed, and lame were healed. And there was great joy in that city. (Acts 8:6–8 NKJV)

PAUL NEEDED POWER

Likewise, the apostle Paul acknowledged His dependency on the power of the Holy Spirit. In his first letter to the church at Corinth, he wrote, "My message and my preaching were not with wise and persuasive words, but with a demonstration of the Spirit's power" (1 Cor. 2:4 NIV). The gospel was never meant to be dependent upon the words of man, no matter how eloquent or well-intentioned. The Holy Spirit has always been God's intended means of bringing a visible demonstration of His kingdom to this earth.

The apostle Luke recounts in the book of Acts how "God did extraordinary miracles through Paul, so that even handkerchiefs and aprons that had touched him were taken to the sick, and their illnesses were cured, and the evil spirits left them" (Acts 19:11–12 NIV). Picture that: Paul's ministry was marked by such supernatural power that God brought healing and deliverance to people who were miles away from where Paul was working his day job as a tentmaker.

All of this shows that we must have the power of God in order to fulfill the Great Commission, disciple nations, and transform society.

AKIKO'S POWER ENCOUNTER

Our Bible study, TAG, went from 150 people when I joined it in 1974 to 2,000 in the next two years, involving many new converts during the Jesus movement on the East Coast of the United States. Without hyperbole, between 100 and 150 came forward each week as the preacher gave the altar call for salvation. The harvest came in like I have never seen before—or ever since.

We didn't see a great harvest during the Toronto Blessing like in the Jesus movement, but we *did* see significant conversions through power evangelism. I remember when someone brought a Japanese student named Akiko, who was studying English at Pasadena City College, to one of our Harvest Rock Church Sunday morning services around June 1994. I knew she was a visitor, so I went up to her during our ministry time and shared the gospel with her. After I shared, I asked if she wanted to give her life to Jesus. She politely said, "I can't. My father is a Shintoist, and my mother is a Buddhist." Later, I found out that her father was a Shinto priest and even had a shrine in his name.

Then I asked Akiko if I could just pray for her. Being a polite Japanese girl, she said yes. I simply placed my hand over her head, an inch from her forehead, and prayed, "Jesus, reveal Yourself to Akiko." The moment I prayed, she slumped to the floor like a cut-off marionette. It was the first time I saw an unbeliever fall under the power of the Holy Spirit. I said to myself, "This is interesting. That was not a courtesy fall!" I continued to minister to other people during this ministry time.

Twenty minutes later, I went to check on Akiko, and she had not moved an inch. I knelt down and whispered into her ear, "Akiko, are you OK?" She nodded her head. I then asked, "Did Jesus reveal Himself to you?" She nodded her head affirmatively. So, I followed up with the bigger question: "Would you like to pray and give your heart to Jesus?" She nodded yes, got up, renounced Shintoism, and gave her heart to Jesus!

The next week, Akiko brought three of her friends to Jesus, and after the service, she came up to me and said, "Pastor, pray for my friends like you prayed for me." So, I did, and all three fell under the power and got up and gave their hearts to Jesus. In the weeks ahead, so many of her Japanese friends were coming up and asking for prayer that I finally said, "Akiko, you can do the same thing as me. Just put your hand over their heads and invite the Holy Spirit to come." When she did, they fell under the power and gave their lives to Jesus.

This is not an exaggeration: Over 30 Japanese students came to know the Lord this way, and Akiko ended up leading a large cell group for us. She went to Fuller Seminary, and I had the joy of sending her back to Japan when her visa expired. What is really remarkable about this testimony is that the Japanese are traditionally one of the hardest people to reach. Less than 2 percent of Japan is Christian, but through the power of the Holy Spirit, we saw a significant harvest among the Japanese. I believe that Gen Z is very much like the Japanese, as only a small percent of them have come to know the Lord, and only 4 percent have a biblical worldview,[78] but I believe that through power evangelism, we will see a great harvest of souls.

HOW TO RECEIVE THE POWER

If we are going to see a harvest through power evangelism, it has to start by receiving the *power* first. So, how do we do that? Let's explore two main components of living a life full of the Holy Spirit's power.

1. Make the Great Commandment and the Great Commission a top priority in your life.

If you want to walk in the power of the Spirit, be sure to put first things first. The Great Commandment (to love God) and the Great Commission (to love others through evangelism and discipleship) are the keys to walking this out.

In the longest book of the Bible, one out of every three Psalms shows God's heart for the nations. One of the most basic but essential truths in all of Scripture is that God loves the world. That is why He sent Jesus to save us—His great love for all people (John 3:16). God's love is the driving force behind everything we do, including power evangelism. Paul put it this way, "The love of Christ compels us" (2 Cor. 5:14 NKJV).

As we prioritize the Great Commission, we must remember that there is no such thing as a closed country, only closed

---

[78] Tracy Munsil. "CRC Study Shows Younger Generations Reject Biblical Worldview…" Cultural Research Center, Arizona Christian University. May 28, 2024. https://www.arizonachristian.edu/2024/05/28/crc-study-shows-younger-generations-reject-biblical-worldview-ushering-in-new-morality/

minds. Right now, the gospel is penetrating even the darkest nations on earth, such as North Korea and Iran. When we keep our eyes on Jesus, we will be reminded of His greatness as we bring the good news to the lost and broken. His supernatural power can redeem any life, heal any sickness, and free any soul from the bondage of addiction or demonic possession. After all, our vision for the Lord determines our vision for the lost.

God provides supernatural power and supernatural grace to fulfill the divine calling on our lives. Prior to 1847, almost half of the Methodist circuit riders did not get married because they knew that half would not live beyond their 30th birthday.[79] They were fully committed to pursuing the Great Commission, and God gave them the grace to live the sacrificial life of His laid-down lovers.

Today, not every believer will become a full-time missionary, but everyone needs to be involved in whatever way they can. For you, that might look like starting to give to missions, or you may plan to go on a short-term mission trip. Whatever you choose to do, keep the love of God central as you stoke the flames of personal revival in your life. Missions have always been driven by revival, and I believe we are on the verge of the most significant mission thrust ever as the Spirit of God continues to move in unprecedented ways.

---

[79] "The Hard Road of a Methodist Circuit Rider." The United Methodist Church. March 21, 2018. https://www.umc.org/en/content/the-hard-road-of-a-methodist-circuit-rider

2. Be continually filled with the Holy Spirit.

The baptism and continual infilling of the Holy Spirit are essential for any believer who wants to "say goodbye to powerless Christianity." When we cease to lead our lives in our own strength, we will step into greater influence and responsibility as we rely on God's supernatural power.

In fact, the apostle Paul encourages us to be filled continually with the Holy Spirit: "Do not get drunk on wine, which leads to debauchery. Instead, be filled with the Spirit" (Eph. 5:18 NIV). The word *filled* in the Greek is in the continual present tense, so the verse really reads: "Do not be drunk with wine. Instead *be continually filled* with the Spirit" or, as one translation reads, "keep on being filled."

Scripture often refers to us as vessels of the Lord (see Jer. 18). The one thing about being living vessels is that we "leak," as Charles Spurgeon liked to say. We need refilling with water and food, joy and love, affirmation and communication. The same is true with the presence of the Lord in our lives through the Holy Spirit.

> But you shall receive power when the Holy Spirit has come upon you; and you shall be witnesses to Me in Jerusalem, and in all Judea and Samaria, and to the end of the earth. (Acts 1:8 NKJV)

The truth is that none of us can obey the commandment to love God and others (Matt. 22:37–39) without His love, grace, and the Holy Spirit dwelling fully in us. God has designed this to be that way. The Bible says in Zechariah 4:6b (NASB1995), "'Not by might nor by power, but by My

Spirit,' says the LORD of hosts." That is why we cannot love God—nor see a powerful revival and reformation—with our might, our power, or our efforts. It can only be by His love, the love of God that has been poured into our life by the Holy Spirit.

The baptism of the Holy Spirit is the key to unlocking this lifestyle of supernatural love. Many people seek the power of the Holy Spirit to be influential in ministry. Being passionate about ministry is a good thing, but we must realize that ministry is simply a byproduct of our relationship with God. As wonderful as our desire to reach nations with the power of the Holy Spirit is, we need to understand that the Holy Spirit gives us His supernatural love for us to fulfill the Great Commission. My encouragement for you is to hunger and thirst after the Holy Spirit so you can be a lover of God and others (Matt. 5:6).

Experiencing the baptism of the Holy Spirit can be described as receiving the baptism of love. Romans 5:5 tells us that "the love of God has been poured out within our hearts *through the Holy Spirit* who was given to us." God's love is the greatest virtue in His kingdom, and it is the very first "fruit of the Spirit" mentioned in Galatians 5:22. The fruit of the Spirit within you is *love,* joy, peace, patience, kindness, goodness, faith, humility, and self-control. The penultimate fruit, *praotes* in Greek, can be translated as meekness, gentleness, or humility. I choose to translate this word as humility because pride is the sin of satan and the opposite of God, who is love (1 John 4:8, 16).

The Holy Spirit gives us power to serve one another through His love (Gal. 5:13). If we "walk by the Spirit," we will be able to carry out God's will, which includes loving others, and turn away from the desires of our flesh (Gal. 5:16). We will cultivate God's love in our life as we cooperate with the Holy Spirit in our daily walk.

HOW TO BE FILLED

Much like receiving the power of the Spirit for power evangelism, we must constantly be filled. Here are some practical ways to keep the fire burning.

1. **Hunger and thirst for the Holy Spirit.** In Matthew 5:6, Jesus promises that if you hunger and thirst after righteousness, you will be filled.

2. **Repent.** As we saw in an earlier chapter, repentance is a necessary precursor of revival—whether that is personal revival or corporate revival (see Joel 2:1–28; Acts 2:38, 3:19, 5:31).

3. **Ask.** If you want more of the Holy Spirit, ask with the expectation to receive. I ask God for a fresh filling every morning. "You do not have because you do not ask" (James 4:2).

> So I say to you, *ask, and it will be given to you*; seek, and you will find; knock, and it will be opened to you. For *everyone who asks, receives*; and he who seeks, finds; and to him who knocks, it will be opened. Now suppose one of you fathers is asked by his son for a fish; he will not give him a snake instead of a fish, will he? Or if he is asked for an egg, he will

not give him a scorpion, will he? If you then, being evil, know how to give good gifts to your children, how much more will your heavenly Father *give the Holy Spirit to those who ask Him*? (Luke 11:9–13 NASB1995)

4. **Receive by faith.** Believing in prayer will set you up to receive what you are praying for.

> And Jesus answered saying to them, 'Have faith in God. Truly I say to you, whoever says to this mountain, "Be taken up and cast into the sea," and does not doubt in his heart, but believes that what he says is going to happen, it will be granted him. Therefore I say to you, all things for which you pray and ask, *believe that you have received them, and they will be granted you.* Whenever you stand praying, forgive, if you have anything against anyone, so that your Father who is in heaven will also forgive you your transgressions.' (Mark 11:22–25 NASB1995)

HOW TO MOVE IN POWER EVANGELISM

First, I want to encourage you to be sensitive to the prophetic voice of the Holy Spirit. If you belong to Jesus, you are one of His sheep, and Jesus said that His sheep hear His voice (John 10:27). God created you with the innate capacity to hear Him. Just as Jesus obeyed everything that He heard from the Father, He set the example for us to follow in His footsteps. That is why Jesus said it would be better for Him to go back to the Father, so the Holy Spirit could come and guide us into all truth.

> When the Spirit of truth comes, he will guide you into all the truth, for he will not speak on his own authority, but whatever he hears he will speak, and he will declare to you the things that are to come. He will glorify me, for he will take what is mine and declare it to you. (John 16:13–14 ESV)

Second, I encourage you to look for those who are hurting physically, and if the circumstance is right, ask if you can pray for them. Hearing God's voice and being led prophetically by Him are keys to seeing healing in power evangelism. Let me share a story with you about what this can practically look like.

One morning, sometime around 2008, I was leaving my house to go to the church office. At that time, the office was by Mott Auditorium in Pasadena. My neighbor Ann, a hospice nurse, called out to me from across the street. Ann and her husband, Andy, were the typical unchurched yuppie couple. Sue and I had often witnessed to them, inviting them over for a barbecue and giving them gifts for Christmas and Easter each year, as we just wanted to love on our neighbors.

Seeing her wave me over, I walked to the driveway across the street to talk with her. "What's up, Ann?"

"Ché, I have a patient who has been in a coma for two weeks," Ann told me. "She's 90 years old, and I think she's going to die any minute now. Could you come and give her the last rites?"

To be honest with you, I had no idea how to give last rites. Ann came from a Roman Catholic background, so she saw me as a priest. I said, "I'll be happy to, but I have a meeting in Altadena."

"The patient is in Altadena," she replied.

"Great, let me drive my car over, and then after I see your patient, I'll head to our church office." Thus was the arrangement. In my mind, I figured I would just say the Disciple's Prayer, quote Psalm 23, and that would be it.

So, I followed behind Ann in my car for the short trek to Altadena. When we arrived at a small two-bedroom bungalow, I got out of the car and was led to the elderly woman's room where a Filipina nurse was attending her. The patient's name was Lois. She was indeed in a coma, by all appearances, shriveled up and connected to an IV and some other basic life support. The moment I walked in the room, I heard the Lord say to me, "Raise her from the coma and preach the gospel to her."

Now, I didn't want to alarm Ann because she had a very traditional expectation of what I was there to do. I turned to her and said, "Do you mind if I pray a different kind of prayer than give the last rites?"

She said, "What do you mean?"

"Do you mind if I pray that God would heal her?"

Ann looked at me like, *I knew you were a religious fanatic.* She said, "You can do whatever you want to do," and then she walked over to the corner of the room where the other nurse was standing.

With that permission, I leaned over the bedside and said a simple prayer: "Father, in Jesus' name, I command Lois to come out of the coma and for her to hear the gospel."

Two or three seconds later, Lois suddenly opened her eyes. Seeing an unfamiliar Korean man standing over her bed, she immediately said, "Who are you?"

I was so stunned by her coming out of the coma so quickly that I just said, "I'm a pastor."

"I can't believe you're a pastor," she said, "because I prayed, 'God, keep me alive until You send a pastor to tell me how I can go to heaven.'"

I told her, "Lois, God has heard your prayers, and I'm going to tell you how you can get to heaven." So, I shared the gospel with her, and she gave her life to Jesus Christ. When I came back later to follow up and read the Bible to Lois, the Filipina nurse also ended up giving her heart to Jesus. A few months later, Ann came to our church service on Easter Sunday, and she was the first one to walk forward when I gave the altar call for salvation. Thus, God brought salvation to all three women as a result of Lois' miracle!

God desires all to be saved. He is constantly speaking—we just have to be listening. When we tune into the voice of the Holy Spirit, we must then be obedient and follow His leading to see supernatural results.

MY BREAKTHROUGH INTO POWER EVANGELISM

I first started to see unbelievers getting healed and saved while I was a student at the University of Maryland. This was around two years after I got radically saved and set on fire for Jesus. One weekend, I was invited to a birthday party at the home of one of my dad's church members. This man was a medical doctor who became a multi-millionaire by investing in real estate in Washington, D.C. He was one of the wealthiest Koreans in the area during the Jesus People days and was a tremendous blessing to our church. He even loaned my dad the money to buy our first house, which my parents eventually paid off.

His daughter Helen, who wasn't saved, was throwing a big birthday party for her sweet 16. I didn't know her well, as she and her family didn't regularly attend my dad's church. Her younger brother and my brother were friends, but they weren't that close. Nevertheless, my brother and I were somehow invited to the party at their beautiful house in Potomac. It was a five-acre horse ranch with a tennis court and a swimming pool, so you can imagine how wealthy the family was. To be honest, I mainly went to experience the luxury and enjoy the catered food at a millionaire's home.

While playing tennis at the party, I suddenly felt a strong prompting from the Holy Spirit. He said, "You've been at this party for an hour, and you haven't even once shared your faith."

I felt so convicted that I stopped playing tennis and called my opponent over to the net. I said, "You know what? I can't continue to play because as I was hitting the ball, I came under this incredible conviction. I recently gave my life to Jesus Christ, and I just felt compelled to tell you how much God loves you." In that moment, the Holy Spirit came upon him, and he gave his life to Jesus in the middle of the tennis court.

All of a sudden, I realized that I had a prime opportunity at this party because it was full of nonbelievers. It sounds funny now, but I made a spur-of-the-moment commitment before God: *I'm going to preach until they kick me out.* So, I started to share the gospel with different people. Finally, the birthday girl, Helen, heard I was preaching. She cornered me and said, "I hear you're evangelizing at my party."

I thought, *OK, here comes the left foot of fellowship...*

But she said, "Listen, why don't I call everyone into the rec room, and why don't you tell all my friends what's happened to you? Because I think they'll be interested."

"You're kidding me," I replied in shock.

"No, I'm serious," she said before calling people over. I watched as everyone there—around 40 of her friends—began to get out of the pool, dismount from the horses, and leave the tennis court behind to meet in the rec room.

Once we were all assembled, Helen introduced me to the group like a speaker. She said, "Ché has had a religious experience, and I thought it would be good for all of us to hear what happened to him." They all knew of me because of my reputation as a drug dealer and addict during high school. Word spread quickly in the Korean community, so that meant people also knew that I had become a Jesus freak in more recent times.

As I stood before this captive audience, I knew this had to be of God because most of the people were not Christians. So, I began to preach and gave my testimony, sharing that not only did God save me, but He also healed me of allergies the first time I walked into a Charismatic Bible study called TAG.

As I was talking about God healing me, a guy sitting in front, an upperclassman at the University of Maryland, raised his hand to interrupt me. "Can God heal me of my knee injury?" he interjected.

I wasn't expecting to field a question like this, but I said, "What's wrong?"

"I was a football player," he said, "and I had knee surgery." The guy was wearing shorts, and I could see a huge, ugly scar running from his thigh all the way down to his shin. (These were the days before arthroscopic knee surgeries, so it was much more obvious.)

"I'm not the healer," I replied, "but let's just pray for you." So, I stopped in the middle of my speech, put my hand on his knee, and prayed that God would heal him. All of a sudden, he looked up with wide eyes and said, "It's gone."

"What?" I asked.

He said, "The pain is gone."

One of his friends behind him said, "I don't believe it." The guy turned around and said, "No, I'm telling you. I had pain, and it just disappeared. It just went away."

At this point I suggested, "Is there something you can do that you couldn't do before without pain?"

"For sure," he replied, "I definitely couldn't do knee bends."

"Why don't you try it?" I encouraged him.

Right away, he got up and started doing knee bends. He called out, "It's gone!" and the Spirit of God fell on the whole group.

Another guy chimed in, "I just sprained my ankle messing around on the ranch. Can God heal me of this?" So, I went over to pray for him, and his ankle was immediately healed.

Seeing the momentum of what God was doing, I then shifted into giving an invitation: "If you want to give your life to Jesus Christ, I'm going to ask you to get down on your knees." Without exaggeration, around 30 out of the 40 people there got down on their knees. They gave their hearts to Jesus Christ as I led them in prayer. Then I gave a brief teaching on being filled with the Holy Spirit, and several started praying in tongues. The Holy Spirit was moving so powerfully among us that I don't think anyone present will ever forget that birthday party!

That encounter was a breakthrough moment into what would become a ministry of power evangelism over the decades as I continued following Jesus. It was part of the overflow of the revival that had broken out during the Jesus Revolution of the 1970s. God gets all the glory for this testimony and for every healing that takes place. I hope you can see now that it is God's desire for us to preach the gospel with signs and wonders following. Power evangelism isn't just for people called to the office of an evangelist—*it is for you, too!*

If you have not yet experienced the baptism of the Spirit, or you simply want to receive a fresh infilling, pray this prayer by faith:

"Father God, Your Word says that You delight to give the Holy Spirit to those who ask You. Right now, I ask You to baptize me with Your Holy Spirit. Fill me with Your Spirit and activate the gifts of the Spirit within me. Empower me to reach the lost, heal the sick, and transform the world—all in the mighty name of Jesus. Amen!"

Chapter 12:

FROM POVERTY TO PROSPERITY

*Beloved, I pray that you may prosper in all things and be
in health, just as your soul prospers. (3 John 2 NKJV)*

The first time I went to Toronto Airport Christian
Fellowship, in October 1994, during their first Catch
the Fire Conference, I was convicted of materialism. It was
the morning session on the second day of the conference,
and the speaker was Mike Bickle, the founder of the International House of Prayer. (As of the writing of this book,
I realize that Mike is no longer in ministry; nevertheless, I
know that his message that day was right on and exactly
what God wanted me to hear.) He emphasized that if we
were drawing security and life from anything other than
Jesus, we were engaging in idolatry. The message ended with
an invitation to the Holy Spirit to show us if we had given
our hearts to anything other than Jesus. After a corporate
prayer, we were all dismissed for lunch.

As other conference participants drifted out of the room, I remained seated in my chair and asked the Holy Spirit if there was anything I was putting security in other than Jesus. I quickly heard a still, small voice: "Son, you have a stronghold of materialism." I immediately rebuked that voice and disagreed with what it said. I thought it couldn't possibly be the real Holy Spirit. After all, we had just started Harvest Rock Church (HRC), and I did not even receive a salary in the first five months. Sue and I had lived by faith for almost a year and a half now. Those were not the actions of a materialistic person!

Then the Holy Spirit spoke to me again: "I want to show you how strong this is in your life. I want you to take your retirement money and sow it into My kingdom." We had depleted our savings to cover our living expenses, but we had a little over $20,000 in our retirement account. When God spoke this to me, I immediately said, "No, Lord!" (Of course, this is the ultimate oxymoron. How can you call Jesus "Lord" and say "no"?) As soon as those words came out of my mouth, I realized how right He was and how deep of a stronghold materialism had on my life. I wept for the next two hours. In part, I was crying because I didn't want to give my retirement money away, but most of my tears were honest weeping over my sins.

Finally, after two hours, I could see that God wasn't going to change, so I said, "OK, God. But this is not just my retirement money. It also belongs to Sue. I have to call Sue and see if she will agree." (To this day, Sue and I do not make any transactions, purchases, or give more than $500 to any ministry without praying and talking to each other about it first.)

I was actually relieved. Sue wasn't at the conference, and this would be a cold call. She would be shocked by the news and never go for it. I'd be off the hook!

So, I called her in Pasadena, California. When I told Sue what I sensed the Lord had said, she paused for a couple of minutes to pray. Then she said, "That is the word of the Lord. Let's do it!" Honestly, I was mad at her at that moment. Here I was in Toronto, experiencing revival, and there she was 3,000 miles away. It took me two hours and a flood of tears before I said yes. She said yes in less than two minutes of praying! But you see, this was not her problem. It was mine.

We didn't know it then, but God was testing our hearts, for in the future, He was going to allow us to manage millions in the various ministries we serve. This was another opportunity to train to reign in God's kingdom.

THE STRONGHOLDS OF MAMMON AND MATERIALISM

> No one can serve two masters; for either he will hate the one and love the other, or he will be devoted to one and despise the other. You cannot serve God and wealth [*Mammon*]. (Matt. 6:24)

Most people don't really understand the word *Mammon*. Even the various translators of the Bible use different words for Mammon, such as *money* (NIV) or *wealth* (NASB). The only translation I have found that recognizes that the word is a proper noun and capitalizes it as "Mammon" is

Young's Literal Translation. When Jesus said that you cannot serve both God and Mammon, it is not a metaphor. Mammon is a major demonic principality under satan. It encourages us to become self-reliant as we put our trust in wealth rather than God.

People deceived by Mammon are obsessed with wealth. They may or may not be prosperous; many poor people struggle with this spirit. The enemy uses Mammon as a pawn to take the place of God. Mammon promises to give us things that only God can give us, like significance, security, identity, power, authority, and freedom. It promises everything and delivers nothing.

Money is not the same as Mammon. Money is an amoral tool, a neutral object that can be used either for good or evil. The Spirit of God or the spirit of Mammon can rest on money. If money is not submitted to God, it is by default dominated by satan and the spirit of Mammon. Money submitted to God and His purposes is blessed and used to advance His kingdom. Money that has the spirit of Mammon is used to manipulate and control people.

One of the most common misinterpretations of Scripture is the saying that "money is the root of all evil." That is not what Scripture says, and it is not how God regards money. The Bible says, "For the *love* of money is a root of all sorts of evil…" (1 Tim. 6:10). It is the love of money—not money itself—that is the root of all evil. This is further clarified in the rest of that verse: "Some people, eager for money, have wandered from the faith and pierced themselves with many griefs" (NIV). Because money is amoral, it all boils down to who has the money and how they are using it. With a hundred-dollar bill, I can either buy drugs or give to my church, and of course, I would never buy drugs.

Materialism is the most common expression of the spirit of Mammon. Materialism consists of the devotion to material wealth and the accumulation of possessions at the expense of anything and everyone else. It is the sensually driven love of excessive comfort.

Our culture is driven by materialism. We are constantly bombarded by a stream of ads on our smartphones, on TV, on billboards—the list is endless. The ads tell us we're lacking if we aren't wearing the latest clothing and hairstyles, don't have the best star athlete-endorsed shoes, and don't own the latest technological gadgets. There is no saturation point. George Otis Jr., in his book *Last of the Giants*, writes that materialism is one of the major spiritual strongholds in the world. Its roots infiltrate every culture worldwide.[80]

I remember when I had lunch with the late David Wang, a major leader of the Church in Hong Kong at that time. He said to me, "Ché, you think you live in a republic in the United States, but you don't. You really have a monarchy in America. Your king is materialism, your queen is entertainment, and your crown prince is sports." I reflected for a moment and knew he was right.

GIVE AS MUCH AS YOU CAN

Throughout church history, when God wants to restore a truth like deliverance, prosperity, or the apostolic, God sovereignly allows imperfect believers to teach it in an unbalanced

---

[80] George Otis Jr., *The Last of the Giants*. Chosen Books, 1991.

way with the view that as the church matures, she will find the right biblical balance. Is there materialism in the church? Of course, there is. The love of money is running rampant in the church throughout much of the world, and it is one of the biggest killers of revival. I hate materialism because God hates it.

Yet, on the other side of the coin, the Bible teaches that God wants you to prosper financially.[81] I have taught over the years that God wants you to *prosper for the purpose* of providing for your family and advancing His kingdom. God desires that the money He gives us should be used for His will to be done on earth as it is in heaven. It takes finances to fulfill the Great Commission.

One of my heroes in church history is John Wesley, a great apostle and founder of the Methodist movement. In 1789, Wesley famously said in his notes on "The Use of Money," *"Earn all you can, save all you can, and give all you can."*[82] I have taught and practiced this truth ever since 1997, when God broke a poverty mindset off my life.

As we look at each aphorism of Wesley's adage, I want to highlight five keys to walking in prosperity with a purpose.

Key #1: Practice Graduated Giving

Years ago, Sue and I began to practice *graduated giving* or living to give. In February 2005, our good friend Ed Silvoso was sharing at Peter Wagner's "Eagles Vision Apostolic Team"

---

[81] See Gen. 12:1–3, 13:1; Deut. 8:18, 28:11; Jer. 29:11; Matt. 7:7–11; John 10:10; 2 Cor. 8:9; 3 John 2.
[82] "John Wesley on giving." Resource UMC. Accessed August 20, 2024. https://www.resourceumc.org/en/content/john-wesley-on-giving

(EVAT) meeting. Ed told us about the 51 Club, which began primarily with Christian businessmen in Argentina who had pledged to sow more than half of their income—51 percent and above—into God's kingdom. He excitedly recounted the ripple effects of revival, reformation, and financial break-through that came in the wake of their graduated giving. While the momentum started in Argentina, anyone could be part of the 51 Club.

After the meeting, Sue and I discussed what this might look like for us. "Why should the businesspeople have all the fun?" I said to her. "Why don't we give 51 percent?"

Sue replied, "51 percent? That's nothing. My goal is that we give away 90 percent and live off the other 10!"

"You have more faith than I do," I said. "Let's begin by shooting for 51 percent."

By then, we had gradually made our way to giving away 40 percent of our income before taxes. That stretch of faith took several years, and we knew we couldn't jump to 51 percent overnight. Regardless of the timing, we made a commitment before the Lord to give away 51 percent. Six years later, in the spring of 2011, we crossed that threshold for the first time and officially joined the 51 Club.

At this stage of our lives, there are some years, by God's grace, where we are able to surpass the 90-percent mark, just as Sue had spoken by faith in 2005. When we sold our home in Altadena in 2022, it was totally paid off, and we gave the proceeds to our church. Now, we put that money in a trust fund to reinvest it in perpetuity, but 100 percent of the $1.85 million went to Harvest Rock Church. In every season of our faith journey, we have learned in real time that God wants us to give as much as we can—all while He provides abundantly beyond what we could ask or imagine (see Eph. 3:20).

Over the years, we have had encounters with the Lord that led to us becoming passionate about giving and growing in generosity. We received a revelation that everything belongs to God, including all the money in our possession. One of the biggest lies in the church is that "it is my hard-earned money, and I can do with it whatever I wish!" But the Bible is clear that "the earth is the Lord's, and all its fullness; the world and those who dwell therein" (Ps. 24:1 NKJV). We ourselves even belong to the Lord—twice. First, God *made* us in His image and likeness (Gen. 1:26–27), and second, He *purchased* us with the blood of Jesus (Acts 20:28b).

When you realize that everything belongs to God and we are just stewards or managers, it is easy to give away your finances when the Lord asks. However, it still takes the grace of God and Christlike character. I personally believe that God instituted the tithe so that we can walk in obedience to Him and demonstrate character aligned with His nature. And the more you grow in Christlike character, the easier it is to give.

MAKE AS MUCH AS YOU CAN

How often do you see the following two words together: "Christian" and "billionaire"? I believe the answer is not often enough. The number of Christians who come to the place of stewarding billions of dollars—think of Hobby Lobby's David Green or Chick-fil-A's Cathy family—are relatively few and far between. I want to propose that *we need more billionaires in the Body of Christ!*

Most of the known billionaires today are non-Christians like George Soros. As a socialist Marxist, Soros gives vast sums of money for extreme Left causes that are, frankly, nothing short of evil. Jesus said, "For the sons of this world are more shrewd in their generation than the sons of light" (Luke 16:8 NKJV). In other words, those walking in darkness are using Mammon to fund the advancement of satan's kingdom, yet it is like pulling teeth for Christian millionaires to give a large portion of their money to advance God's kingdom.

A couple of years ago, I had lunch with a multimillionaire in Scottsdale, Arizona (the Beverly Hills of the Phoenix area). He boasted that he had seven cars in his garage, including a Rolls-Royce, and had purchased his one-of-a-kind house with $2.1 million in cash. After listening to him, I asked an important question: "How would you like to move from success to significance?"

"What do you mean?" he replied.

"I mean, all you have done is share how many toys you have."

"I tithe," he said defensively.

"I'm not talking about tithing. Have you heard who George Soros is?"

"Of course. Who hasn't?"

"Why don't you become a Christian version of George Soros?" I went on, "Do you know that Soros has a Super PAC? Why don't you start a Super PAC and support conservative believers who are running for office?"

He paused and finally said, "Jesus just told me to do that."

And so, he did. He paid thousands of dollars in legal fees to apply to the Federal Election Commission (FEC), and the FEC gave America Upheld Super PAC the license to operate on August 22, 2022. Please note the numbers of that date. I don't think it was a coincidence that God granted the PAC status in the eighth month, on the 22nd day, in the year 2022. Eight is the number of new beginnings, and "2222" represents Isaiah 22:22: "I will give him the key to the house of David—the highest position in the royal court. When he opens doors, no one will be able to close them; when he closes doors, no one will be able to open them" (NLT).

Getting the PAC off the ground has been a game-changer. As soon as the Federal PAC (Super PAC) status was confirmed, America Upheld's treasurer, Tom Montgomery, applied for the California PAC status and obtained it soon after. Subsequently, a PAC was established in New Jersey. The goal of America Upheld is to start a PAC in every state where we can support conservative Christian candidates with a biblical worldview or Judeo-Christian values.

In my book *The Grace of Giving*, I go deeper into various topics related to making as much as you can and stewarding the money for God's kingdom. Here in this section, I will share the next two keys to walking in prosperity with a purpose.

Key #2: Have at Least Five Sources of Revenue

First, *your personal income* is typically what comes to mind when you think of your revenue sources, but it should not be your only one! Many people get discouraged or stuck in a rut when they try to wrap their heads around living off only one stream of income, especially in expensive cities like Los Angeles or New York City. The good news I want you to grab hold of is that God wants to bless you with multiple revenue sources, including but not limited to your full-time job.

Second, for married couples, *your spouse's income* counts as another source of revenue. That being said, I also believe that if a wife is called to take care of the home and home-school her children, that is a full-time job in itself, and there is no shame in that. My daughter Grace is doing that with her four children. However, if there is something you can do on the side, like multi-level marketing, I encourage you to go for it.

Third, *passive revenue sources*, such as investments, are important to add to the mix. Isaiah 60:11 says, "Your gates will be open continually; they will not be closed day or night, so that people may bring to you the wealth of the nations." This prophecy promises that even while you are sleeping, wealth will be brought to you. I like the sound of that! Proverbs 13:11 (ESV) adds, "Wealth gained hastily will dwindle, but whoever gathers little by little will increase it." These scriptures remind me of the way in which wise investments bring in a good ROI over time. The idea is to work smarter, not harder. As mentioned above, having a great financial manager will take your investment journey to the next level.

Fourth, *rental income* is an opportunity you should not pass up. For years, Sue and I always had a single person living in our home after our kids started leaving the nest. It was a win-win situation. We were able to gain monthly income from unused space in our house, and the young person was able to rent a room for a much lower price point than the normal going rates in LA. One of my daughters followed suit and began renting out a cute back house on their property to Airbnb guests.

Key #3: Start Your Own Business

The third key—and fifth revenue source I want to highlight—is to start your own business. A major advantage of having your own business is the ability to make tremendous tax write-offs if you do it correctly. Another benefit is the unlimited potential for growth. If you've ever watched the TV show *Shark Tank*, you will know there is no shortage of new ideas for businesses. Some start off strong but soon fizzle out. Others build a strategic business that continually grows with a view for long-term success.

Could God give you the download of a brilliant business idea that no one else has ever thought of? Absolutely. I believe there will be greater occurrences of disruptive technology—affecting not only the business world but also medicine and science—that will be discovered by Christians who are inviting the Holy Spirit to be the number-one partner in their business.

As I mentioned in a previous chapter, my wife and I started an S Corp in 2010 called Joseph's Storehouse LLC. My honoraria from speaking engagements and royalties from book sales are all included under Joseph's Storehouse. Whenever revenue comes in, we invest it through our financial manager, Tony Amaradio, especially in real estate.

Around the time we created Joseph's Storehouse, I had a prophetic dream. In the dream, I was standing in front of a mountain of gold as high as the Empire State Building. A young missionary couple came up to me and asked for financial support for their mission work. I pulled out a large harvest knife and cut out a chunk of gold. I asked them, "Is this enough? If you need more, let me know." In a lot of ways, the essence of this dream has come true over the past 14-plus years, as we have been able to give generously to many ministries that are actively advancing the kingdom of God all over the world.

SAVE AS MUCH AS YOU CAN

Along with giving and making all you can, I believe the habit of saving as much as you can is not only beneficial but biblical.

The Bible has given us instructions for providing for our family. For example, 1 Timothy 5:8 says, "But if anyone does not provide for his own, and especially for those of his household, he has denied the faith and is worse than an unbeliever." This is a strong word from the apostle Paul. Unbelievers don't know any better because the god of this age has blinded their eyes (2 Cor. 4:4), but Christians should understand that God's priority for your life is first Jesus and second your family, beginning with your spouse. Notice that the verse specifies your "household," which also includes your grandchildren. If you can go beyond the nuclear family and help your extended family members, that is wonderful, but God expects you to provide primarily for your nuclear family.

One of my favorite verses is Proverbs 13:22 (NASB1995): "A good man leaves an inheritance to his children's children, but the wealth of the sinner is stored up for the righteous."

As of this writing, I have nine grandchildren, and Mary, my youngest daughter who served as the Vice President of Harvest International Ministry (HIM), is with her fourth child—in reality, a baby in the womb—so we consider her the tenth grandchild. And we are praying for more.

According to God's Word, if we are a righteous couple, Sue and I should leave an inheritance for all our grandchildren. So, that is where our savings are going. We have already given our children part of their inheritance, and each is using the funds to purchase a home in LA Another portion, allotted for our grandchildren, is part of our savings program. The rest of our savings is our six-month reserve for emergencies. All these funds are invested with our financial planner, Tony Amaradio. This brings us to the next key to being a godly steward.

Key #4: Surround Yourself with Experts

Drawing from our own experience, I highly recommend the following experts for your life so you can prosper to another level for the purpose of advancing God's kingdom.

First, you need a great *financial manager*. Tony Amaradio is not only our personal manager but also manages money for HRC and HIM.[83] He has introduced brilliant ways to steward our finances for God's glory, resulting in us saving more money and using it for more creative purposes.

Second, you need a great *accountant*. Robert Kiyosaki, in his classic book *Rich Dad, Poor Dad*, writes, "Accounting is possibly the most confusing, boring subject in the world,

---

[83] https://www.tonyamaradio.com

but if you want to be rich long-term, it could be the most important subject."[84] I have the very best accountant in Philip L. Liberatore, a covenant friend and the President of America Upheld.[85]

Third, you need a great *lawyer*. My personal lawyer is Victoria Ko, one of our pastors at HRC Orange County and a spiritual daughter. She is also our in-house counsel for all the ministries I am involved with.[86]

Fourth, you need a great *personal doctor*. Ideally, this is a medical professional who loves you and can take care of you beyond your insurance policy. I have two doctors: my younger brother, Dr. Chae Ahn, a member of HRC, and Dr. Todd Lyon, one of our church elders.

Key #5: Get Out of Debt and Stay Out of Debt

The final key to saving as much as you can is to deal aggressively with debt. The sad reality is that we are a debt-ridden society in the U.S. As of August 2024, our national debt reached a record high of $35.2 trillion,[87] with outstanding personal consumer debt at a whopping $17.8 trillion (including credit, mortgage, auto, and other

---

[84] Robert T. Kiyosaki. *Rich Dad Poor Dad*. Plata Publishing, LLC. Kindle Edition, p.66.

[85] https://www.liberatorecpa.com

[86] https://www.victoriakolaw.com

[87] "Public debt of the United States from August 2013 to August 2024." Statista. Accessed September 24, 2024. https://www.statista.com/statistics/273294/public-debt-of-the-united-states-by-month/

debt).[88] If you are currently in debt, your priority should be to do whatever it takes to get out of debt as soon as possible. If you are fortunate to already be debt-free, your priority should be to stay out of debt as you continue stewarding your financial health.

Romans 13:8 (NIV) says, "Let no debt remain outstanding, except the continuing debt to love one another." The Word of God also specifies in Proverbs 22:7 (NKJV), "The rich rule over the poor, and the borrower is servant to the lender." I don't know about you, but I believe God has called us to be the head and not the tail—to be lenders and not borrowers (see Deut. 28:12–13). There is no condemnation if you are struggling with your finances, but if you want to prosper, you must strike debt at its roots.

Defeating debt requires changing your habits in very practical ways. One example is to have a budget—and not only have one but stick to it! Living within your means is crucial to being free of debt. Resolve not to buy anything unless you can afford it; refuse to resort to credit cards if you tend to spend more than your monthly paycheck. To be abundantly clear, I classify credit card debt as bad debt. "Good debt," on the other hand, would be the mortgage on your home (to build equity) and college expenses (to provide a quality education for yourself or your children).

The further you distance yourself from debt, the more you can save. And the more you save, the more you can bless

---

[88] David Straughan. "Americans Are Carrying Record Household Debt in 2024." MarketWatch. September 25, 2024. https://www.marketwatch.com/guides/banking/american-debt-2024/

your family, sow into the next generation, and invest in the kingdom of God.

THE GREAT TRANSFER OF WEALTH IN THE LAST DAYS

The second half of Proverbs 13:22 emphasizes that the wealth of the sinner is stored up for the righteous. The last book Peter Wagner wrote before he graduated to heaven in 2016 was *The Great Transfer of Wealth*. He prophesied in his book that we will be coming to a Haggai 2:7–9 (NASB1995) period in church history:

> 'I will shake all the nations; and they will come with the wealth of all nations, and I will fill this house with glory,' says the LORD of hosts. 'The silver is Mine and the gold is Mine,' declares the LORD of hosts. 'The latter glory of this house will be greater than the former,' says the LORD of hosts, 'and in this place I will give peace,' declares the LORD of hosts.

I agree with Peter that in a time of global economic shaking, God is going to supernaturally provide by transferring wealth from the unrighteous to the righteous. This will begin with God's called-out ones, His *ekklesia*, who are committed to His house and the purposes of God for revival and reformation. By all accounts, we have been in a time of global shaking since 2020 when COVID-19 shook over 200 nations. But it is beyond the virus; it has been the unnecessary lockdowns, whereby over 16,000 businesses went bankrupt in California[89] and one in four restaurants closed down in the U.S.[90] We then entered a perfect storm of bad economic policies: shutting down oil production in the name of climate change, open borders, 40-year-high inflation, and national debt that has increased by $1 trillion every 100 days under the Biden-Harris administration.[91] These policies have been criminal because the people being impacted the most are the poor. America's citizens are paying significantly higher prices for essential household items than they did under President Trump.

Yet, in the midst of this global economic shaking, God is getting ready to bring about the greatest revival and reformation in church history. God "shouts to us in our pain," as C.S. Lewis wrote in his book *The Problem of Pain*[92]—first, for believers to repent and turn back to God, and second, for unbelievers to give their hearts to Jesus. When things are going great, people will say, "Who needs God?" But when you go through one trial after another, you begin to call upon

[89] Kelly McCarthy, "Nearly 16,000 restaurants have closed permanently due to the pandemic, Yelp data shows," *ABC News*, July 24, 2020, https://abcnews.go.com/Business/16000-restaurants-closed-permanently-due-pandemic-yelp-data/story?id=71943970

[90] Jefferson Graham. "One in 4 restaurants won't re-open after pandemic, says exec." USA Today. May 14, 2020. https://www.usatoday.com/story/tech/2020/05/14/your-favorite-restaurant-may-not-reopen-post-covid-opentable-study/5193994002/

[91] Michelle Fox. "The U.S. national debt is rising by $1 trillion about every 100 days." CNBC. March 1, 2024. https://www.cnbc.com/2024/03/01/the-us-national-debt-is-rising-by-1-trillion-about-every-100-days.html

[92] C.S. Lewis, *The Problem of Pain* (San Francisco: HarperSanFrancisco, 2001), p.91.

God, and "everyone who calls upon the name of the Lord will be saved" (Rom. 10:13).

Along with the revival, Haggai says, "They will come with the wealth of all nations" (Hag. 2:7b). God is going to bless and prosper His people who will use the wealth for His purposes in these last days. In order to prepare for this extraordinary wealth transfer, we must free ourselves from the grip of Mammon and the spirit of poverty. On a personal level, we must first deal with these spiritual strongholds in our own lives so we can step into the fullness of our God-given calling to transform society.

BREAKING THE SPIRIT OF POVERTY

In October 1997, our church was hosting our annual prophetic conference in Pasadena. Cindy Jacobs—a major prophet in the Body of Christ, one of my dearest friends, and a board member of HIM—was our keynote speaker. Between the lunch break and the start of the afternoon session, one of our church members named Patricia walked over to me with an envelope in her hand. She began to tell me how she had just gone through the worst week of her life. She lost her job at the start of the week, and a few days later, her husband lost his job as well. They had emptied their savings account, and she was bringing $2,000 as seed money to sow into the church.

Their generous and sacrificial gift touched me, but I was concerned about their financial predicament. "Patricia," I said, "you and your family will need this money to hold you over until you find a job." I thought my response to her at that time was wise and pastoral. I gave her back the envelope and walked away feeling "spiritual" for refusing the offering.

I didn't realize it, but Patricia walked away frustrated. She went into our resources center, where Cindy Jacobs was doing some last-minute shopping before her afternoon session started. Patricia shared the whole story with Cindy, how she and her husband lost their jobs, and how she brought seed money to me, which I had refused.

Cindy came running out of the bookstore—in high heels, mind you—with Patricia running right behind her. I have never seen Cindy so mad in my life. She came storming up to me, got right in my face, and asked, "Did you refuse this woman's offering?"

"Well, yes, but she lost her job, and her husband lost his job, and they will need this money to hold them over," I replied, feeling confused and a little sheepish.

Cindy asked, "Ché, do you believe in the Bible?"

I didn't know where she was going with this line of questioning, but I simply said, "Yes."

"I don't believe you really do," she replied. "The Bible says that it is more blessed to give than to receive (Acts 20:35). If you really believed, then you would have received this woman's offering and not deprived her of her blessing. You see, she was giving out of her need. Now, you receive this offering!"

I obediently received the offering. Then Cindy went on, "I think you have a spirit of poverty, and I bind and break the spirit of poverty, and I command that spirit of poverty to leave you right now, in Jesus' name!"

Not only were people watching this take place, but once the afternoon service began, Cindy proceeded to share the whole incident with everyone at the conference. I wanted to find a hole somewhere to crawl into! Then she had Patricia come up, and Cindy took up a spontaneous offering for her. More than $18,000 came in that afternoon, and the whole amount was given to Patricia. Later that week, Patricia got a better job, and her husband also found a better-paying job.

My life was forever changed that week—it was a pivotal step in breaking the spirit of poverty off my life. I didn't even know I had the spirit of poverty operating behind the scenes, but in retrospect, I realized that I used to apologize for taking offerings. I needed to learn an important truth about how God uses money for His kingdom purposes. Not long afterward, I would need to raise $10 million for TheCall (2000–2003) and then $4.5 million within four months as a down payment to buy the Ambassador Auditorium (May 14, 2004). In recent years, I have personally been raising money to support conservative political candidates championing biblical values.

It takes money to transform society, which is why God wants to set us free from a poverty mindset and the spirit of Mammon.

Pray this with me as we start nearing the end of our journey together:

"Heavenly Father, I give You my whole heart, all that I am and all that I have. In the name of Jesus, I repent of and renounce the spirit of poverty and the stronghold of Mammon. I break off the poverty mindset from my life and my bloodline. Thank You for prospering me with the purpose of advancing Your kingdom. Help me to be a wise steward of the resources You have given me, all for Your glory. In Jesus' name, amen."

ESSAY: HOW THE PROTESTANT REF- ORMATION BROKE THE SPIRIT OF POVERTY

Along with souls being saved, we are seeing nations being transformed economically, a sign of reformation. In the *New York Times* bestseller *Culture Matters*—edited by two Harvard professors, Lawrence Harrison and Samuel Huntington— the premise of the book is that where Judeo-Christian values have penetrated a nation, that nation will prosper economically. Quoting another Harvard professor, David Landes, the text explains:

> Protestant merchants and manufacturers played a leading role in trade, banking, and industry ... The heart of the matter lay indeed in the making of a new kind of man—rational, ordered, diligent, productive. These are virtues, while not new, were hardly commonplace ... Two special characteristics of the Protestant reflect and confirm this link. The first is to stress on instruction and literacy. This was the byproduct of Bible reading. (By way of contrast, Catholics were catechized but did not have to read, and they explicitly discouraged from

reading the Bible.) ... The second was the importance accorded to time.[93]

This passage refers to how Christians steward time and
not just money. Ephesians 5:15–17 (NKJV) is a key passage
to consider: "See then that you walk circumspectly, not as
fools but as wise, redeeming the time, because the days are
evil. Therefore, do not be unwise, but understand what the
will of the Lord is." I have found that when I see myself not
as an owner but as a steward in life, I have prospered and
helped my children and my church prosper.

History confirms the assertion that where Judeo-Christian values are inculcated into a society, it brings economic
blessings. Huntington and Harrison use Korea as an example. In 1960, South Korea was declared by the U.N. as one of
the poorest nations in the world. Today, it is one of the rich-
est. They won't say that it is because of spiritual revival, but
they say it is because of the Protestant values of "hard work,
honesty, seriousness, the thrifty use of money and time."[94]
Values shape the culture, and having a Christian (biblical)
culture will transform a nation.

Unfortunately, the Protestant Reformation and her biblical values never broke into countries in Latin America, the
Philippines, other Roman Catholic nations, and Africa until
the last 50 years, when revival started to break out in some
of these countries. Economists and social scientists like Huntington and Harrison believe that where Protestant values

---

[93] Lawrence E. Harrison and Samuel P. Huntington. *Culture Matters: How Values
Shape Human Progress*. Basic Books, 2000, p.12.
[94] Ibid., p.11.

got inculcated into a nation, they shifted from a Marxist or a totalitarian regime to more democratic rule, which is again the byproduct of the Protestant Reformation.

But the question they ask is why it took so long: "Why after more than 150 years of independence has Latin America, an extension of the West, failed to consolidate democratic institutions?"[95] That is a good question. By contrast, they recognize how prosperous we are in the United States with our free market values, our Protestant work ethic, honesty, and relatively less corruption in the government than most poor nations. (However, remaining under the Democratic party's administrations for 12 of the last 20 years, we have seen more evil enacted by a corrupt government than ever before. Biblical culture does matter!)

The authors don't assert this, but I believe that satan has kept these nations poor under a principality of the spirit of poverty. Peter Wagner would often teach, "If God wants us to prosper, then it stands to reason that satan wants to keep us poor." Indeed, satan is the thief that comes to steal (money and wealth), kill (lives and destinies), and destroy (anything that would keep people blessed and prosperous, including a free market economy). But Jesus came to give us life and life to the fullest (John 10:10)!

I had the privilege of sitting under Dr. Donald McGavran, the founder of Fuller Seminary's School of World Mission and Peter Wagner's boss and mentor. He taught "redemption and lift," the observation that wherever Christianity has flourished, it has lifted people out of

---

[95] Ibid., p.xix.

poverty. I believe that our greatest weapon to defeat satan's kingdom and his minions is to advance God's kingdom through the gospel, dismantling demonic ideologies and principalities with prayer, and declaring God's truth that will set the captives free, including taking authority over the spirit of poverty. Jesus said, "You will know the truth, and the truth will set you free" (John 8:32).

One of the greatest injustices in society is systemic poverty (see Appendix A). Ed Silvoso says, "The premier social indicator that transformation has taken place is the elimination of systemic poverty."[96] According to what the Bible teaches, "the Son of Man [Jesus] has come to seek and to save that which was lost" (Luke 19:10). Please note that the New American Standard Bible does not say that Jesus came "to save the lost," but "to save *that which* was lost." Jesus came to restore the blessing of Paradise, the Garden of Eden. Through the gospel of the kingdom, I believe God will specifically restore the economic blessings of Paradise. That is what revival and reformation look like.

INFILTRATING COMMUNIST CHINA

I hate Communism because it is a demonic, socialistic economic system that will keep a nation poor. Just look at North Korea, Cuba, Venezuela, and other Marxist nations. In my view, the devil wants to keep nations in poverty because he is doing everything possible to hurt God and thwart God's purposes on earth. China is the exception because of the

---

[96] Ed Silvoso. *Transformation*. Ventura, CA: Regal Books, 2007, p.29.

explosive growth of the church, thus bringing Judeo-Christian values and a policy shift toward the free market in spite of Communism.

Some years back, I had the privilege of meeting with the apostles of the five largest underground churches in China, thanks to Peter Wagner. Also through Dr. Wagner, I met one of the leading economists in China, who taught economics at Beijing University and was an economic consultant to the Central Committee. I have to withhold his name because he left the Communist Party and became a believer in Jesus.

Before he made his conversion public, he wrote a white paper to the Central Committee, at that time under President Hu. This man was a reformer in China. His paper was entitled "Why Christianity Is Good for the Chinese Economy." He highlighted some of the core values of Protestant Christianity like honesty, hatred of corruption, and hard work ethics, explaining that when Christians are working for a higher authority than the state, they do their work unto Jesus. This paper had such an impact on the church that President Hu gave the underground church more freedom to meet, although such meetings were still illegal.

Unfortunately, Hu stepped down as President and Xi Jinping took over—at which point, in my opinion, the Marxist principality that was under Mao came back with a vengeance in China. Religious persecution and human rights abuses against the underground church, followers of Falun Gong (an offshoot of Buddhism and Taoism), Uyghurs, and other Turkic Muslims have returned with a renewed zeal. Even the Three-Self Church, the government-sanctioned church, has suffered persecution by President Xi.

In spite of every opposition, revival is breaking out in the underground church once again, and the kingdom of God is making advances. We know how the story ends: "The kingdoms of this world [will] become the kingdoms of our Lord and of His Christ, and He will reign forever and ever" (Rev. 11:15 NKJV).

Conclusion:

PERSONAL TRANSFORMATION LEADS TO SOCIAL TRANSFORMATION

When Jesus saw the crowds, He went up on the mountain;
and after He sat down, His disciples came to Him.
He opened His mouth and began to teach them…
(Matt. 5:1–2 NASB1995)

I am the vine, you are the branches; he who abides in
Me and I in him, he bears much fruit, for apart from
Me you can do nothing … If you abide in Me, and
My words abide in you, ask whatever you wish, and it will
be done for you. My Father is glorified by this, that you
bear much fruit, and so prove to be My disciples.
(John 15:5, 7–8 NASB1995)

On September 2, 1982, I had an extraordinary dream that would change the trajectory of my life and my family forever. In the dream, a black man appeared to me. The man looked like he was in the NFL—he was 6 feet 5 inches tall and 300 pounds of chiseled muscles. "Come to Los Angeles," he said to me, "for there will be a great harvest."

When I awoke from this dream, I heard what seemed to be an inner audible voice ringing in my mind, "The time of revival is at hand!" I looked at the digital clock on our lamp table, and it was exactly 4:00 a.m. I woke up Sue next to me. I couldn't wait till the morning. "Honey, I had the most amazing dream," I told her. "It was more like a vision than a dream. A black man appeared to me and told me to come to LA for a great harvest."

Immediately, the presence of God that I was experiencing came upon Sue. She said, "This dream is of God. Let's get down on our knees and pray and dedicate this dream to the Lord and ask for confirmation." It was extraordinary for Sue to say, "This is of God," because she had never been to Los Angeles and knew no one there. I had been out to Westwood once to speak at UCLA and knew no one personally in LA.

I will never forget what we prayed next while we were on our knees: "Father, if this is of You, please have our pastor Larry confirm it by asking me to lead a church-planting team and let him ask, 'Where would you like to go?' In Jesus' name."

Six months went by, and Larry Tomczak took me out for lunch one day when he finally said, "Ché, I have been sensing that it is time for you to be sent out to plant a church. If you had the choice of going anywhere, where would you like to go?"

I replied, "Larry, I have been waiting six months for you to ask." I told him about the dream, but when I said, "LA," he almost fell out of his chair.

"LA?! I was thinking maybe Fairfax, Virginia, or Philadelphia, or a major city nearby, but LA?"

"I know, Larry. This sounds crazy because we know no one there. All of our relatives and family members are in the D.C. area, but we know that God is calling us to LA."

Larry told me to take a weekend off to pray and fast for a confirmation. I called my Uncle Mark, who owned a condo in Ocean City, Maryland, and he gave me the keys so Sue and I could drive there for the weekend in February 1983.

Once we got to the condo, Sue and I put down our suitcase, and before we even unpacked, we knelt in the hallway and dedicated the weekend to the Lord. We prayed, "Father, we have been sent by our pastors to pray and fast for a confirmation that would be the biggest decisions of relocation from our church, family, and friends. We ask that You confirm if we are to move to LA or not over this weekend. In Jesus' name we pray, amen."

As soon as we finished praying, this thought came into my mind, which I believe was a word of knowledge: *Turn on the television, turn to* The 700 Club, *and Pat Robertson will give you a word about moving to LA.* This sounded crazy. First of all, I didn't know if the cable TV was even working. It was the off-season for Ocean City, and most people turned off their TV subscriptions during those months. Secondly, what are the odds that *The 700 Club* would be on at that time?

I turned to Sue and said, "Honey, I think God just told me to turn on the TV. He said *The 700 Club* would be on, and Pat Robertson would give us a word!"

I got up to turn on the TV, and it worked! I didn't have a TV guide, so I started to channel surf with the remote, and sure enough, *The 700 Club* was on with Pat Robertson and co-host Ben Kinchlow praying over a stack of letters. I turned the volume up as they were giving out words of knowledge for people to be healed of specific ailments. Then Pat paused and said, "There is a pastor who is praying about starting a church and is looking for a confirmation. The Lord says, 'This is the confirmation, and if you go out in harmony and unity, I will give you great success!'" You can't make this up!

Sue and I looked at each other. A second thought came into my mind: *This particular show will be aired again later, and I need to record it with my microcassette recorder.* I went downstairs, found a newspaper stand, and bought that day's paper. I quickly scanned the TV guide and saw that the show would be on several times that day. We recorded Pat's prophetic word, and I told Sue, "We got the confirmation we need! We don't have to fast. Let's go and celebrate!" We went to Phillips Crab House that night and enjoyed a marriage weekend away on the church. God is so good! I played the recording that Tuesday at our weekly pastors' meeting. The Spirit of God fell, and all the pastors said, "This is of God. You are to go to LA!"

After getting the blessings of all the pastors and transitioning out of my duties in Maryland, Sue and I—along with our young family, Lou and Therese Engle, David and Nikki Warnick, and others—were sent out in April 1984 to plant Abundant Life Community Church in Pasadena. Honestly, I thought revival would break out the first time I walked through Pasadena Mall. I read how Charles Finney walked through a factory in Rochester, New York, and the Spirit of

God fell on the workers and how revival had broken out. After all, God gave me a supernatural dream of a "great harvest." But nothing happened.

The next ten years were the hardest years of my life. Everything came easy before I moved to California. But after seven years, our church was having trouble breaking the 500 barrier. Knowing that 80 percent of the churches in America are under 200 people, you would think I would be grateful, but remember, I was sent out of a church that would grow beyond 3,000. And, after all, God did say "a great harvest." We were only seeing a handful come to know Jesus, and most of the growth was through transfer growth.

As I look back, in some ways, they really were some of the best years of my life. Not only did I enroll at Fuller Seminary for two degrees, but this was the time that Peter Wagner would become my mentor, apostle, and a dear friend. More importantly, I grew tremendously in Christlike character through the ten years of "tribulations."

CHRISTLIKE CHARACTER: GOD'S HIGHEST PRIORITY FOR US

"For whom He foreknew, He also predestined to be conformed to the image of His Son, that He might be the firstborn among many brethren." (Rom. 8:29 NKJV)

God, in His wisdom, allows us to go through hardships, difficulties, unmet expectations, and persecution so He can use these trials to help us become more Christlike in character. Paul says in Romans 5:3–5 (NKJV), "And not only that, but we also glory in tribulations, knowing that tribulation produces perseverance; and perseverance, character; and character, hope. Now hope does not disappoint, because the love of God has been poured out in our hearts by the Holy Spirit who was given to us."

James gives us a similar exhortation: "My brethren, count it all joy when you fall into various trials, knowing that the testing of your faith produces patience. But let patience have its perfect work, that you may be perfect and complete, lacking nothing" (James 1:2–4 NKJV).

God was using my first ten years in California to break off my pride and selfish ambition. He was also teaching me to be a loving husband, as our marriage hit a major crisis nine years into our time in SoCal.

By the end of 1993, I was desperate for God. I needed a breakthrough. I had stepped down as Senior Pastor of ALCC in 1992, went through a marriage crisis in 1993, and I was on the verge of quitting vocational ministry altogether. I was out of a job, financially broke, and ready to take on a marketplace job in order to support my family of six in one of the most expensive cities in the world, Los Angeles.

The breakthrough process began to take place on January 20, 1994, in Toronto. A revival broke out called the Toronto Blessing. A week later, John Wimber was hosting his annual healing conference in Anaheim, and he announced that revival had broken out in one of their churches in Toronto when the Spirit fell on their Sunday evening service just a few days before the conference. He was basically prophesying that this conference would be a life changer, and it was for me.

The first night during worship, Lou Engle, my prophet friend, saw holy laughter hitting different sections of the packed, 4,000-seat auditorium. As we were sitting near the far end of the top of the auditorium, Lou had a bird's eye view of how the Spirit of God was moving. He shoved his elbow into my body and said, "The laughter is coming toward us."

My immediate response was, "Well, I am not going to laugh!" In fact, I was miserable and depressed. 1993 was the worst year of my life. But because of God's great love and mercy (Eph. 2:4)—even when I had a bad, sulking attitude—the laughter hit our section, and I suddenly felt myself getting inebriated. I could not stop laughing, even though I didn't want to laugh! Everything was funny, and everyone around me looked funny. A man sitting in front of me was totally bald, and for some reason, his bald head looked outrageously funny, to the point that I put my hand on his head and began to buff his head with my hand. I was drunk in the Spirit! He didn't care, as he was drunk in the Spirit, too, and we both fell out of our seats laughing. The laughter lasted a good 20 minutes, and I realized that my depression was now gone! And by God's grace, I have never been depressed again!

JOURNEY OF PERSONAL TRANSFORMATION

"...the Spirit of truth, whom the world cannot receive, because it neither sees Him nor knows Him; but you know Him, for He dwells with you and will be in you. I will not leave you orphans; I will come to you." (John 14:17–18 NKJV)

Through these seasons of walking by faith, I have learned so many lessons in my journey of personal transformation. God has blessed me with the opportunity to share these insights with others, including the ones highlighted in this chapter. When it comes to stewarding our personal revival, I want to highlight three lessons that will help you fan the flames of transformation in your walk with Jesus.

Lesson #1: Be continually filled with the Holy Spirit.

One of biggest revelations that I received from the Toronto Blessing is that there is always more of the Holy Spirit. We are to be continually filled with the Holy Spirit. In Ephesians 5:18 (NKJV), the Word says, "And do not be drunk with wine, in which is dissipation; but be filled with the Spirit." The word *filled* in the Greek grammar is in the continuous present tense, which translates to "be continually filled with the Holy Spirit."

The reason why we are to be filled with the Holy Spirit continually is not just for the gifts of the Spirit to manifest (1 Cor. 12) but for the fruit of the Spirit to come forth (Gal. 5:22). One of the key verses to be revelatory in my life during this season was Galatians 5:16 (NKJV), "I say then: Walk in the Spirit, and you shall not fulfill the lust of the flesh." We are not only saved by grace but we are sanctified by the grace of God (Titus 2:11) through the power of the Holy Spirit abiding within us.

Lesson #2: Do only what you see the Father do.

"Then Jesus answered and said to them, 'Most assuredly, I say to you, the Son can do nothing of Himself, but what He sees the Father do; for whatever He does, the Son also does in like manner.'" (John 5:19 NKJV)

Jesus only did what He saw the Father do, and He only spoke what He heard the Father say. My problem was that God never called me to grow a megachurch. Still, because I came out of a megachurch in Maryland, my assumption was that in order for me to fulfill the dream of "coming to LA for a great harvest," that automatically meant pastoring a megachurch. However, they are not the same word. I began to see how my pride and ambition were getting in the way of being true to the prophetic dream. Unfortunately, it wasn't until years later that I also realized it is not about me. It is all about Jesus and His kingdom. Humility became a big deal in my life. I started to hate pride and value humility. It took years of breaking to start to see this sin in my life. I also came to the realization that this journey to walk humbly before God will be a lifelong one.

Lesson #3: Walk in the fear of the Lord.

"The fear of the LORD is to hate evil, pride and arrogance and the evil way and the perverse mouth I hate." (Prov. 8:13 NKJV)

The Lord gave me several dreams beginning in 2012, when He started teaching me the fear of the Lord. It went to another level in 2022 when I heard John Bevere teach on the fear of the Lord and read his book *The Awe of God*, which I highly recommend. One sentence that John said rocked me: "If you fear the Lord, you will love what He loves, and you will hate what He hates."

When he said this, Proverbs 6:16 came into my mind. This verse is one that I had memorized in order to give biblical basis why God hates abortion. He hates "hands that shed innocent blood."

> These six things the LORD hates, yes, seven are an abomination to Him: a proud look, a lying tongue, hands that shed innocent blood, a heart that devises wicked plans, feet that are swift in running to evil, a false witness who speaks lies, and one who sows discord among brethren. (Prov. 6:16–19 NKJV)

God highlighted the rest of the passage that I didn't take seriously, but as I began to go over the list, I came under the conviction that I had, at one time or another, violated all seven abominations, even including "hands that shed innocent blood." The Lord showed me that when I was 16, one year before my conversion to Christ, I had gotten my girlfriend pregnant. Her mom wanted her to get an abortion, and in fear, I supported her decision to get the abortion. The Lord told me I was complicit by supporting and agreeing with the shedding of innocent blood as she went through with that decision. As the saying goes, "It takes two to tango," but the church has been so fixated on the woman's choice to abort the baby and hardly ever speaks out on the role of the boyfriend or husband, many of whom urge and pay for the abortion.

When God showed me this sin, I realized I had never once confessed that I was also complicit in the "shedding of innocent blood." From then on, whenever I would speak out on abortion, I would also include my part of this story with the hope that men would also take responsibility for their sins. This is not to condemn anyone. The moment the Lord showed me my part in this going back to 1972, I knew I was forgiven and that the blood of Jesus had cleansed me from all sin. This would not have happened if I had not received a revelation of the fear of the Lord.

I believe the fear of the Lord has helped me to walk in holiness and righteousness. I know theologically that I am positionally righteous the moment I give my heart to Jesus (2 Cor. 5:21). But the fear of the Lord has helped me to walk in righteousness. A key verse is "work out your own salvation with fear and trembling" (Phil. 2:12). John Bevere illustrated this by sharing that when you are married, you are "positionally" a married person. You can prove it to anyone by showing them your marriage license. But that doesn't mean your marriage is good and healthy. Anyone who is married knows they have to work on their marriage for the rest of their lives to have a successful and healthy marriage.

So, too, is our walk with God. That is why we need the Holy Spirit and the fear of the Lord to be righteous and holy as He is holy (1 Pet. 1:16). The fear of the Lord and the Holy Spirit give us God's grace to help us be conformed into His image with Christlike character.

A HOLY, RIGHTEOUS LIFE WILL TRANSFORM THE WORLD

"Give me one hundred preachers who fear nothing but sin, and desire nothing but God, and I care not a straw whether they be clergymen or laymen; such alone will shake the gates of hell and set up the kingdom of heaven on Earth." — John Wesley[97]

God has always used a remnant of holy people to usher in a move of God that transformed their world. The 120 in the Upper Room come to mind. The 300 members of the famous Clapham Group during the Great Awakening in England, led by William Wilberforce, is another great example. Keep in mind that the First Great Awakening began in 1738 when the Holy Club, made up of Charles Wesley, John Wesley, and George Whitefield, experienced the baptism of fire on January 1, 1739, at an all-night prayer meeting at Aldersgate.[98]

Of all the "apostolic strategies" that the Lord has given me to be a reformer, the most important is that I am to pastor and raise up a holy remnant from our church and the apostolic network that I lead to be radical lovers of Jesus and walk in the fear and reverence of God. When you have a company of laid-down lovers of God, they will hear what the Holy Spirit is saying to the church and will obey whatever God asks them to do to transform their world.

I find it arresting that Jesus begins the Beatitudes in Matthew 5 with character qualities that He loves:

- The poor in spirit—that is, a humble person who is totally dependent on God (v.3).

- Those who mourn over their sins and repent (v.4).

---

[97] Dr. Rick Vance. "Lessons from John Wesley." March 29, 2021. United Methodist Men. https://www.gcumm.org/news/lessons-from-john-wesley/

[98] John Wesley, *The Journal of the Rev. John Wesley* (London: S. Thorne, 1828), 72.

- A meek person—that is, one with strength under control (v.5).

- A person who is hungry for God, which is indispensable for being continually filled with the Spirit (v.6).

- One who walks in love and compassion (v.7).

- A person who is pure and holy (v.8).

- A peacemaker who is walking in reconciliation with believers (v.9), and as far as it depends on us, to be at peace with unbelievers (see Rom. 12:18).

- Even when they persecute you (v.10–11), we are to bless them and do good to them (see v.43–48).

In all these areas, we are allowing our Christlike character to shine to a dark world (Isa. 60:1–2). Then Jesus shifts His teaching to focus on His character, since He is all that the Beatitudes espouse. For example, He says, "Learn from Me, for I am gentle and lowly of heart" (Matt. 11:28). In this verse, *gentle* is the same Greek word (*praus*) as *meek* in Matthew 5:4.

Following the Beatitudes, Jesus highlights how we are called to transform the world by being salt and light.

BEING THE SALT AND LIGHT OF THE WORLD

You are the salt of the earth, but if salt has lost its taste, how shall its saltiness be restored? It is no longer good for anything except to be thrown out and trampled under people's feet. You are the light of the world. A city set on a hill cannot be hidden. Nor do people light a lamp and put it under a basket, but on a stand, and it gives light to all in the house. In the same way, let your light shine before others, so that they may see your good works and give glory to your Father who is in heaven. (Matt. 5:13–16 ESV)

Two of the most transformational agents are salt and light. Each of these changes the environment. You put salt on bland food, and it changes into a gourmet dish. You bring a match into a dark cave, and it lights up the whole thing. God has called each one of us to transform our world by calling us as salt and light.

Both salt and light were very valuable to Israel during the time of Christ. Besides adding much-needed flavor to one's food, salt was used to preserve it and mixed into fertilizer to help agriculture grow. In his book *Salt: A World History*, Mark Kurlansky reminds us that salt is the only rock that we eat, and its importance has shaped civilization in all sorts of important ways. He says, "From the beginning of civilization until about 100 years ago, salt was one of the most sought-after commodities in human history."[99] Kurlansky goes on to say that Roman soldiers were given the option of being paid with Roman coins or salt. That is why we have the idiom, "He is not worth his salt." In other words, he is not doing the job he is being paid to do.

---

[99] Mark Kurlansky. *Salt: A World History*. Knopf Canada, 2011, Ebook.

After calling us "the salt of the earth," Jesus teaches that we "are the light of the world" (Matt. 5:14a). Note His progression: From the macro view of the world, "the light of the world," next He says we are to transform our cities. "A city set on a hill cannot be hidden" (Matt. 5:14b). Finally, and in reality, it begins with us being a light to our family and home. "Nor do people light a lamp and put it under a basket, but on the lampstand, and it gives light to all who are in the house" (Matt. 5:15). It is roughly the reverse order of when He gives the Great Commission in Acts 1:8 (NASB1995), "But you will receive power when the Holy Spirit has come upon you, and you will be my witnesses in Jerusalem and in all Judea and Samaria, and to the end of the earth."

The end goal is to be salt and light to the ends of the earth, but it begins in your home and your Jerusalem. For me, it is my home and Los Angeles, and specifically Pasadena.

LET YOUR LIGHT SHINE BEFORE OTHERS

The question remains: How are we to shine as light? Jesus gives us two final instructions. First, we have to do good works. It is not just talking about love, but we are to love in deed and in truth. "Little children, let us not love in word or talk but in deed and in truth" (1 John 3:18 NASB1995). Second, our good works have to be done in the name of Jesus or with the gospel associated with them "so that they may see your good works and give glory to your Father who is in heaven" (Matt. 5:16 NASB1995). There are a lot of humanists who do charitable works in society, but for the kingdom of God to come to earth as it is in heaven, our good works must be associated with the gospel of the kingdom.

I remember when Sue and I were newly married, we rented a house that my parents owned on Georgia Ave. in Silver Spring, Maryland. Almost a year into our marriage, we were going through a heat wave in the nation's capital. It was June, but the temperatures were in the 90s, and with the D.C. humidity, it was unbearable to be outside.

On this particular morning, I was in my office, studying the Word, when I heard the trash collectors coming up our road. I heard the Holy Spirit whisper into my heart, "These workers are extremely hot. Give them something cold to drink." One of the ways I know that the Holy Spirit is speaking to me is that the word comes out of left field; in other words, I had never thought about giving trash collectors something cold to drink before.

So, I quickly went downstairs and asked Sue if we had anything cold to drink. She said no and asked why. I quickly told her, and she thought it was a great idea. She said, "Why don't you flag down the guys and bring them to our house, and I will quickly make some frozen orange juice and bring some cups outside?" By now, the collectors had gone past our house, so I ran up to them and said, "Hey guys, it's really hot out today. My wife is making some cold orange juice down at our house, a few houses away. Why don't you guys come down and take a little break?"

They looked at me as if I was from Mars. Who gives trash collectors anything? Still, they walked down to our house. My car was parked under a big oak tree that provided shade, and I used the hood as a table. The timing was impeccable.

Sue walked outside with the orange juice and cups, and I poured the juice and passed it out to the four workers, who gratefully gulped down the drink.

All of a sudden, the Sermon on the Mount came into my mind, specifically Jesus' words in Matthew 5:16. I didn't want them to think I was just a nice, humanistic guy. I wanted Jesus to receive all the glory, so I began to share my testimony.

"A number of years ago, I would never have taken the time to do something like this. I was a drug addict, totally selfish, never thinking about others, just looking out for number one, me," I said as I pointed my thumb to my chest. "But then I gave my life to Jesus, and He delivered me from drug addiction in just one day. And I want you to know that God loves you and told me to give you guys something cold to drink!"

They all thanked me and went back to work. I didn't ask them to pray to accept Jesus, but I did do a good deed that gave glory to Jesus, so I went into the house knowing that I had obeyed.

Three months later, in early September, Sue and I bought our first house in Wheaton, Maryland. Gabriel, our firstborn, was about due in two weeks. We moved to the other side of Wheaton, and God bless my parents; they helped us buy our first home. After we finished unpacking, we had a large number of boxes and trash accumulating on the side street in front of our house that needed to be picked up. I knew the trash collectors were scheduled to pick up the trash the next day, but I thought they would never take all we had piled up. So, I decided to do a "Korean" thing and bribe them to take everything. I decided to go to Dunkin Donuts and buy a dozen assorted donuts, make some coffee, and set everything up on our outdoor patio to await the trash collectors.

When the collectors arrived, I rushed up to them and asked, "What's your policy for picking up trash beyond the two-can limit when someone just moves in?" The person in charge said, "Our policy is to take everything, not just the two-can limit."

Wow, I thought. *I didn't have to buy the donuts and make the coffee after all.* But since everything was set up, I asked the guys, "Why don't you take a break? I have some donuts and coffee set up on our patio table." I didn't have to ask them twice. They quickly went to the table and helped themselves.

Then, the Lord reminded me of what happened when we gave out orange juice only a few months prior, so I thought I would use this opportunity to preach the gospel. I began sharing my testimony. As I was speaking, one of the collectors interrupted me: "Did you used to live on Georgia Avenue in Silver Spring, Maryland?"

"Yes," I said. "How did you know?"

"You were the guy who gave us orange juice when we went through that heat wave."

"Yes," I answered.

"I want to thank you and shake your hand!" he said, reaching out his hand toward mine. "What you did made such an impression on me that a few weeks later, a friend of mine invited me to a Christian meeting. I went and gave my life to Jesus there. I wanted to come by your house and thank you, but I was transferred to this new neighborhood. I can't believe you moved into my new route. I want to thank you for planting that seed in my life."

Again, you can't make this up! I wonder how many people we have witnessed to that ended up becoming followers of Jesus. I know we will find out when we get to heaven, but this time, God allowed me to see this fruit on this side of glory. But the realization from that day still hit me: *What if I had given them orange juice without sharing the gospel through my testimony?*

So, why am I concluding with this story? Well, out of everything shared in this book thus far, I am convinced that *the most important* apostolic strategy for transforming the world is for transformed Christians to transform their world by demonstrating and declaring the gospel in Jesus' mighty name!

APPENDICES

Appendix A:

ADDRESSING THE GREATEST INJUSTICES OF OUR DAY

*T*he greatest injustices today are actually the same as those during the time of Christ, although I would place them in a different order of gravity.

Number one on the list in Christ's day would have been *the poor*, no question about it. The majority of the people in the first century A.D. lived in abject poverty. That context helps us understand the prophecy Jesus fulfilled when He said, "The spirit of the Lord is upon me; He has anointed me to preach good news to the poor," because that was the greatest need of His day. The poor were in abundance, and good news to the poor is that you don't have to be poor anymore. God will bless you and meet your needs as you put your trust in Him (Phil. 4:19).

Number two would have been *slavery*. Slaves were ubiquitous throughout the Roman Empire and really all of the ancient world. The book of Philemon offers us a small glimpse of God's heart, as Paul presents the countercultural appeal to set a slave named Onesimus free and to treat him like a brother in Christ (Philem. 16).

Number three would have been *infanticide*. This was essentially a form of abortion, where they would abandon a newborn child that they did not want to live. We do not have exact numbers on each of these injustices, but we know they were rampant in Christ's day.

Today we have statistics to highlight the social injustices that are most evident. The love of Christ compels us to respond to these issues and make a difference in as many lives as possible. I will briefly address them in ascending order of magnitude.

#3: Systemic Poverty: Nine million people die of hunger and malnutrition each year.[100] This statistic shows how far we have come,[101] as we have eradicated the levels of starvation and poverty that marked the days of first-century Rome. But at the same time, we have our work cut out for us to meet the needs of millions of poor individuals and their families, not just by giving handouts but by bringing reformation to transform lives and societies to be prosperous.

#2: Human Trafficking: According to a 2022 report, an estimated 50 million people are human trafficked or in situations of modern-day slavery on any given day of the calendar year. That comes out to around 1 in every 150 people in the world.[102]

---

[100] David Beasley. "In world of wealth, 9 million people die every year from hunger…" World Food Programme. September 24, 2021. https://www.wfp.org/news/world-wealth-9-million-people-die-every-year-hunger-wfp-chief-tells-food-system-summit

[101] Max Roser. "We Need a New Global Measure for Poverty." *New York Times*. September 24, 2024. https://www.nytimes.com/interactive/2024/09/24/opinion/global-poverty-rates

[102] "Global Estimates of Modern Slavery: Estimation Method." Counter-Trafficking Data Collaborative (CTDC). Accessed August 2, 2024. https://www.ctdatacollaborative.org/story/gems2022

#1: Abortion: The number-one injustice issue in our world today is abortion. The unfathomable number of 73 million abortions take place around the globe *every single year*. That translates to 29 percent of all pregnancies—almost one out of every three babies—and 61 percent of unintended pregnancies ending in abortion.[103]

Why California Desperately Needs Reformation

Of all the issues facing Americans today, abortion is one of the most polarizing. Even though *Roe v. Wade* was overturned on the historic date of June 24, 2022, abortion is still a hot issue on the state-by-state level. As a case in point, California remains the number-one abortion state and is in desperate need of reformation.[104]

On January 1, 2023, California's legislature added this to her laundry list of evil: Proposition 1 codified late-term abortion until the last day of the ninth month into our state constitution. We have become a sanctuary state for abortion, which grieves me to write and undoubtedly grieves the heart of God even more. Before Prop 1 was passed, Gov. Gavin Newsom paid for billboards in seven red states in 2022, advertising that anyone can come to California and have an

---

[103] "Abortion." World Health Organization. May 17, 2024. https://www.who.int/news-room/fact-sheets/detail/abortion

[104] Nadine El-Bawab. "Illinois, Florida, California saw largest increase in abortions…" ABC News. February 28, 2024. https://abcnews.go.com/US/illinois-florida-california-largest-increase-abortions-15-months/story?id=107651669; "#WeCount Report: April 2022 to March 2023." Society of Family Planning. June 15, 2023. https://societyfp.org/wp-content/uploads/2023/06/WeCountReport_6.12.23.pdf#page=9

abortion at California's expense.[105] All of these things have serious ramifications for our nation as we watch a Pandora's box of evil being opened up on California's soil.

On the same day Prop 1 came into effect, Senate Bill (SB) 107 also turned California into a sanctuary state for transgender individuals.[106] Any person 17 years or younger could now come to California and receive transgender medical treatment without parental notification and at Californians' tax dollars.

Again, we are only scratching the surface of the corruption enacted by Californian officials. As of September 2020, SB 145 declared that having sex with a minor between the ages of 14 and 17 no longer requires the perpetrator to be registered as a sex offender in California "if the person is not more than 10 years older than the minor."[107]

Another egregious bill is SB 357, signed by Gov. Newsom in 2022. Once SB 357 became law, California police officers could no longer question a teenager loitering for the purpose of prostitution. Thus, we have seen the acceleration of teen

---

[105] Lara Korte "Gavin Newsom promotes California as abortion sanctuary on red-state billboards." Politico. September 15, 2022. https://www.politico.com/news/2022/09/15/gavin-newsom-california-abortion-sanctuary-red-state-billboards-00057060
[106] "Senator Wiener's Historic Bill To Provide Refuge For Trans Kids And Their Families Signed Into Law." California State Senate District 11. Accessed May 15, 2024. https://sd11.senate.ca.gov/news/20220930-senator-wiener's-historic-bill-provide-refuge-trans-kids-and-their-families-signed-law
[107] "SB-145 Sex offenders: registration. (2019-2020)." California Legislative Information. September 14, 2020.
https://leginfo.legislature.ca.gov/faces/billTextClient.xhtml?bill_id=201920200SB145

prostitution and human trafficking in California since the start of 2023.[108]

We must remember that these are all bills passed by State Senators and State Assembly members, and all were signed into law by Governor Newsom. If our *elected* officials are making these kinds of decisions on our behalf, it is high time for Californians to wake up and vote these same officials out of office. My frequent prayer is this: "God, save them or remove them!" Reformation, as we see throughout this book, can be sparked in many ways, including prayer, but especially so at the voting booth.

A Trio of Prophetic Dreams

As I was finishing writing this book, I had three successive dreams in one night that I felt compelled to add to the manuscript.

In my first dream, I was about to speak at a meeting that was full, but the atmosphere wasn't anointed, even though I knew I had a word from the Lord. The people were glad I was there and were looking forward to what I had to share, but I knew it wasn't about me. I was dressed in my gym shorts, a T-shirt, and tennis shoes. As I walked into the lobby, I saw a grown man lovingly holding a five-year-old child asleep peacefully in His arms. I knew immediately that this man was Jesus. It was clear that the dream was all about Jesus and

---

[108] "Prostitution Surges in CA After Decriminalization of Loitering." California Family Council. October 23, 2023. https://www.californiafamily.org/2023/10/prostitution-surges-in-ca-after-decriminalization-of-loitering/

His heart for children, emphasizing the need to bring about righteousness and justice for His children around the world.

In the second dream, I was seated at a table with five marketplace leaders or apostles who were faceless and nameless. Although I didn't recognize them, I felt a strong connection to them. I sat down and told them I was going to give them the keys to become super successful billionaires, but to avoid sounding like I was exaggerating, I said "multi-millionaires" instead. I revealed that the key to our success was the "Don't Mess with Our Kids" movement, spearheaded by Jenny Donnelly (see Appendix B).

In the final dream, I was again with the same five men, but this time, I was at a Chinese restaurant. We were on a conference call using my iPhone, but because the company we were speaking with was a Christian tech company, they had activated a Zoom call with each person on their own device. The company was interested in investing in the "Don't Mess with Our Kids" movement but had concerns after attending one of our meetings during their due diligence. They complained that our meetings were too political, with people waving flags, dressed in red, and wearing MAGA hats. They also pointed out that a mother was changing her baby's diaper in the front of the room instead of in the restroom, and they found the meeting too loud and disorderly. As a result, they were hesitant about investing. My response in the dream was firm: *This is who we are, and we are not going to change.* I told them they would need to change their values if they wanted to partner with us.

When I woke up, I immediately went to prayer about what I had dreamt. I believe God gave me these dreams to reinforce that our mission is centered on Jesus and His heart for children, no matter how unconventional or challenging it may appear. They served as a reminder that we must stay true to our values and calling, even if it means standing firm in the face of opposition or misunderstanding. We must continue to fight for reformation because the next generation is at stake!

Appendix B:

MODERN-DAY REFORMER
MOVEMENTS

Don't Mess With Our Kids

"In 2017, a million and a half people marched in the streets of twenty-six cities in Peru with banners warning, 'Don't Mess With Our Kids' (*Con Mis Hijos No Te Metas*). The marches, originally proposed by a young man named Christian Rosas, were in opposition to the public gender development policies of the Peruvian government in education and other areas of public administration. Nothing arouses the righteous anger of parents and grandparents more than when their children and grandchildren are attacked," James Garlow writes in his book *Reversed: From Culturally Woke to Biblically Awake*.[109]

What started in Peru spread like wildfire throughout Latin America and has reached American soil—just in time, too. The attack on the family has been driving many Christians to their knees in prayer in recent years, as radical progressive

---

[109] James L. Garlow. *Reversed: From Culturally Woke to Biblically Awake*. Well Versed Publishing, 2024, p.15.

Left agendas have been gaining ground in the mainstream media, government legislation, and school systems. "Our nation is in a crisis—families are being ripped apart at the seams by an agenda determined to sexualize our kids," the Don't Mess With Our Kids website states. "ENOUGH IS ENOUGH … We're committed to seeing America turned back to God through united prayer, fasting, and taking a stand in the public square for righteousness and truth."[110]

Her Voice Movement and A Million Women Gathering on the Day of Atonement: October 12, 2024

Jenny Donnelly, founder of Her Voice Movement[111] and a commissioned apostle under Harvest International Ministry, has been spearheading the American chapter of this movement. In 2022, Jenny joined forces with my covenant brother, Lou Engle, to see one of his prophetic dreams come to pass. Five years prior, Lou had a dream of an immeasurable crowd of women gathering to hear the book of Esther being read. God was calling him to be a Mordecai to help mobilize the realization of that dream: "A righteous women's movement that is going to gain authority in America over principalities and powers, ideologies that are seeking to destroy the children of this nation."[112]

---

[110] https://www.dontmesswithourkids.us
[111] https://www.hervoicemvmt.com
[112] Lou Engle. "A Million Women - An Esther Call On The Mall - October 12, 2024." February 27, 2024. https://www.youtube.com/watch?v=1DAznDpAmfc

That is why they strategically planned an event called "A Million Women: An Esther Call to the Mall" in Washington, D.C., on October 12, 2024, the Day of Atonement on the Jewish calendar. Along with many other leaders in the Body of Christ, we gathered at this crossroads of history, daring to believe that God will shift the trajectory of our society and save our nation. Find out more at *amillionwomen.org*.

To get involved with other like-minded movements, revisit Chapter 10 for a list of more organizations that are bringing reformation today.

Appendix C:

GIVE HIM 15 BY DUTCH SHEETS

"Changing America"
August 23, 2024

*G*od wasted no time before introducing the all-important concept of government in Scripture, doing so in the very first chapter: Genesis 1:26-28. Government is vital. Whether it be in a home, city, nation, or any other grouping of people, God's intent for government was that it serve people by providing protection (covering), instruction, justice, appropriate and loving discipline, peace, and more (Luke 13:34; 19:44; 1 Timothy 2:1-4; Romans 13:1-4). Righteous rule (government) is God's primary method of releasing these necessary actions and outcomes on earth. Proverbs 29:2 tells us that this brings joy to people; when it does not occur, the result is mourning. No wonder He told us to pray first for those in government! (1 Timothy 2:1-4)

The Hebrew word used for "mourn" in Proverbs 29:2, that which occurs when the wicked rule, is a strong word. *Anach* means not only to mourn, but to moan and groan, even to gasp. Moaning, groaning, gasping, and mourning—that's what wicked rulers produce. Proverbs 14:34 adds that the sin these rulers produce causes shame and disgrace to a nation.

The controlling element of America's current ungodly government has brought disgrace and mourning by believing it has the right to:

- Kill babies and make those who believe this is murder pay for the abortions.
- Approve the selling of the aborted babies' body parts (are you gasping yet?).
- Allow babies born alive during failed abortions to lay unattended until they die.
- Redefine what it means to be male and female.
- Reject the first covenant God established on earth, marriage, and redefine it using activities He forbade (and celebrate this rebellion with cheering, flags, nudity, and lit-up government buildings).
- Take ownership of children from their parents; they indoctrinate them using pornography and drag queens, even to the point of encouraging the children to be sterilized by drugs or castration (are you mourning yet?).
- Open our borders to drugs that kill tens of thousands every year, to criminals, rapists, and terrorists, and to millions of illegals annually who are never taught our laws, history, and values (all for votes to stay in power).
- Promote Marxism and socialism.

- Rewrite America's history, attempting to steal our Judeo-Christian roots.
- Redefine our Constitution.
- Remove our freedom of speech.
- Lie to us at will.
- And much more.

What if I told you the American church could easily change all of this? Yep. You see, approximately half of evangelicals aren't registered to vote, and half of those who are still don't vote. It is an accepted fact that if all evangelical Christians voted and did so according to biblical values, we could control every national election and place godly, Bible-believing leaders in office. This means that in one election cycle, we could begin reversing every evil I just listed. Every one. In America, "we the people" have the amazing right to place in power who we want to rule over us; "we the believers" have the numbers to ensure they'll be leaders who possess God's biblical values.

Let me be more specific. Yours and my votes, based on biblical truth, could save the lives of babies, the reproductive future of children, God's plan for marriage and the family, and America's freedoms—almost overnight.

But "we the believers" don't do so. We empower evil by not voting or by voting inappropriately. Why? Complacency—not voting; a dislike and distaste for the political process and political spirit; succumbing to the political spirit and voting based on party affiliation; and compromising biblical truth by voting based on party affiliation, personalities, and promises of personal benefits, rather than voting based on truth and the good of all.

How can we change this? Here is a helpful tool.

MyFaithVotes.org is an informative website that has done the work for you! It is a wonderful one-stop-shop website where the Christian voter can be educated, informed, prepared, and ready to go to the polls. There, you can find information concerning upcoming elections, articles about upcoming bills in Congress you need to be aware of, and much more. If you follow their prompts, you can even find out if you are registered to vote, info on absentee voting, where to vote near you; and if you are NOT yet registered to vote, their links will take you directly to the right link in YOUR state where can register to vote online, right then! Additionally, they provide simple ways to engage with those who represent us in our State and U.S. Congresses. You can do all of this from home!

Here are a few of the many tools the MyFaithVotes.org website offers:

> **My Voter Hub** — check your registration, receive a text voting reminder, order an absentee ballot, see your ballot ahead of time - who is on it, what they stand for - and mark your sample ballot to take to the polls with you, and more.

> **Contact Your Elected Officials** — simple instructions for composing an email regarding your concerns and the ability to send it with one click to whichever of your representatives you would like to contact.

Think Biblically — a 6-week Bible study course on topics in the public square, presented by Christian influencers, such as Voddie Baucham on Justice, and Abby Johnson on Abortion...

Let's all do our part to encourage people to vote for leaders with traditional and biblical values.

Pray with me:

> Father, we thank You for the awakening happening in the church. The sleeping giant is stirring. Cause the alarm clock to become louder and louder. Make it impossible for Christians in America to silence the alarm or override it with other activities and thoughts.
>
> Our hearts, though breaking over many issues, are also filled with faith that You are changing things dramatically. The conscience of a nation is being brought back to life. The heart of a complacent and passive church is being, and will continue to be, awakened. Thank You for Your grace and Your mercy.
>
> And Father, as believers awaken from complacency and lethargy, motivate them to vote. Give organizations like My Faith Votes great participation and success as they implement Your creative ideas. We ask You to lead many people to participate in their efforts. Thank You for turning

this nation around. We are very grateful that You have not given up on America. And since You have not given up on her, we won't either. Your verdict has been rendered: America shall be saved! So be it. And we, Your family, will do our part to see this occur. In Christ's name, we pray this. Amen.

Our decree:

We declare that we, the church, will involve ourselves at every level and in every facet of government, releasing the authority and blessing of God into the earth through our prayers and actions.[113]

---

[113] https://www.givehim15.com/post/august-23-2024?mc_cid=f8b8228294&mc_eid=faa09acb09

Appendix D:

START YOUR NEW LIFE
WITH CHRIST

*Y*ou can have real, lasting peace today through a relationship with Jesus Christ. *Start your four-step journey now!*

Step 1 – God's Purpose: Peace and Life

God loves you and wants you to experience peace and abundant, eternal life.

- The Bible says: "We have peace with God through our Lord Jesus Christ." (Rom. 5:1)
- "For God so loved the world, that He gave His one and only Son, that whoever believes in Him should not perish but have eternal life." (John 3:16 ESV)

Why don't most people have this peace and abundant life that God planned for us to have?

Step 2 – The Problem: Sin Separates Us

God created us in His own image to have an abundant life. He did not make us as robots to automatically love and obey Him. God gave us a will and freedom of choice, but we choose to disobey God and go our own willful way. We still make this choice today. This results in separation from God.

- The Bible says: "For all have sinned and fall short of the glory of God." (Rom. 3:23)
- "For the wages of sin is death, but the free gift of God is eternal life in Christ Jesus our Lord." (Rom. 6:23 ESV)

Our choice results in separation from God. People have tried in many ways to bridge this gap between themselves and God... **But no bridge reaches God... except one.**

Step 3 – God's Remedy: The Cross

Jesus Christ died on the cross and rose from the grave. He paid the penalty for our sin and bridged the gap between God and people.

- The Bible says: "For Christ also suffered once for sins, the righteous for the unrighteous, that He might bring us to God." (1 Pet. 3:18 ESV)
- "But God shows His love for us in that while we were still sinners, Christ died for us." (Rom. 5:8 ESV)

God has provided the only way... Each person must make a choice...

Step 4 – Our Response: Receive Christ

We must trust Jesus Christ as Lord and Savior and receive Him by personal invitation.

- The Bible says: "If you confess with your mouth that Jesus is Lord and believe in your heart that God raised Him from the dead, you will be saved." (Rom. 10:9 ESV)

Will you receive Jesus Christ right now? Here is how you can receive Christ:

- Admit your need. *(I am a sinner.)*
- Be willing to turn from your sins *(repent)* and ask for God's forgiveness.
- Believe that Jesus Christ died for you on the cross and rose from the grave.
- By faith, surrender your whole life, all that you are, and all that you have to Jesus.
- Through prayer, invite Jesus Christ to come in and control your life through the Holy Spirit. *(Receive Jesus as Lord and Savior.)*

We suggest a prayer like this one:

> **"Dear God, I know I am a sinner. I want to repent of my sins, and I ask for Your forgiveness. I believe that Jesus Christ is Your Son. I believe He died for my sins and that You raised Him to life. I want Him to**

come into my heart and take control of my life. I surrender and give my life to Jesus. I want to trust Jesus as my Savior and follow Him as my Lord from this day forward. In Jesus' name, amen."

*Based on "Peace With God" by the Billy Graham Evangelistic Association

ABOUT THE AUTHOR

*D*r. **Ché Ahn** and his wife, Sue, have been the Senior Leaders of Harvest Rock Church in Pasadena, California, since 1994. Ché serves as the President of Harvest International Ministry, a global apostolic network equipping leaders, multiplying churches, evangelizing, and bringing revival and reformation to more than 70 nations. He is also the International Chancellor of Wagner University, an international educational institution equipping believers for practical ministry.

Ché received his M.Div. and D.Min. from Fuller Theological Seminary and has played a key role in many strategic local, national, and international outreaches. He has authored numerous books, including *Spirit-Led Evangelism*, *Say Goodbye to Powerless Christianity*, *The Grace of Giving*, *Modern-Day Apostles*, and *Turning Our Nation Back to God Through Historic Revival*. Ché ministers extensively throughout the world, teaching and equipping people for revival, healing, and evangelism. He is also using media to reach the world through his TV show on PTL and Faith TV. His greatest desire is to see society transformed through Christians who understand and fulfill their destiny.

Ché and Sue have been married for over 45 years. They have four wonderful children and the ten cutest grandchildren in the world.

For more information about Ché Ahn, his ministries, and his resource materials, visit: cheahn.org, harvestim.org, wagner.university, and harvestrock.church.

MORE TITLES BY CHÉ AHN

Turning Our Nation Back to God Through Historic Revival
Modern-Day Apostles
God Wants to Bless You!
The Grace of Giving
Say Goodbye to Powerless Christianity
When Heaven Comes Down
Spirit-Led Evangelism
How to Pray for Healing

Find these and more at cheahn.org

www.ingramcontent.com/pod-product-compliance
Lightning Source LLC
Chambersburg PA
CBHW060857120626
46553CB00001B/119